Extreme Photoshop CS

Matt Kloskowski

friendsof
DESIGNER TO DESIGNER™
an Apress® company

Extreme Photoshop CS

ISBN (pbk): 1-59059-428-2

Printed and bound in the United States of America 9 8 7 6 5 4 3 2 1

Distributed to the book trade in the United States by Springer-Verlag New York, Inc., 233 Spring Street, 6th Floor, New York, NY 10013, and outside the United States by Springer-Verlag GmbH & Co. KG, Tiergartenstr. 17, 69112 Heidelberg, Germany.

In the United States: phone 1-800-SPRINGER, fax 201-348-4505, e-mail orders@springer-ny.com, or visit http://www.springer-ny.com. Outside the United States: fax +49 6221 345229, e-mail orders@springer.de, or visit http://www.springer.de.

For information on translations, please contact Apress directly at 2560 Ninth Street, Suite 219, Berkeley, CA 94710. Phone 510-549-5930, fax 510-549-5939, e-mail info@apress.com, or visit http://www.apress.com.

Credits

Commissioning Editor
Gavin Wray

Technical Reviewer
Michael Hamm

Editorial Board
Steve Anglin, Dan Appleman, Ewan Buckingham, Gary Cornell, Tony Davis, Jason Gilmore, Chris Mills, Dominic Shakeshaft, Jim Sumser

Project Manager
Beckie Stones

Copy Edit Manager
Nicole LeClerc

Copy Editors
Kelli Crump, Nicole LeClerc

Production Manager
Kari Brooks-Copony

Production Editor
Laura Cheu

Compositor
Dina Quan

Proofreader
April Eddy

Indexer
Michael Brinkman

Artist
Kinetic Publishing Services, LLC

Cover Designers
Matt Kloskowski, Kurt Krames

Manufacturing Manager
Tom Debolski

*I dedicate this book to my adoring wife, Diana,
and my children, Ryan and Justin.*

*The patience they had while I was locked away for many hours
writing this book is above and beyond the call of duty.*

Thank you.

CONTENTS

About the Author . . . . **x**

About the Technical Reviewer . . . . **xi**

Acknowledgments . . . . **xii**

PART ONE: PHOTOSHOP AND REALISM . . . . **XX**

Chapter 1: Photoshop and Realism: Tools and Concepts **1**

Different types of realism 2
   Faking realism with Photoshop 3
Photorealism: What's the difference? 4
Tools of the trade 8
   Color modes 8
   Pen tool 10
      Drawing paths 12
      Stroking paths 14
      Filling paths 15
      Simple path exercise with the Pen tool 15
      Advanced paths with the Pen tool 17
Concepts of realism 22
   Linear perspective 24
      Horizon line 24
      Vertical lines 24
      Vanishing point 25
   Atmospheric perspective 25
   Shadows 26
   Reflection 27

Refraction 28
Depth 29
Summary 30
Expert Interview 31

Chapter 2: Brushing Up On Reality **37**

Looking at history 38
Brushes and the toolbox 39
Liquify filter 39
Stuck in the rough? 40
Creating fire 50
Summary 64

Chapter 3: Realism and 3D **67**

3D techniques and concepts in Photoshop 68
Clipping groups 68
Reflections and highlights 70
Refraction 70
Texture mapping 71
Texture map 71
Bump map 71
Reflection map 71
Techniques and concepts wrap-up 72
Creating a 3D glass fishbowl 72
Summary 101

Chapter 4: Photorealism Techniques **103**

Why photorealism? 104
Product shoot modifications 104
Accessory additions 104
Photo quality 104
A photograph doesn't exist 106
It's just plain cool 106
Reference images 106
Layer comps 126
Summary 129

PART TWO: CARTOONING IN PHOTOSHOP **130**

Chapter 5: More Power to the Pixel **131**

Setting up 132
Pencil tool 132
Marquee tools 133
Magic Wand tool 133

Zooming and navigating 134
ImageReady 137
The mathematics of pixel art 138
Isometric perspective 138
Breaking the rules 140
Lighting 150
Shading 151
Text 166
Anti-aliasing 166
Pixel fonts 167
Building your pixel empire 173
Extending your pixel art illustration 185
Building a library of reusable pixel art 189
Summary 192

Chapter 6: Icons and Emoticons **195**

Icon overview 196
Emoticons 198
Conceptualization 200
Sketches 200
Guidelines 200
Designing and illustrating icons 201
Creating the actual icon file 226
Summary 226

Chapter 7: Cartoon and Comic Book Art **229**

Getting your drawings into Photoshop 230
Scanning 230
Using the Levels adjustment 231
Color palettes 231
Saving and using swatches 231
Various cartoon and comic book styles 232
Comic book art 232
Japanese manga/anime-style art 234
Summary 251

PART THREE: ADVANCED ILLUSTRATION **252**

Chapter 8: Silhouette Illustration **253**

What is a silhouette? 254
Why use a silhouette illustration? 254
Mood 254
Picking an image to silhouette 255
Complexity 255
Viewing angle 256

Composition 257
Creativity 257
Extracting your image 258
Summary 269

Chapter 9: Wireframe Illustration 271

What is a wireframe? 272
Wireframe history 272
Picking an image to wireframe 273
Complexity 274
Viewing angle 274
Creativity 275
Creating outlines 276
Summary 305

Chapter 10: Stylizing Photographs 307

Stylizing techniques 308
Picking a photograph 308
Complexity 308
Hair 308
Copyright issues 309
Getting started 309
Bringing out highlights and shadows 309
Summary 327

PART FOUR: RETRO AND VINTAGE ART 328

Chapter 11: Retro and Vintage Art Styles 329

A sampling of retro styles 330
Pop art 330
Art deco 330
Bauhaus/constructivist 331
Research and inspiration 331
Summary 361

Chapter 12: Building a Reusable Retro Library 363

Shapes 364
Reasons for creating shapes 366
Starting a library of retro custom shapes 367
Opening third-party custom shape sets 367

Fonts 367
    Font preview 370
    Creating font sample files 370
    Symbol fonts and repurposing 372
Patterns 375
Color palettes 378
The Adobe Illustrator connection 379
Inspiration and material 380
    Building a library of inspiration 383
        Starting out 384
        Finding and sorting through your inspirational
        files with File Browser 384
Backing up your work 385
Summary 387

Index **389**

ABOUT THE AUTHOR

 **Matt Kloskowski** is a writer, instructor, illustrator, and graphic designer based out of Tampa, Florida. As well as being an Adobe Certified Expert, he holds certifications in Macromedia Flash, is a Microsoft Certified Solutions Developer (MCSD), and is an expert in dynamic- and database-driven website development. In addition, he writes columns for the National Association of Photoshop Professionals (NAPP), *Mac Design* magazine's website, and *Create Magazine*. He is also the course developer and instructor for an advanced Photoshop course at Sessions.edu (http://sessions.edu) and is president of an Adobe user group (www.adobetampa.com) in the Tampa Bay area. Matt is a 1995 graduate of the University of South Florida, with a degree in computer information systems and marketing. He hosts a Photoshop (www.extremephotoshop.com) website, among other sites, where he provides tutorials on all aspects of using the program. His tutorials have been used in over 15 schools throughout the United States and have been translated into seven languages.

In his spare time, Matt enjoys jogging, golfing, playing video games, and spending time with his wife, Diana, and two toddler sons, Ryan and Justin, in their Tampa home.

ABOUT THE TECHNICAL REVIEWER

Michael Hamm is a freelance designer and illustrator living in Houston, Texas. He started www.ergodraw.com in 2001 as a way to teach others about Adobe Illustrator and digital illustration through a series of in-depth tutorials. He is a 1996 graduate of the Art Institute of Houston. Michael also teaches a number of illustration classes to students worldwide at Sessions.edu (http://sessions.edu) online school of design and, on occasion, enters the real world of classroom instruction as well. You can reach Michael at his website, http://looktwo.com.

ACKNOWLEDGMENTS

This is the part of the book where I get to thank everyone who has helped me along my journey as a writer, instructor, and graphic artist. I've seen many acknowledgments pages before and always thought it was a cliché when an author writes about how there isn't enough room to thank all of those involved. The funny thing is that after writing two books, I no longer think it's a cliché—in fact, it's true. This is such a large undertaking, and there's no way to give thanks to all of those who deserve it in such a short space. However, I'll try my best.

First off, I'd like to thank the technical editor for this book, Michael Hamm. He's a very talented graphic designer and has kept me honest throughout this entire process. Although this was only my second experience writing a book, I can't imagine having anyone else review my work. He has truly contributed a huge amount to the quality of this book. I'd also like to thank the editor from friends of ED, Gavin Wray, for believing in this book and providing much needed feedback and guidance along every step. In addition, I'd like to acknowledge the entire team at Apress: Beckie, Steve, Pete, Laura, Kelli, Nicole, Dina, and everyone else who helped in getting this book published.

Next, I'd like to thank those who have directly or indirectly inspired and helped me throughout the writing of this book and my career, specifically Roger Kohler, Robin Barna (my high school English teacher), and Bill Moore (my college writing professor). I'd also like to thank Stewart Sandler (www.fontdiner.com) and Brad Nelson (www.braineaters.com) for contributing some of the fonts used in this book and allowing them to be included on the download website so you can follow along. In addition, thanks to Val and Denise at www.photospin.com for providing many of the photographs used in this book.

Also, thanks to my friends at NAPP, Jeff Kelby, Stacy Behan, and Jodi Nizin—you have given me great opportunities and have been a pleasure to work with.

To my family, I can't express my appreciation enough. Mom and Dad, you've always been an inspiration and encouraged me to do whatever I wanted to in life. Your guidance continues to be something that I depend on constantly. You are two of the finest people I know, and I couldn't ask for better parents. To my older brother and sister, Ed and Kristine, and your spouses, Kerry and Scott, you've been siblings that I've always looked up to and respected. Thanks for giving me something to strive for. And to my nephew Jay, thanks for being my biggest fan and thinking this stuff is "so cool."

As for my sons, Ryan and Justin, thank you for making me remember two of the most important things in my life: both of you. In other words, thanks for doing your best to divert me from getting any work done. Those forced breaks were often the most necessary things, and they always helped keep things in perspective for me.

And finally, to my beautiful wife, Diana, words cannot express the love, respect, and appreciation that I feel for having you in my life. Writing this book has been a dream come true for me, one that I wouldn't have been able to realize without your help and guidance. You are truly the most wonderful wife and mother I could have ever hoped to find. The work you have put toward helping me write this book can never be repaid.

PART ONE PHOTOSHOP AND REALISM

Adobe Photoshop has become to graphic design and illustration what Coke has become to soft drinks, Kleenex to tissues, and Xerox to copiers. It's all too often that the word "Photoshop" is used as a verb these days. How many times have you heard, "Can you Photoshop this picture?" or someone say, "That picture was Photoshopped?" Often, the context of these types of questions is centered on an image that looks very realistic. In fact, Photoshop has become a key piece of software used in creating, enhancing, and manipulating reality.

Photographers use Photoshop to retouch photographs and make them appear just as good, or better, than the subject looks in real life. Product designers use Photoshop to help design products when an image of that product, or the product itself, doesn't yet exist. Illustrators use it to create a scene that cannot be captured by a photograph. Of course, there are many other uses for Photoshop, but one common theme is **realism**.

Photoshop is an ideal program for conveying reality in graphic design. It's a program that allows its users to wield ultimate power over an image by working right down to the pixel level. However, it's broad enough that it allows many fast and powerful adjustments to an image at a high level.

Whatever your interest in Photoshop, the chances are you'll be faced with creating a design someday that looks realistic or modifying something to look more realistic. Chapter 1 is the first of four to introduce you to this subject. In this chapter, I'll cover two different concepts of realistic work in Photoshop:

- Basic realism techniques
- Photorealistic artwork

You'll explore the various tools, techniques, and concepts essential to working with realism and Photoshop. By the end of Chapter 1, you'll have a good foundation to begin work on the following three chapters and a good introduction to the techniques that professional designers and illustrators use in their everyday workflow.

Different types of realism

As I mentioned, realistic work in Photoshop can be separated into two categories: *realism* and *photorealism*. Realism involves creating designs and illustrations that carry on the basic principles of perspective, lighting, reflections, shadows, and texture. On the other hand, photorealism involves creating artwork that looks like a photograph. Although the two approaches may sound similar, working with realism in Photoshop doesn't necessarily entail creating photorealistic artwork. The two methods utilize the same concepts, but not every design requires the degree of detail of a photorealistic illustration. Often, as long as a design adheres to the basic principles of perspective, lighting, and shading, it's fine for its intended audience. If your goal is to make people believe that a picture was taken of a product that doesn't exist, then a photorealistic illustration may be a better choice.

Faking realism with Photoshop

Faking realism with Photoshop involves taking some key concepts into consideration, such as perspective, lighting, shading, and reflections, which will be discussed further later in this chapter. My goal here is to show you the difference between this concept and the concept of photorealism. For example, this image was created in Photoshop and conveys several aspects of realism. It isn't photorealistic, but you do get the idea that basic concepts such as perspective and depth were used heavily to make this scene look somewhat realistic.

Another example is this picture of my kids and an Apple Powerbook.

With a few Free Transform commands in Photoshop, this image is created.

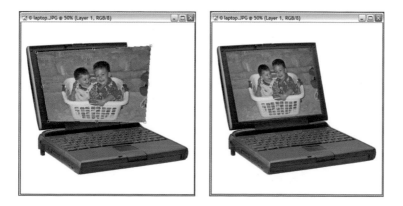

Again, the purpose here, and with this category of realism, is not to make people think that you painted this image from scratch in Photoshop. There are many photos of laptops out there or you can usually take one yourself to keep from having to do this task. The idea is to make viewers see the picture on the laptop and forget about the fact that perhaps the photograph really wasn't originally captured that way.

Photorealism: What's the difference?

As defined by Artcyclopedia.com, "photorealism is a movement which began in the late 1960's, in which scenes are painted in a style closely resembling photographs. The subject matter is usually mundane and without particular interest; the true subject of a photo-realist work is the way we unconsciously interpret photographs and paintings in order to create a mental image of the object represented."

The key difference between creating realism in Photoshop and photorealistic artwork hinges on the word "photo" in photorealistic. Simply put, photorealistic works attempt to re-create reality down to every excruciating detail—almost to fool the viewer into thinking a photo has been taken of the scene. In fact, the ultimate compliment to a photorealistic illustrator is when someone asks the question, "Are you sure that's not a photograph?" However, this type of illustration can be expensive. It requires many hours and a keen eye to produce illustrations that can elicit this type of reaction.

The leading members of the Photorealist movement, using traditional media such as pen, pencil, and paint, are Richard Estes and Chuck Close. Estes specializes in street scenes with elaborate reflections in window glass.

Close does enormous portraits of neutral faces. Other photorealists typically specialize in a particular subject matter: trucks, horses, diners, etc.

Today, many computer graphic designers and illustrators have adopted this style as well. However, the way in which the artwork is created has changed significantly. Photoshop has become one of the primary tools of choice when creating photorealistic artwork.

This program, coupled with a computer and all of the accompanying tools, allows artists to re-create reality on a computer screen.

Some notable artists today are Bert Monroy, Colin Smith, Felix Nelson, and Robert Dennis. Bert Monroy is one of the pioneers of digital art. His fine-art, photorealistic works are considered among the best in the world.

1

Monroy uses a combination of custom brushes, Channels, Paths, and the Pen tool, among others, to create his illustrations in Photoshop.

Colin Smith (www.photoshopcafe.com) is another digital illustrator making waves in the industry today. He has caused quite a stir in the design community with his stunning, pho-torealistic illustrations. These illustrations are composed 100% from within Photoshop and he uses no scans, photos, or 3D applications to help.

Smith's camera is perhaps his most popular photorealistic illustration and it won him a Photoshop Guru award at the 2001 PhotoshopWorld convention. It has also been used by many instructors and speakers to demonstrate the power within Photoshop.

One of his more recent photorealistic images, an Ibanez electric guitar, won a Guru award in 2002 and is featured in *New Masters of Photoshop: Volume 2* from friends of ED.

Look at the detail Smith managed to convey within this illustration.

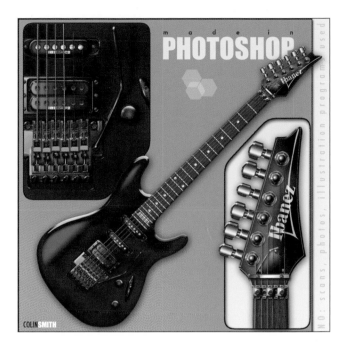

Upon closer examination, you can see that the illustration only gets better. Even the strings look real. Chrome is always a good candidate for a Photoshop effect. As you can see, Smith has this technique mastered.

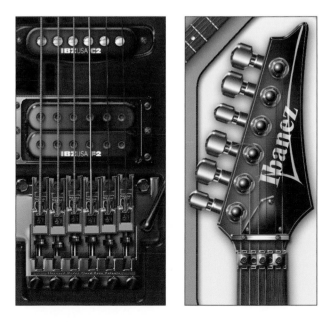

Finally, look at a sample of the work of Robert Dennis. This image is titled "Reflections".

Dennis used a combination of techniques in Photoshop and Illustrator to create this incredibly realistic illustration. His work paid off, as this image took first place in the Illustration category at PhotoshopWorld 2004 in San Francisco. You can read more about Dennis and his techniques in the interview at the end of this chapter.

Tools of the trade

It's time to go over some key tools of the trade. However, this section doesn't only apply to realistic artwork, but to many of the techniques and styles examined throughout this book. In fact, you'll find that the theory and concepts covered in individual chapters will often apply to other chapters as well.

Color modes

There are roughly eight color modes in Photoshop with which to work. However, for the most part, you only need to concern yourself with two:

- RGB (Red, Green, Blue)
- CMYK (Cyan, Magenta, Yellow, Black)

The discussion of color, and in which color mode to work, can often take on the tones of a religious or political debate. I'll spare you that controversy and convey a brief understanding of why you should work in the various color modes and when it's appropriate to switch between the two most popular ones.

First, how do you choose a color mode in which to work? Well, before you can create a new canvas in Photoshop, you must choose File ➤ New or *CTRL/⌘+N*. Within the New dialog box is a drop-down menu called Color Mode where you can choose between five different color modes: Bitmap, Grayscale, RGB Color, CMYK Color, and Lab Color. To switch color modes in an existing Photoshop document, choose Image ➤ Mode.

Next, concerning the definitions of the various color modes, there are plenty of resources that go into detail about RGB and CMYK color modes. For the purposes of this book, the RGB color space is what's displayed on your computer screen and CMYK is used in print work. However, if you'd like a good description of the color modes in Photoshop, the Photoshop Help file contains a fine one. See Working with Color or search color modes in the Help file as a starting point.

Most of the time, I tend to use the RGB color mode for several reasons:

- Nearly 100% of my work starts on the computer screen. Monitors use the RGB color mode to display pixels onscreen. Therefore, working in this mode means my onscreen colors will more accurately match what the computer screen is displaying.

- Much of my work's final destination is a computer monitor. If most of your work is bound for computer monitors, then it makes sense to use the color space most native to those monitors—in this case, RGB.

- Photoshop warns you when a color is out of gamut and won't convert properly or reliably from RGB to its CMYK equivalent.

Not only does Photoshop display an exclamation point when a color is out of gamut, but it also displays a small square color swatch with the nearest in-gamut color. The Info palette also contains a notification when a color is out of gamut. Note the appearance of exclamation points after the numerical values next to the C, M, Y, and K fields.

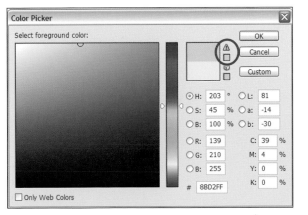

> A **gamut** is the range of color encompassed by a color space. Therefore, **out of gamut** means that the chosen color isn't in the color space in use. For example, as in the previous screens, when a color is picked that isn't inside the RGB color space, Photoshop presents an out-of-gamut warning. This indicates that the chosen color is not included in the RGB color space.

The most popular alternative to working in the RGB color mode is CMYK. CMYK more closely matches color used in print, which is why many choose to work in this color space from the start of an image. This is a perfectly logical choice, as many designers need total control of their final printed output and they feel that starting out in the CMYK color mode gives them additional control. Working in CMYK produces slightly larger source files, but with today's high capacity storage devices and low prices, this is no longer a reason to avoid this color mode.

The next logical question is what color mode should you use? This choice is entirely up to you. With a growing number of designers primarily creating works for the Web, RGB seems like a good choice. RGB is the primary color space used throughout this book as well. If used correctly, you can produce work that looks good and is consistent in color for multiple outputs.

Pen tool

The Pen tool and paths are essential to any realistic or photorealistic illustration. I urge you to read through this section no matter what type of digital artwork you intend to produce; I can't stress the importance of paths and the Pen tool enough. I truly feel that once you get a good handle on using them, you can take your Photoshop skills, abilities, and artwork to an entirely different level.

A primary reason for gaining a solid understanding of these features is that there really is no other way to draw accurately in Photoshop. You could use the Marquee tools, but unless you're drawing a rectangle or an ellipse you won't be able to draw smoothly. Take a look at these three illustrations of a heart-shaped selection created with the Lasso tool for an example of what I mean.

You can see just by looking at the outlines that it isn't easy to control the Lasso tool. The resulting shape has jagged edges, and it gets even worse when filled with a color. Sure, there are ways you can smooth the edges out a little, but these methods aren't controlled and would leave you guessing as to the quality and shape of the final object.

Now, if I use the Pen tool for this task, I can draw the same shape with smooth edges.

If this isn't a good reason for you to use the Pen tool, then let me try to convince you with a few images of toolbars in other digital design and illustration-related programs, such as Illustrator, InDesign, and Flash MX 2004. The point is that the Pen tool (or some form of it) is found within many graphic design, illustration, and animation programs. If the tool palettes from FreeHand MX and CorelDRAW were included, they would also contain a Pen tool. However, unless you've used vector-based drawing programs in the past, such as Illustrator (Photoshop's slightly less popular, but equally powerful sibling), you may have avoided the Pen tool until now. As you can see, it's the universal method of drawing on the computer and essential to understand.

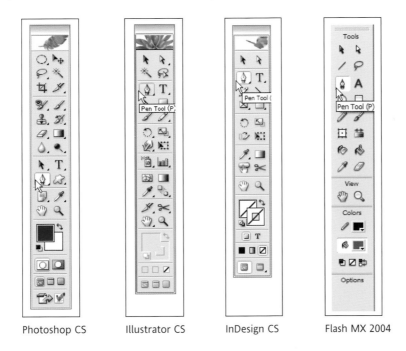

Photoshop CS   Illustrator CS   InDesign CS   Flash MX 2004

If the Pen tool is so amazing, then why it is so misunderstood and shunned? I'll try and answer this with a story. While attending a recent PhotoshopWorld event in San Francisco, I watched an instructor ask how many people use the Pen tool; only about half the people in the room raised their hand. He then explained that although the Pen tool is the most accurate way of drawing in Photoshop, it virtually defies the way we think about drawing.

Many people open up Photoshop and begin by creating selections and shapes with the Marquee tools or painting with the various brush tools. Well, how do you make selections and shapes in Photoshop? You click and drag. When you're done dragging, you have a selection or shape. The same holds true for painting. You select a brush, and then you click and drag. In the end, you have a brush stroke.

However, it's totally different with the Pen tool. If you click and drag with the Pen tool, you produce an **anchor point** with a **handle**.

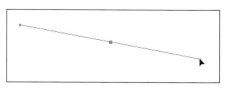

Wow! An anchor point with a handle! Great, huh? I know, not really. But if this is your first experience with the Pen tool, what are you likely to do? Switch to the next tool and work with what you know. Hence, the vicious cycle begins and the Pen tool gets all the bad press. So, if you're one of those people who wouldn't have raised their hand at the conference, follow along and learn how to come to grips with the Pen tool.

Drawing paths

Paths are what you create when you use the Pen tool. The Photoshop CS Help file says, "A path consists of one or more straight or curved line segments." Placing two anchor

points on the canvas using the Pen tool creates a line segment. Once you have those two anchor points, you have a path. Most of the time, you'll create more complicated paths, but this is a simple example.

OK, that was really straightforward, wasn't it? For those of you not familiar with paths or the Pen tool in Photoshop, follow along over the next few paragraphs for a quick lesson.

First, you can find the Pen tool halfway down the toolbox. For those new to Photoshop, Adobe tends to group related tools together in the toolbox, using small horizontal separators to set them apart. For example, the highlighted group here is all path-related tools.

The Pen tool is selected in this illustration. Just above it is the Path Selection tool, as well as the Direct Selection tool located in the flyout menu. These tools are used to modify and select paths after they're created.

The Type tools are to the right of the Path Selection tool. Text created in Photoshop is actually a vector- or path-based object, hence its placement in this area of the toolbox.

Finally, below the Type tools are the Shape tools. This flyout menu is comprised of the Rectangle, Rounded Rectangle, Ellipse, Polygon, Line, and Custom Shape tools. These all create path-based objects, which is why they're placed in this category of the toolbox.

The next area of interest is when you click the Pen tool or one of the shape tools. Notice the tool options bar that appears at the top of your window just beneath the menu bar. It contains three small icons.

Only the first two icons apply to the Pen tool. The first instructs Photoshop to create a shape layer. A **shape layer** is basically a layer with a mask in the shape of whatever path you draw. Photoshop will fill the entire layer with the foreground color, but only the area within the mask is displayed in color.

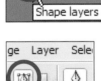

The second icon creates **paths**.

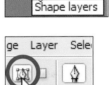

This process alone does nothing but create the actual path. A path really isn't art until you stroke or fill it. Go ahead and try using the Custom Shape tool. With the Paths button selected in the tool options bar, drag out a shape on the canvas. I used the Animals custom shape set included with Photoshop CS to create the fish path, which you can load from the flyout options in the Shape drop-down menu in the tool options bar.

Stroking paths

If you only want to put a stroke around a path, first create a new layer on which it can be painted. Next, select the Brush tool (*B*), open the Brushes palette (press *F5*), and change your settings to those in this illustration. Here we are defining a brush with which to stroke the path.

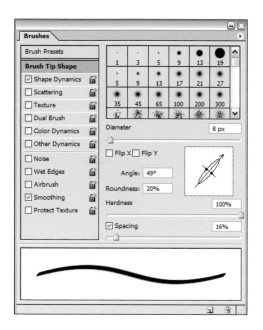

Be sure that your new layer is active by selecting it in the Layers palette (a small paintbrush icon next to the layer indicates that the layer is active and ready for painting). Then, switch over to the Paths palette (Window ➤ Paths) and click the Stroke path with brush button at the bottom of the palette. This will stroke the path with the current foreground color.

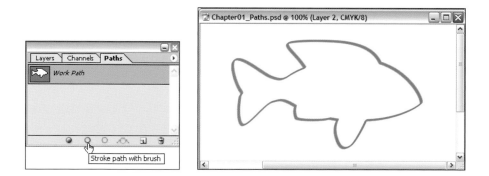

If you don't get the desired effect, the Brush tool may have been inadvertently deselected. This stroke method relies on having the tools and/or settings currently selected with which you'd like to stroke the path.

Filling paths

You can also fill the path, which is actually easier than stroking it. Create a new layer to hold the filled shape. Switch over to the Paths palette and click the Fill path with foreground color button at the bottom of the Paths palette.

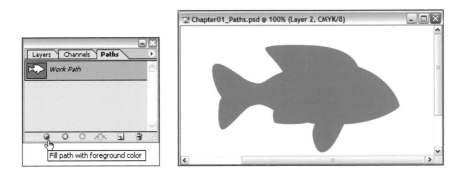

Simple path exercise with the Pen tool

Now that the basics of paths are covered, the next steps show you how to begin using the Pen tool.

1. Create a new canvas (File ➤ New or *CTRL*/⌘+*N*). Choose the 640 x 480 canvas preset size from the Preset drop-down menu. I use this setting often to create quick and consistent test files in which to practice a technique.

2. Select the Pen tool and choose the Paths option in the tool options bar.

3. Click once on the canvas to create the first anchor point.

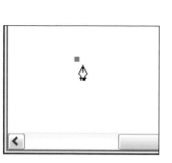

4. Click where you would like to place the second point, but don't yet release the mouse button. If you do, you'll create a straight-line segment. Since you're going to draw a curved object, keep the mouse button depressed, as this allows you to manipulate the anchor point handles in the next step.

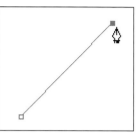

5. Drag the cursor to the right while holding the *SHIFT* key down and let go when the point on the direction line appears vertically above the first anchor point you made.

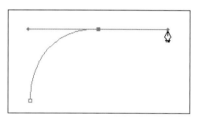

The SHIFT key constrains the angle in which you can drag to 45-degree increments.

6. Next, click once where you would like to place the third point. In this example, I placed it horizontally across from the original point to form a semicircle.

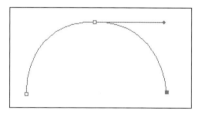

7. Click once again to place a fourth point and drag it across just as you did in step 5.

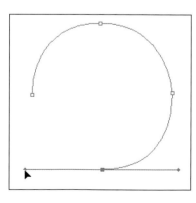

8. Finally, click the original point to close the path. Note the small circle that appears over your cursor to inform you that the path is closed.

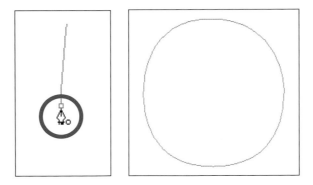

Great, you drew a path! Simple, right? I know, you're thinking to yourself that this is only a circle—and probably not even a symmetrical one at that—but keep following along and let's try a few more advanced tricks with the Pen tool.

Advanced paths with the Pen tool

1. Open `Chapter_01_PathOutline_Start.psd` from the download files for Chapter 1. Notice that this file contains two layers: a BACKGROUND layer and an OUTLINE layer. The OUTLINE layer contains the outline of a dolphin that you'll use as a guide for this exercise.

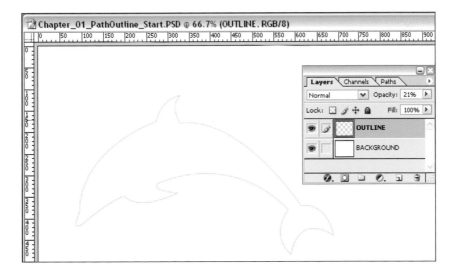

2. Select the Pen tool and click once on the canvas to create the first point. Then click a second time and drag to the right.

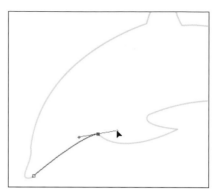

3. Hold down the *ALT/OPTION* key and click the second anchor point to turn it into a corner point. Notice how the cursor changes to let you know that the Convert Point tool is now active.

4. Click again at the edge of the fin and drag up and to the right.

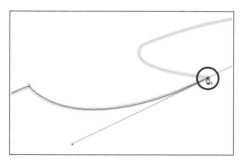

5. Once again, press the *ALT/OPTION* key and click that anchor point to convert it to a corner point.

6. Next, let's try something a little different. Click the point at which the fin meets the body. This is about halfway around the slight curve shown in the outline. However, before letting go of the mouse button, first set up the curve for the fin, and then hold down the *ALT/OPTION* key and drag the handle to the right, so it aligns with the outline of the body. This is another way to add a corner point.

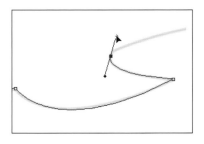 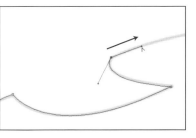

7. Click at the tail fin and drag down and to the right.

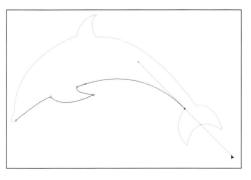

8. Turn this anchor point into a corner point by pressing the *ALT/OPTION* key and clicking in it.

9. Click the edge of the tail fin and drag down and to the right. Without letting go of the mouse button, hold the *ALT/OPTION* key and drag the handle up and to the right to produce another corner point.

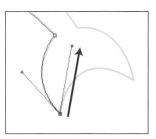

19

10. Click the other edge of the tail fin to place another anchor point. Notice how the curve already closely matches the curve needed for the tail fin. This is because of the way we dragged the handle in the previous step.

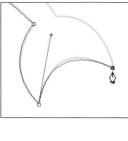

11. Click where the tail fin meets the body and drag down and to the left. Release the mouse button and *ALT/OPTION* click this point to convert it to a corner point.

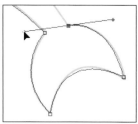

12. Click and drag to the left to produce the curvature along the body meeting up with the top fin. Convert this point to a corner point as well.

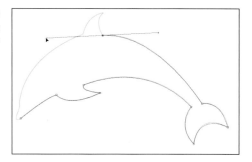

13. Click at the top of the fin and drag up and to the left. Use the same technique as in step 6 to convert this anchor point to a corner point and drag the handle down and to the left. Notice how the initial direction of the handle you just dragged matches the slope of the curve it's about to produce.

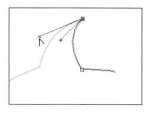

14. Click once where the fin meets the body to place another anchor point.

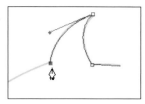

15. Click and drag down just before the dolphin's nose area. Hold the *ALT/OPTION* key down and drag the handle back up toward the nose to begin the curved segment you'll need to finish in order to produce the rounded front of the dolphin.

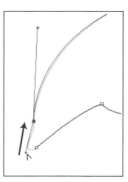

16. Finally, click the first anchor point you made to close off the path and drag to the right slightly to complete the rounded nose.

Hopefully, even if you're new to the Pen tool, you had no problems following the previous steps. You'll finish this exercise off by adding some color.

17. If you're following along using the download file, hide the OUTLINE layer and create a new layer named DOLPHIN.

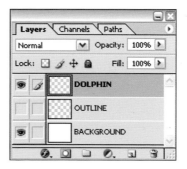

18. Make sure this new layer is selected and switch over to the Paths palette. Click the Load path as selection button at the bottom of the Paths palette to turn the original path into a selection (note that the original path will remain intact).

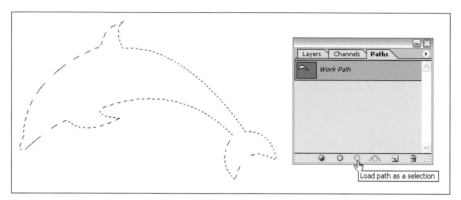

19. Now go back to the Layers palette. Set your foreground color to R:136 G:189 B:236 and your background color to R:13 G:74 B:224. Select the Gradient tool and, using the Foreground to Background gradient, drag a linear gradient across the selection.

I realize drawing with the Pen tool can be a difficult technique to master. Although it's consistently referred to as "drawing", it's far from the traditional association most people have with that term. However, mastery of this process is essential for any graphic designer or digital illustrator who wishes to take their skills to a professional level. One thing that helped me as I was learning to use the Pen tool was to trace one moderately complex object each day for about two weeks. Your hand, a Nintendo Game Boy, a shoe, a car— these are all great objects with which to start. At the end of those two weeks, I guarantee that you'll no longer fear using the Pen tool.

Concepts of realism

In everyday life, our eyes are constantly scanning the world and the objects within it, whether you realize it. Through this constant process, our minds build up what's known as **experience data**. There's no mythical definition or breakthrough revelation to what experience data is. Basically, it's data about our experiences and much of it deals with how we see objects and scenery. Our minds begin to form a mental understanding of what we have seen. However, this mental image can never correspond to what was actually experienced. This is because we have learned to take only key aspects of an experience away with us. Things such as form, color, place, position, or size may all be some of those qualities that we remember. But there's much more—perspective, lighting, shadows, and reflections are some of the qualities that we may not store in our minds about an experience.

For example, if you see a red sports car, you may remember some key characteristics of that car: its size, color, or perhaps even its make and model.

However, what you may not remember is the perspective in which you saw the car, any shadows or highlights surrounding the car, and any reflections off of the surface of the paint. So, if you commissioned me as an artist and said that you saw a red Porsche and must have a realistic painting of it, what would you think if I showed you this as the end result?

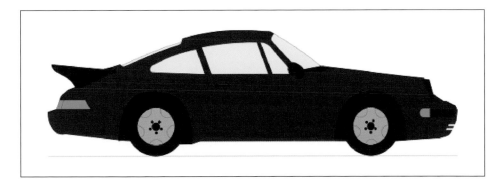

You'd say I was crazy and would probably refuse to pay me. At that point, I may become agitated and an all-out brawl may ensue. OK, maybe this is an extreme example, but I hope my point is clear—how we express what we see may not actually represent how we have really seen it. It's those inexpressible qualities of realism that make a design or illustration come to life. These are the qualities of which you must be aware when working in Photoshop if you wish to incorporate realism into your work.

With this said, let's examine some key concepts in realism and how they relate to our work in Photoshop.

Linear perspective

Linear perspective is a method for creating the illusion of space and distance on a flat surface. It's a system based on a scientific study from the 17th century intended to help translate 3D space into two dimensions. Since all of the objects that we view in the world are in some way three dimensional, it's important that we learn how to translate them onto a two-dimensional canvas in order to re-create reality. Linear perspective helps us do this though some basic elements.

Horizon line

Determining the **horizon line** is one of the key steps in using linear perspective. The horizon line is always at eye level. If you were standing on a beach and looking out at the ocean, you would notice that the water meets the sky at your eye level. This never changes. You can jump up in the air and they will still meet at your eye level at that exact moment. You can lie down on the sand and, although you may look silly, the water and sky will still meet at your eye level. If you were ten stories high in a building looking at the same ocean and sky, they would still meet at your eye level. I'm sure you get the point here.

Vertical lines

Vertical lines stay vertical. Various horizontal lines used to aid in determining linear perspective may not be perfectly horizontal as you begin to apply the rules of linear perspective to them. However, vertical lines will *always* remain vertical.

Image by www.PhotoSpin.com. © All rights reserved.

Vanishing point

The **vanishing point** is the point at which all the lines that are parallel to the viewer recede or converge. A good way to think of this is to imagine that you're standing in the middle of a long straight highway. The edges of the highway would appear to move at an upward angle until they meet the horizon or the vanishing point.

As you can see from these example perspective images, red lines are on top of the original artwork to help translate the effects of perspective for you. You can create these lines in Photoshop with the Pen or Line tools and just as easily use them as guides in your artwork to maintain proper perspective. If you put these on a separate layer, these perspective lines can really help the speed and accuracy of your work. They can be hidden easily at a later point in the project.

Image by www.PhotoSpin.com.
© All rights reserved.

Atmospheric perspective

Atmospheric perspective (also known as atmospheric volume) is the phenomenon that causes objects to blend with the environment as their distance increases. Mountain ranges are a perfect example. Up close, mountains are usually brighter and more saturated with color, yet mountains in the distance are less saturated with color and appear lighter, blurry, and hazier.

Images by www.PhotoSpin.com. © All rights reserved.

Atmospheric perspective occurs as a result of several factors, with dust and moisture particles in the air as the most prevalent reason. In Photoshop, it's important to re-create this phenomenon when trying to add realism to your designs because it helps them make the jump from flat designs to realistic 3D ones. It's the observation of blurry and clear objects that allows us to judge their distance. We're confident that objects that are less saturated with color and blurry are farther away in the distance. Conversely, we also know that clear, crisp objects are close to us. Therefore, making this association and using it in Photoshop is very important.

Shadows

Light directed on an object causes shadows to be cast on the surface opposite the side of the light source. Viewing these shadows provides information regarding the object's position in space and is an integral part of the way we perceive depth.

Here is the well-known aqua button with a Drop Shadow layer style applied to it in Photoshop. Both buttons are casting shadows, but each shadow is noticeably different for each button.

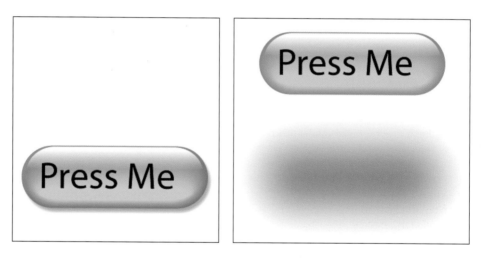

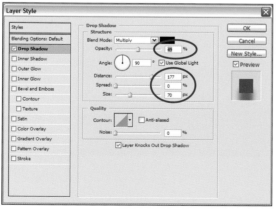

The light source is the same (directly above the button), so why does one button look as if it's just over the surface while the other looks suspended in mid-air?

This is mainly due to the placement of the shadow. By varying the Distance setting in the Drop Shadow Layer Style dialog box, you can lift the button up off the surface. By decreasing the Opacity and increasing the Size setting, you can make it even more realistic as shadows become more spread out and less defined as the object casting them moves farther away.

Reflection

A **reflection** is a mirror image of an object and occurs when you view an object on or near a glossy or shiny surface, such as glass, water, or polished metal. Reflections are a key component to keep in mind when creating realistic designs and illustrations.

A key characteristic concerning reflections is that they're a product of light. Without a light source on or around a reflective surface, we wouldn't see anything reflected. In some ways, a light source produces a reflection much the same way it would produce a shadow. Thus, a reflection follows some of the same rules as shadows.

For example, the aqua button displays a shadow that becomes less intense as the button is moved farther away from the surface. Reflections follow similar rules. Take a look at this car and its associated reflection.

Image by www.PhotoSpin.com.

The light source is positioned behind the car. Therefore, the front of the car is farther away from the light source. Notice how its reflection, while longer in that area, fades away at the ends farthest from the object causing the reflection.

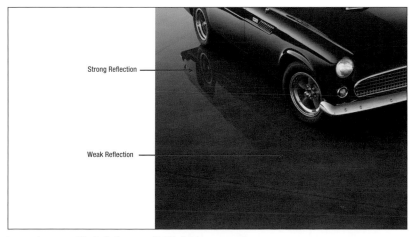

Strong Reflection

Weak Reflection

Image by www.PhotoSpin.com.

Another key component of reflections is that they depend largely on the angle at which the viewer sees them. Water is a perfect example, as shown in this photograph. The viewing angle is quite shallow. The photographer was almost at the same level as the water. As such, notice how the water is almost 100% reflective and you can't really see anything underneath it.

Now examine this photograph. The angle is steeper and the photograph was taken from a higher point. Notice how you can see through the water slightly. For example, if you look at a pool from up above, say from a hotel balcony, you can see straight to the bottom. If you lie on the ground next to the pool, it's most likely you won't see under the water at all.

Refraction

Refraction is very similar to reflection. It deals with how light interacts with transparent objects. Depending on the transparency of the object, light is visible through it at various levels. In addition, this light is refracted and causes visible distortions throughout the transparent object. A perfect example of this phenomenon is a fish bowl.

Notice how the inner front area of the fish bowl, the area closest to you, is mostly clear and the transparency of the glass and water is fairly pure. However, if you view the outside edges of the fish bowl, you'll see that it becomes darker and less transparent. This is because the angle at which you're viewing that surface becomes steeper. The area toward the front of the bowl is flatter from your perspective and therefore won't refract light as much as the side areas with a greater angle.

Your next question may be: "How can these phenomena be controlled in Photoshop?" The answer is a few common techniques using gradients and masks. See the fire text tutorial in Chapter 2 and the iPod exercise in Chapter 4 for examples on creating faded reflections with masks. Also, see the fish bowl exercise in Chapter 3 for an example using gradients to add refraction to a rounded transparent object.

Depth

In many ways, depth can be encompassed or explained by nearly each of the concepts I just described, yet it has so many forms that it makes sense to go into a little more detail. This illustration shows a set of cubes tumbling and taking on some key properties relating to depth as they get farther away from the viewer.

This illustration can be applied to realism in several ways:

- **Size of objects.** Smaller objects seem farther away from the viewer.
- **Overlapping or superimposing.** Partially covering one object with another gives the appearance of depth. In Photoshop, placing each cube on its own layer allows you to place objects in front or in back of each other.

- **Texture.** Texture density increases as an object gets farther away. This was accomplished by scaling down the cubes earlier in Chapter 1.

- **Focus.** Objects lose detail as they recede into space. Decreasing the opacity and/or adjusting the Hue/Saturation settings (*CTRL/⌘+U*) helps accomplish this effect. One key point to remember is to always start with a crisp version of your object to place close to the viewer. You can always take away detail, color saturation, and brightness for receding objects later, but it's difficult to add it to an object that didn't originally start out crisp.

- **Brightness.** Objects tend to be brighter and more saturated with color when they're closer to the viewer. Brightness is similar to focus. Once again, decreasing the opacity and/or adjusting the Hue/Saturation settings (*CTRL/⌘+U*) helps accomplish this effect.

- **Shade and shadow.** Darker shadows seem closer especially when overlapping other shadows. Reducing the opacity of shadows and blurring them slightly as they recede will help accomplish this task.

- **Upward angular location.** This creates depth if juxtaposed to ground and skylines, for example, tall buildings. Use the Move and Free Transform tools to reposition objects as they recede into the vanishing point.

- **Color.** Color intensity is much greater closer to the viewer and tends toward medium-gray as it recedes. Once again, start with a crisp object and reduce its detail as it recedes from the viewer.

Summary

In wrapping up Chapter 1, it's likely your head is swimming with a good deal of both Photoshop and non-Photoshop information. Up until this point, you may have survived using Photoshop without any formal art training or, if you have had some form of training, you may not have known how to translate those concepts into the digital world and Photoshop.

In fact, as computers have become more affordable and popular, many digital artists have little traditional or formal training in art. Of course, this is fine and bound to happen. Some of the best digital artists out there today have never taken a class in art, but knowing the concepts of reality and how they relate to Photoshop are a vital part of becoming a professional designer. It will not only help you with your everyday work in Photoshop, but it will help you take your use of this incredible piece of software to the next level.

This book is named *Extreme Photoshop* for a reason. After reading it, you should be left with the knowledge and real-life artwork to help you take Photoshop to the extremes and go beyond your current use of the program. This first chapter and the chapters to come are the stepping stones to help you achieve this goal.

Expert Interview

Name: Robert F. Dennis

Residence: Burbank, CA

Occupation: Retoucher and Graphic Artist

Primary Software Used: Photoshop, Illustrator, and Dreamweaver

Hardware/OS: Dennis uses both platforms, but tends to work mainly in the PC environment. A Wacom tablet is always at hand. He never considers retouching without it.

Robert Dennis is a computer graphics artist concentrating in Photoshop retouching, manipulation, and compositing. He graduated from the Pennsylvania State University in 1986 with a BFA degree in Theatre Design and Production. After spending several years working for professional Regional theatre and opera companies around the country, he moved to Los Angeles to work in film and television.

After a few years working freelance and also with a prop house, he decided to move into computer graphics. Following a few classes in digital imaging and desktop publishing, Dennis began working for a photography studio doing layouts and retouching. Additional classes in graphic and Web design, motion graphics, traditional photography, and darkroom techniques contributed to his specialties in retouching, compositing, and photo restoration.

When working in digital imaging, Dennis brings years of traditional art techniques and disciplines with him. During his years of theatrical and film work, he was called upon to do a variety of tasks including: carpentry, welding, sculpting, mold-making, sewing, and set decorating. Also, his experience in lighting design has played an integral part in his photography and Photoshop work. Understanding the principles of light and color are vital in the production of realistic rendering of digital images, whether it be on film or in a digital environment. Additionally, knowledge in painting and sculpture help bring life and dimensionality into an otherwise flat, 2D situation.

Dennis primarily uses Photoshop for his work at a portrait studio. He spends much of his time retouching portraits and specialty work. The specialty work ranges from making vignettes and photo edges, to spot work due to dirty CCDs from the digital cameras, to colorizing black and whites, and making sepia conversations. Also, he makes panorama composites of large groups consisting of anywhere from 30 to 1,000 people.

Recently, Dennis won the Photoshop Guru award at the world famous PhotoshopWorld seminar in San Francisco. His illustration, "Reflections from the Ground Up", took first place in the Illustration category. While the creation of the illustration was a combination of work done in Photoshop and Illustrator, Dennis found Photoshop the essential place to start. "I had to do a few preliminary breakdowns, or pre-visualizations, in Photoshop," explained Dennis. "This was done to show where major areas of color lay. I wanted to see how each color blended into its neighbor, and to find the major and minor areas of color."

This approach also served another purpose in giving him a working color palette. Using the Eyedropper tool, he built a new Color Swatch palette that would travel with the file.

First, Dennis started by using the Cutout filter (Filter ➤ Artistic ➤ Cutout) on the source image. "It gave me the breakdown of colors and shapes I was seeking," said Dennis.

"Using the appropriate maximum and minimal settings gave the best fidelity you can hope for in this approach." Dennis also notes that it made a less intimidating roadmap for the work left in this detailed photorealistic illustration.

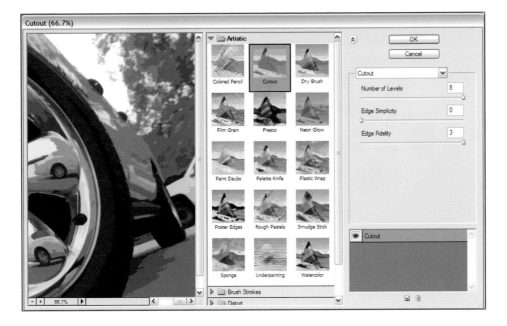

His next step was to pump up the midtones.

This process was done using a Curves adjustment. By taking the mid-level point and pulling it up several points he was able to show the necessary detail in the shadow areas.

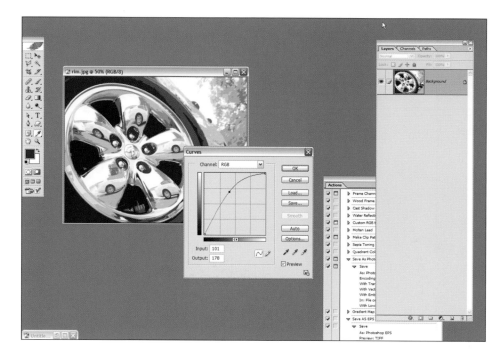

These two breakdowns and the source image were all he needed to create the photorealistic image. Once in Illustrator, a new document was created using the same dimensions as the source image. Three template layers were created, which had the original source photo, the cutout version, and the high-mid versions inserted. As he attacked each area of the image, new layers were created and named to tell them apart. In the end, there were 19 layers, including the three source images and countless sub-layers.

As you may guess by its title, Chapter 2 is about using brushes to help create or enhance reality. The key to unlocking your potential and mastering many realistic techniques lies in Photoshop's brush engine. It gives you an entirely new way to think about brushes and presents unparalleled control over the angle, size, shape, and direction of your brushes. This is a broad topic and there are more techniques than could possibly be covered. However, this chapter will present several key techniques that will get you thinking about how brushes within Photoshop can be used for realism purposes. In addition, I'll touch on nearly all of the advanced capabilities available to you when using brushes. When you're finished with Chapter 2, you'll have two highly realistic designs and a strong understanding about how mastering brushes is essential for any professional designer to push their skills to the extreme.

Looking at history

First, let's go over a little bit of history relating to brushes and Photoshop. Before Photoshop 7, the Brushes palette was similar to the basic palette view you get when you select a brush tool and access the Brushes palette through the tool options bar. While there was a degree of control over your brush shape, the brush engine in no way came close to offering what Photoshop 7 and CS do. By accessing the expanded view (click Window ➤ Brushes or press *F5*), you can see the Brushes and Expanded Brushes palettes in all their glory.

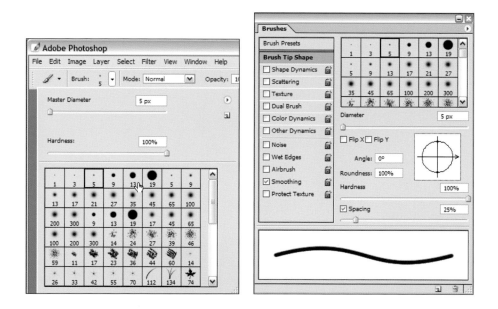

As you can see, the Brushes palette is similar to the Layer Style dialog box first mentioned in the Shadows section of Chapter 1. Much like styles, you can check the boxes in the left column of the Brushes palette check boxes to apply specific Brush attributes or click the name in the left column to apply the option and view its associated settings in the right area of the palette.

Brushes and the toolbox

If you recall from the Pen and Path topic in Chapter 1, Photoshop groups similar tools in the toolbox and separates them with a small horizontal divider. This holds true for the painting tools as well.

Nearly all of these tools are used for painting in Photoshop. The only exception is the Gradient and Paint Bucket tools; it seems Adobe needed a place for them and they fit best near the painting tools. The remaining tools in this section of the toolbox all use a brush in some way and you'll be better equipped to use them by gaining a deeper knowledge of the Brushes palette.

2

Liquify filter

There is one more place that contains a brush: the Liquify filter. Yep, I'm not kidding. A filter has a brush. The Liquify filter is actually a special type of filter. Instead of just clicking the filter and adjusting a few settings to apply it, you must actually use a brush in this filter to accomplish anything. Sure, you can leave the default settings, but the Liquify filter is such a powerful Photoshop tool that you can benefit from a better understanding of brushes and their properties when using it.

Here's a quick view of what you see when you choose Filter ➤ Liquify.

The top-left area of this dialog box includes all of the tools that can be accessed by using the Liquify filter. Although they aren't called brushes, that's essentially what these tools are. This is apparent by selecting these tools at the left and examining the Tool Options area at the right. Note the labels for each setting; they all begin with the word "Brush". The Liquify filter offers power and flexibility matched nowhere else in Photoshop. It could just as easily be called the wood-water-liquid-fire-smoke filter. This is mainly because most of these effects rely on randomization when created in Photoshop. Without the Liquify filter, it would be very difficult to make those effects look so realistic.

The Liquify filter is truly a one-of-a-kind tool and worth adding to your skill set. The best part is that when you learn how to better use brushes in Photoshop, you automatically learn many key areas of this tool. This filter, combined with the expanded Brushes palette, gives you unprecedented options and accuracy for creating realistic designs in Photoshop CS.

Stuck in the rough?

The following exercise will help build a great foundation for using the Brush tool. You can build up a whole range of textures, objects, and effects simply by using a brush. Adobe stepped up this area in version 7 by totally re-creating the brush engine and giving designers more options when creating and using brushes. In Photoshop CS, they have carried this part of the program through and it has become a must have for any professional designer's toolbox.

Before beginning, take a look at the illustration of the golf ball. This section of the book is about realism and this is a great effect to demonstrate this topic. The subject of this exercise is a close-up shot of a golf ball in the rough, a term golfer's use for the long grass on a golf course. Besides using brushes to create reality in this illustration, you'll incorporate a few other concepts mentioned in Chapter 1. For example, **depth of field** is a key element. The focus of this illustration is the golf ball, so the ball and grass immediately surrounding it will be in focus. However, the grass between the hypothetical camera and the ball will be slightly blurred. Also, the grass that's a good distance behind the ball will be blurred too. In addition, the objects further away will be affected by **atmospheric perspective**. This includes the grass as well as any clouds. Finally, the clouds will be affected by depth of field and blurred because they are very far away and our focus is on the golf ball.

1. Create a new RGB canvas. As mentioned earlier, it's good practice to create a canvas larger than you really need. I would normally create this illustration at a high resolution suitable for print—most likely at least 1600 × 1200 pixels in size and 300 dpi. However, all of the PSD files created in this book will be included in the download files from www.friendsofed.com so to keep them at a manageable download size, I'll create a 640 × 480 pixel canvas at 72 dpi resolution.

2. Let's start by placing the golf ball in the scene so there's a reference point. Open Chapter_02_GolfBall.psd.

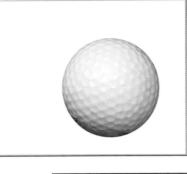

3. Drag the GOLF BALL layer from the Chapter_02_GolfBall.psd file into your current working PSD using the Move tool (press *V*). Click the original golf ball and drag it onto your new canvas. Once there, you can position it as shown in this reference image.

4. Now create a new layer by clicking the Create a new layer button at the bottom of the Layers palette (or press *SHIFT+CTRL/⌘+N*). Name this layer SKY and position it below the GOLF BALL layer.

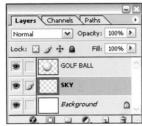

5. Create a new gradient for the sky. Select the Gradient tool in the toolbox, and then click the Gradient picker in the tool options bar to open the Gradient Editor dialog box. Now you can create your own gradient by double-clicking the color stops and choosing a color. Set the left color stop to R:133 G:187 B:255 and the right color stop to R:76 G:134 B:206.

6. Click OK and use the Gradient tool to drag a linear gradient from the bottom to the top of your canvas.

Great. Now the sky and the golf ball are in place. This should give a good reference for creating the other elements in the scene.

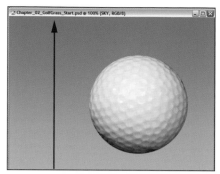

7. Next, create a **custom brush**. Select the Brush tool and open Photoshop's extended Brush palette by choosing Window ➤ Brushes (press *F5*).

8. Click Brush Tip Shape at the top left of the palette to display the following brush options. This view allows you to select a brush and modify its diameter, angle, roundness, and spacing.

9. Start off by selecting the Grass brush. Fortunately, this brush ships with Photoshop 7 and CS, so you don't need to create it.

10. After you've selected the brush, change the Diameter setting to 100 px and set the Spacing to 34%.

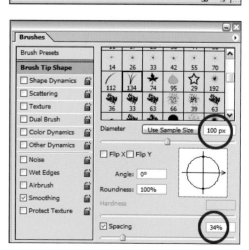

11. Next, select Shape Dynamics in the left side of the palette. Be sure to click the name rather than only checking the check box to select the item. By doing this, you'll not only turn Shape Dynamics on, but also display the settings for this option. Enter the settings shown here. If you've got a stylus pen, feel free to set the Controls setting to Pen Pressure.

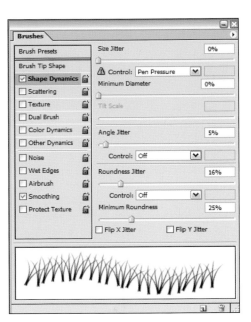

12. Select Scattering and enter these settings.

13. Finally, select Color Dynamics and use the settings in the illustration.

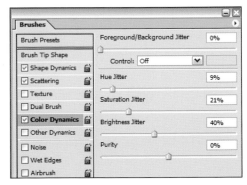

A good habit to get into is to create a **Tool Preset** *from this brush. This saves you the hassle of re-entering these settings every time you want to use this brush. To do this, choose* Window ➤ Tool Presets. *Then click the palette options arrow and select* New Tool Preset. *Give it a name and your brush is now ready use whenever you need it.*

OK, we're done creating the brush. The Brushes palette can be a confusing place if this is the first time you've really used it. Photoshop's help file (press *F1*) is an invaluable resource of which you should take advantage. For a good explanation of the various settings in the Brushes palette, view Contents ➤ Painting ➤ Working with brushes ➤ Specifying brush (shape, scattering, or color) dynamics.

14. Set your foreground color to R:33 G:94 B:32 and your background color to R:37 G:128 B:35. This step is necessary because the Color Dynamics options set in step 13 use the current foreground and background colors.

15. Create a new layer named FRONT GRASS above the GOLF BALL layer. This layer holds the slightly blurred grass that will be in front of the golf ball.

16. With the Brush tool selected, brush across the canvas to create some grass.

17. Now create a new layer below FRONT GRASS, but above GOLF BALL named FRONT BALL. This layer holds the in-focus grass that will be directly in front of the ball.

18. With the Brush tool selected, open the Brushes palette once again and change the Diameter setting of the modified grass brush to 137 px. Remember to first select Brush Tip Shape in the palette to locate this setting.

19. Drag the custom brush across the center of the scene in front of the golf ball. However, don't apply as much grass as you did on the FRONT GRASS layer. A couple of quick brush strokes should be fine.

20. Create a new layer named BEHIND BALL directly below the GOLF BALL layer. This layer holds the in-focus grass that will be behind the golf ball.

21. Brush across the entire scene with the custom brush. This time, the grass should be slightly denser than it was for the FRONT BALL layer, but not as dense as on the FRONT GRASS layer. I hid the other grass layers so you can see how the brush is applied.

22. Open the Brushes palette once again (press *F5*) and click Brush Tip Shape. Change the Diameter setting to 50 px.

> *If your Brushes palette is grayed out, you probably don't have the Brush tool selected. This tool needs to be selected in order to make changes in the Brushes palette.*

23. Create a new layer below BEHIND BALL but above SKY and name it MID GRASS. This grass will be the transition between the grass in front of the scene and the grass toward the background. You'll barely see it when you're done, but it's small enhancements like these that contribute to the overall realism of an illustration.

24. With the Brush tool selected, brush across the canvas a few times to create the grass you see in this reference image. Note that I hid the other grass layers again so you can see the ideal end result.

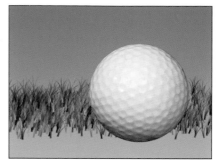

25. Create another layer directly below MID GRASS named DISTANT GRASS.

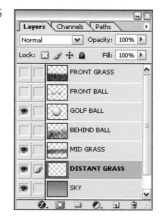

26. Open the Brushes palette again and change the Diameter setting to 25 px.

27. Apply this brush to the canvas liberally. To make the top of the grass horizontal, use the *Shift* key while dragging the brush across the canvas a few times. Once again, I hid the other grass layers so you can clearly see where to brush.

All of the layers are now in place. Next, you'll use some techniques to make this scene even more realistic. At the beginning of this exercise, I mentioned that depth of field was an important concept for this illustration. The ball and the grass immediately surrounding it (the FRONT BALL and BEHIND BALL layers) will be in focus and won't require any modifications. However, the grass in front of the scene needs to be blurred a little to take depth of field into account. The same principle holds true for the grass in the distance.

28. Make the FRONT GRASS layer active. Choose Filter ➤ Blur ➤ Gaussian Blur, set the Radius setting to 1.5 pixels, and click OK to apply the blur.

29. Make the MID GRASS layer active and choose Filter ➤ Gaussian Blur (press *CTRL/⌘+F*) to reapply the same filter as used in the previous step.

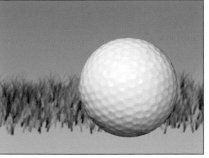

Your scene should now look similar to this illustration.

30. Now make the DISTANT GRASS layer active and apply a Gaussian Blur filter to this layer as well. This time, use a Radius of 2 pixels.

> The keyboard shortcut CTRL/⌘+ALT/OPTION+F will reapply the same filter previously used, but it presents you with the dialog box first, in case you want to make any changes.

Now that you've applied the depth of field effects to the scene, you need to account for **atmospheric perspective**. If you recall from the discussion in Chapter 1, atmospheric perspective is the phenomenon that causes objects to blend with the environment as their distance increases. In the case of our golf ball scene, this means that the grass in the distance will lose color saturation and begin to fade to a blue/gray background. There are two ways you can accomplish this in the illustration. The first is to decrease the opacity of the MID GRASS layer, so it begins to show the DISTANT GRASS layer underneath it. The second is to use the Hue/Saturation adjustment on the DISTANT GRASS layer to desaturate some of the green color.

31. Make the MID GRASS layer active and change the layer opacity to 75%.

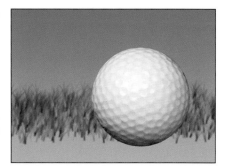

32. Then make the DISTANT GRASS layer active. Choose Image ➤ Adjustments ➤ Hue/Saturation (press CTRL/⌘+U). Reduce the Saturation to –35 and click OK.

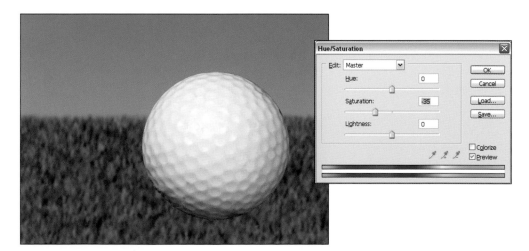

Make all the layers visible. Here's how the final scene should look.

You could always take this a step further and add some clouds. You could add real clouds from a photo or build them using the Brush tool as well. Here are some sample clouds that were created using the Brush tool.

Creating fire

1. Start off by creating a new 800 ✕ 600 pixel canvas with File ➤ New (press *CTRL/⌘+N*).

> *Your intended final output will control the settings that you enter into this* New *dialog box. As I mentioned in Chapter 1, you'll primarily work in RGB color mode for this book. Where size is concerned, I tend to prefer to start out larger than I need and scale down later if necessary. This gives you more flexibility, as it's always easier to scale down than it is to scale up.*

Before we get too far, there's a quick trick I learned which has become a habit of mine. By default, when you create a new file, Photoshop assigns it a Background layer automatically. You cannot change the stacking order, blending mode, or opacity of this layer, which is one of

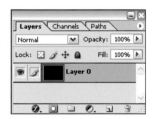

those things that annoyed me time after time over the years. Also, the Background layer is locked by default and you can't unlock it. If I had a dime for how many times I tried to edit that layer only to receive this error message, I'd be a rich man.

You may think you can just select this layer and unlock it, but because the layer is named "Background" you can't. So, the first thing I do when creating a new file in Photoshop is to hold down the *ALT/OPTION* key and double-click the Background layer. This turns it into a real layer named Layer 0 and you can now perform all of the operations on it.

2. Hold *ALT/OPTION* and double-click the Background layer to turn it into Layer 0. Press *D* to set your foreground and background colors to their defaults (black and white, respectively). Then fill this layer with black by pressing *ALT/OPTION+BACKSPACE*.

Select the Type tool (press *T*) and enter some appropriate white text. It's a good idea to start with a small word first because much of the time spent on this technique is dependent on how many letters with which you're working. In this example, I used Times New Roman set at 130 pt.

4. With your type layer active, duplicate it by choosing Layer ➤ New ➤ Layer via Copy (*CTRL/⌘+J*).

2

CTRL/⌘+J is a huge timesaver and is used often throughout this book. If you don't have anything selected, this shortcut will duplicate the entire layer. If you do have something selected, it will make a copy of the selected area on a new layer. It's also good to learn the sister shortcut to this one, which is SHIFT+ CTRL/⌘+J. This shortcut creates a new layer from anything that's selected, but cuts it out of the original layer.

5. Name the topmost type layer ORIGINAL TEXT and drag this layer below Layer 0 in the Layers palette.

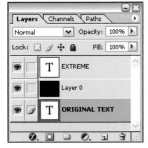

6. Make the EXTREME text layer active and merge it down with Layer 0 by choosing Layer ➤ Merge Down (*CTRL/⌘+E*). Note that this will also rasterize your type layer, so it can no longer be edited. Rename Layer 0 to FIRE BASE.

7. Next, rotate the entire canvas counterclockwise by choosing Image ➤ Rotate Canvas ➤ 90 Degrees CCW.

8. Make the FIRE BASE layer active and choose Filter ➤ Stylize ➤ Wind. Be sure **Wind** is selected as the method and set the Direction setting to From the Right and click OK to apply the filter.

9. Next, press *Ctrl/⌘+F* three more times to reapply the Wind filter again automatically.

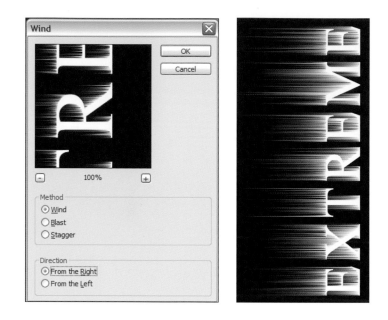

10. Now rotate the canvas back around by choosing Image ➤ Rotate Canvas ➤ 90 degrees CW.

11. Make the FIRE BASE layer active, choose Filter ➤ Blur ➤ Gaussian Blur. Set the Radius to about 4 pixels. However, this setting can change depending on the size of your text and overall image. The larger the text you have, the more you'll need to blur the text. The aim is to make the text look slightly ghostly. It will be blurred, but you should still be able to discern the letters easily.

12. On the same layer, choose Image ➤ Adjustments ➤ Hue/Saturation (*CTRL/⌘+U*). Check Colorize first and then set the Hue to 40 and Saturation to 100. This should give a slight orange-yellow appearance to the text.

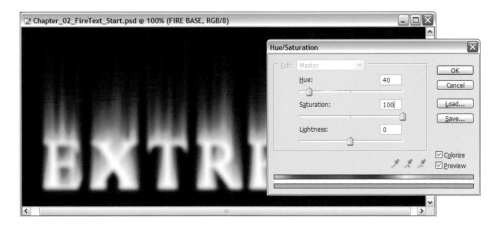

13. Duplicate the FIRE BASE layer by selecting it and pressing *CTRL/⌘+J*.

14. With the duplicate layer active, apply another Hue/Saturation adjustment (*CTRL/⌘+U*). This time don't check Colorize and simply enter –30 for the Hue setting.

15. Change the blending mode of the duplicated layer to Color Dodge.

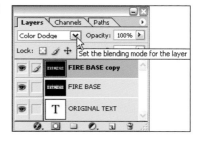

16. Merge the two FIRE BASE layers together by selecting the duplicate layer and pressing *CTRL/⌘+E*.

OK, now for the fun part. You'll use the Liquify filter to create flames. The base is already there (the FIRE BASE layer), as you can start to see the tops of the text begin to take on the appearance of flames. The rest is just a matter of manipulating the top of the text into flamelike shapes. The primary tool is the **Forward Warp tool**. However, once your flames are at a good point, you'll add some finishing touches with the **Turbulence tool**.

17. With the FIRE BASE layer active, choose Filter ➤ Liquify. The following dialog box appears. Choose the Forward Warp tool from the toolbox at the top left of the Liquify dialog box and, in the Tool Options area, set the Brush Size to 45, Brush Density to 90, and Brush Pressure to 40. Also, check the Show Mesh check box in the View Options area of the Liquify dialog box.

18. Now start brushing above each character from the bottom upward. Use curved brush strokes as you do this to simulate the appearance of flames as they rise. Depending on the width of each letter, you may need to use more than one brush stroke above them.

This is one of those circumstances I mentioned in Chapter 1 where a graphic pen tablet can really come in handy. Note the setting in the Liquify dialog box Tool Options area that allows you to control the brush pressure with a stylus pen.

19. Also, don't just distort the streaks at the top of the text, but try to bring up some of the hot areas (yellow to white) as well.

20. Once you feel comfortable with the overall shape of the flames, decrease the Brush Size to 25–30 and the Brush Pressure to 30. Use this brush to fine-tune the flames and add some extra detail.

21. The last step in the Liquify process is to use the Turbulence tool. Select this tool and set the Brush Size to 40 and the Brush Pressure to 30. Move the brush horizontally across the top of the flames to produce a ripple effect and further randomize the flames. Continue this randomization process by moving the brush in the opposite direction across the middle and bottom of the flames. Experimentation is the answer when trying to produce a random and believable effect.

22. Once you're done, click OK to apply the filter. Your flames should look very realistic at this point.

23. Next, duplicate the FIRE BASE layer with *Ctrl*/⌘+*J* and name it GLOW.

24. Set the GLOW layer blending mode to Screen.

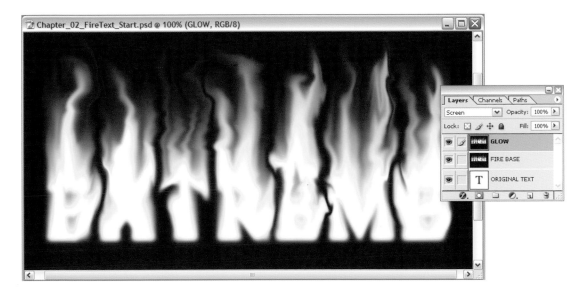

25. Choose Filter ➤ Blur ➤ Gaussian Blur. Enter 13 pixels for the Radius setting. You really want to blur this layer because it will serve as a glow for the fire. However, this setting also depends on how large you made your text in the beginning.

26. Change the opacity of the GLOW layer to 65%.

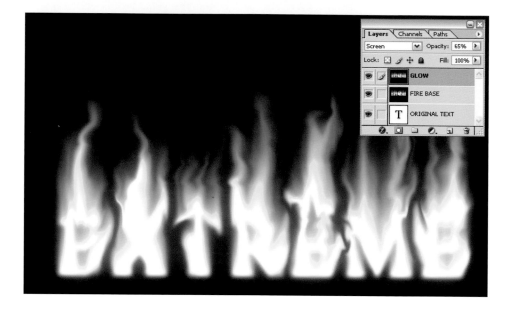

OK, the fire is pretty much done. The last few steps are just some touching up steps that will help enhance the overall effect.

Remember when you renamed the FIRE text layer to ORIGINAL TEXT and moved it below all the other layers? That's because you need a clean copy now. The FIRE BASE text has pretty much been destroyed from all of the blurs, wind, and liquefies that have been applied to it. You may be able to tell what the text says because you know what it said originally, however others may not. This original text layer will serve to enhance the effect because you'll place it on top of the fire. Then you'll simulate real fire by adding a mask that makes the top of the text inherit the flames at the hottest point in the flames. As you move toward the bottom of the text, you'll keep some of the black in there where the flames are not as hot.

27. Drag the ORIGINAL TEXT layer to the top of the Layers palette.

28. Set your foreground color to black by pressing *D*. Fill this ORIGINAL TEXT layer with black by pressing *ALT/OPTION+BACKSPACE*.

29. Double-click the text layer to display the Layer Style dialog box.

30. Reduce the Fill Opacity to 0%, but don't yet click OK.

31. Click the Gradient Overlay layer style. Black should already be your foreground color, so pick the foreground to transparent gradient and change the Scale setting to 115%. Click OK.

This is what your fire text should look like at this point.

32. Finally, all you need is a reflection. Make the FIRE BASE layer active and use the Rectangular Marquee tool (press *M*) to draw a square selection from the top of the flames to the very bottom tip of the text. Now choose Edit ➤ Copy Merged (*SHIFT+CTRL/⌘+C*). This will merge a copy of your current view and selection into one merged image on the Clipboard.

33. Create a new layer named REFLECTION at the top of the Layers palette and make it active.

34. Choose Edit ➤ Paste (*CTRL*/⌘+*V*) to paste the copy into the REFLECTION layer.

35. Choose Edit ➤ Transform ➤ Flip Vertical and drag the copy down until the top of the REFLECTION layer is even with the bottom of the FIRE BASE text.

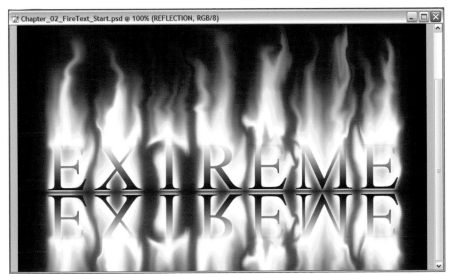

36. Select the REFLECTION layer and add a layer mask by clicking the Add Layer Mask button at the bottom of the Layers palette.

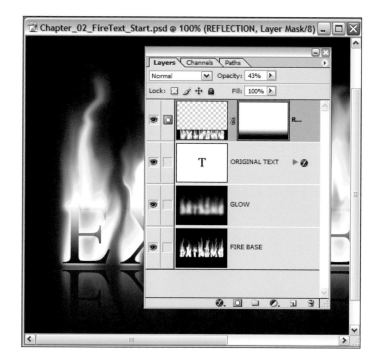

37. Select the layer mask icon in the Layers palette and use the Gradient tool (press *G*) to drag a white to black linear gradient from the top of the reflected text to the bottom. This will fade the reflection as it gets farther away from the base of the text. You can also reduce the opacity of this layer if you find you need to lessen the effect of the reflection.

OK, that's it. You may now shout "I have created fire!", just as Tom Hanks did in the movie *Castaway*. Here is the final image.

Also, please keep in mind that you're not limited to text for this effect. You can use just about any shape, but it may require a little more creativity and some shapes may work better than others. For example, text works well because of the detail it contains. This illustration is a heart shape with the same effects applied to it.

As you can see, even though the fire looks good the illustration begins to lose the characteristics of a heart. However, you could just as easily create the fire effect for one letter and eliminate the text altogether. This image of a match was created from the letter "I", but I made sure to remove any details that tied the fire to a letter with the Liquify tools.

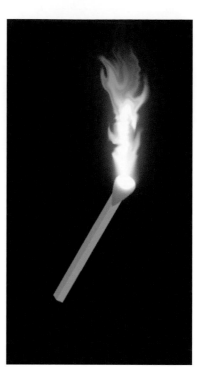

Summary

As you can see, if you'd like to push your skills to the extreme in Photoshop, then using brushes in Photoshop is an essential technique to master. Many times, this is a key crossing point from an intermediate-level Photoshop user to a professional-quality graphic designer. You must learn to make the available tools do the work for you. The Brush tool in Photoshop is one of those tools that can accomplish a great deal of work in a small amount of time. It may require some practice to learn, but the results will make you a better, efficient, and versatile graphic designer.

Part of making the transition from an intermediate-level user to a professional-level user of a piece of software is learning to not accept the traditional capabilities of the software. A common characteristic among professional-level users of Photoshop is that they learn the program, they learn the program's rules and limits, and then they learn how to break those rules and limits.

This philosophy holds true in the area of 3D. Although typically a 2D painting and illustration tool, Photoshop can be an incredibly useful aid for 3D art as well. This chapter will introduce you to the importance of 3D in realistic designs and how you can incorporate it in Photoshop.

3D techniques and concepts in Photoshop

3D concepts not only play an important part in many animations, movies, and special effects that you see in movie theaters today, but also have an impact on realistic graphic design. A design or illustration doesn't need to be created in a 3D application such as Maya or LightWave to use 3D concepts. Photoshop offers many ways to incorporate the third dimension into artwork, in addition to aiding the 3D artist.

Before you begin this chapter's exercise, I'd like to discuss some key techniques and concepts that you'll use throughout this tutorial, including clipping groups, reflections and highlights, refraction, and texture mapping. They're the key not only to re-creating the realistic 3D scene you'll design, but also to understanding the reasoning behind some of the steps that you'll take when working on this illustration.

Clipping groups

Many times in this book, I'll mention **reusability**. I come from a programming background where this concept is crucial. You have to be able to create snippets of code that you can easily use over and over again. This allows you the ability to work smarter and faster when new projects arise. Instead of re-creating the same work for each new project, you can reuse existing work and finish the project in a fraction of the time.

I've learned over the years that reusability is just as important in the graphic design business. You want to be able to quickly reuse or modify your artwork at a later date in case your client desires changes. One way to accomplish this task is to not permanently change the pixels within your designs when you don't need to. Photoshop offers many ways to do this, including layer styles, adjustment layers, masks, and clipping groups.

A **clipping group**, as its name implies, is a group of layers. At least two, to be specific, but it can contain more. In a clipping group, the lower layer acts as a mask for the layer above it, so that only portions of the upper image show through the mask. The transparent contents of the bottom layer in a clipping group mask (or clip) out the contents of the layers above it. Since neither image is actually modified, you can easily modify the position, orientation, and other attributes of the image(s) after you create the clipping group.

As with many techniques in this book, clipping groups aren't limited to realistic-based designs. However, I've found that many Photoshop users don't use clipping groups as much as they could; therefore, I wanted to cover this topic early in this book. The subject also lends itself very well to texturing objects, so it fits right into this chapter on Photoshop and 3D realism.

Let's take a look at a common example of clipping groups. Say you'd like to create some text that uses a photograph as its fill instead of a solid color or pattern. You could create the text, put a marquee selection around it, and then copy that area from the photograph. Finally, you could paste the area over the text. However, this can get messy, and it doesn't offer much flexibility. If you wanted to change the text, its position, its font size, or even its font type, you would have to redo the preceding steps. Enter clipping groups. By creating your text layer below the photograph and grouping the photograph with the text layer, you can quickly and easily restrict the photograph to appear only over the active pixels of the text layer. As you can see from the Layers palette in the following image, neither the text layer nor the photograph layer has been modified, and all pixels are left intact.

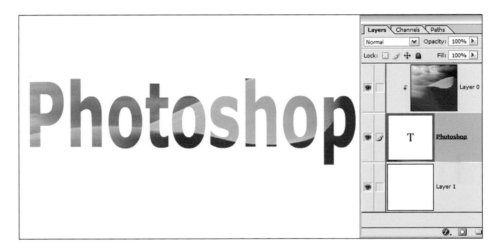

This means that you can close your Photoshop document, open it again a year from now, and still be able to change your text layer if you desire. Also note that you if you don't like the area of the photograph that is showing over the type, you can simply select the photograph layer and drag the image around to reposition that active area that shows through.

As you'll see in this chapter, clipping masks are a great tool to use while working on realistic images and applying textures to objects. They save you the time of selecting and deleting unwanted pixels, and they allow you to quickly make modifications to your designs at a later time if needed.

Reflections and highlights

Reflections and **highlights** are core 3D concepts. Nearly all 3D modeling programs have settings that let you adjust the reflectivity of an object. They're also a key factor in reproducing reality in a 3D illustration. This is especially true when you try to re-create highly transparent or shiny objects.

In this chapter, you're going to re-create a realistic fishbowl. Since the bowl is made of glass, reflections will play an important role in breathing life, depth, and volume into a somewhat flat object. Take a look at the difference when I turn off all reflection layers (in the left image). The bowl appears flat and unrealistic. However, when I turn the reflection layers back on (in the right image), the bowl becomes noticeably more realistic.

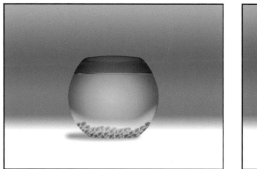
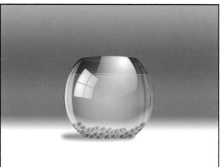

Refraction

If you've ever submerged part of a straight stick into water, you probably noticed that the stick appears to bend at the point where it enters the water. Even better, have you ever looked through a glass object of some sort and noticed that the background you see behind it is distorted (as in the following image)? This optical effect results from something known as **refraction**. As light passes from one transparent object to another, it changes speed and bends. How much bending occurs depends on something known as the **refractive index** of the object and the angle at which the light penetrates the surface of the object. Refractive objects such as plastic, water, and glass each have a different refractive index, and thus each bends light in a different way. When you

work with Photoshop and 3D, refraction is an important concept to keep in mind, since it contributes greatly to the appearance of reality in design.

Keep the concept of refraction in mind as you work through this chapter's exercise. It will come into play at the end when you need to distort the background of the fishbowl to take refraction into account.

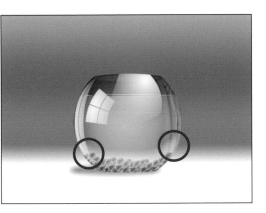

Note the red circles in the following image of the glass fishbowl that you'll create in this chapter. Since your view of the background is being affected by two transparent surfaces—the water and the glass—the blue and white background appears slightly distorted. You'll notice in the image that the background appears to curve upward due to refraction. This is an important element of refraction to grasp, and mastering it will really help breathe life into your realistic illustrations.

Texture mapping

The concept of **texture mapping** is important in 3D programs and design. Adding textures makes all the difference between creating a flat, rendered 3D object and a realistic, lifelike object. In Photoshop, you can not only create textures to later use in 3D programs, but also map textures to objects right within the program. The exercise that you're going to complete in this chapter uses three different types of maps: texture, bump, and reflection.

Texture map

A **texture map** is probably the easiest map type to comprehend. A texture map is simply an image of a texture that is created, scanned, photographed, or imported into Photoshop. Once the texture is in the program, you can save the image as a file for texture mapping in a 3D program, or you can use it as a texture map within Photoshop itself.

Bump map

As odd as it sounds, a **bump map** is exactly what its name implies: a map that, when applied, determines bumps on a surface. Essentially, a bump map is a grayscale image used to create a texture. Gray values of 50% have no effect on the surface to which the bump map is applied. White tones make the surface appear to be raised, and black values make dents appear.

Reflection map

A **reflection map** is an image used on a shiny or glossy surface to simulate a reflection. To apply a reflection map so that the effect is realistic, you should use a picture of the scenery around an object. This way, the object will accurately reflect what is around it. However, it's often acceptable to use a picture of nearly anything. Many times, reflection maps are distorted and faded so much that what's actually in the reflection isn't distinguishable. Just the fact that some sort of image was used to serve as a reflection map usually suffices.

Techniques and concepts wrap-up

I've presented you with a lot of nontutorial-specific material at the beginning of this chapter. I feel it's important for you to become familiar with these concepts, as they'll help you take your Photoshop skills to the next level. These concepts aren't covered in Photoshop manuals, but they're essential for you to understand once you've reached an intermediate to advanced level of skill with the program. This is mainly because there's more to graphic design and illustration than the associated software applications. Having a better overall understanding of the artistic concepts that are a part of nearly any design will help set you apart from your competition. Also, they'll help you take the exercises in this book and customize them. Perhaps creating an ordinary fishbowl isn't of practical use to you. But if you find yourself needing to create highly transparent objects or 3D illustrations, this chapter's exercise will teach you the key concepts behind doing so.

OK, enough discussion—let's move on to the fun stuff!

Creating a 3D glass fishbowl

Now that you understand some basic techniques and concepts you'll use when working with realistic 3D objects and Photoshop, you're ready for an exercise. The fishbowl you're going to create is a perfect candidate for a Photoshop 3D exercise. It uses many techniques and concepts of working with 3D that can be re-created in Photoshop. In the end, you'll be left with an illustration worth bragging about and something you can put directly into your portfolio.

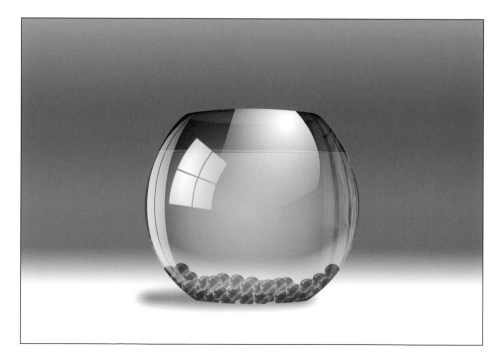

As you can see from the preceding image, you can barely tell that the fishbowl wasn't photographed. As you proceed through the exercise, I'll give you tips on how to achieve this quality of artwork in your realistic designs and how you constantly need to consider 3D concepts if you want to fully re-create reality in your illustrations.

Exercise: Creating a fishbowl

1. Create a new 1600 × 1200-pixel Photoshop canvas and select the RGB color mode.

> *When you work with large files, it's a good practice to make liberal use of the Navigator palette* (Window ➤ Navigator). *The Navigator palette is a great alternative to using the scrollbars to maneuver around your canvas.*

First, you need a background—something with nice blue colors will do fine. You'll need a surface as well.

2. Remember one of my favorite layer-renaming tricks? Hold down the *ALT/OPTION* key and double-click the Background layer to turn it into Layer 0. Rename this layer BACKGROUND.

3. Create a new linear gradient using the color values in the following screenshot as a guide.

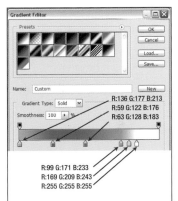

4. On the BACKGROUND layer, drag your new gradient from the top to the bottom. You can see that the transition from blue to white is where the surface begins.

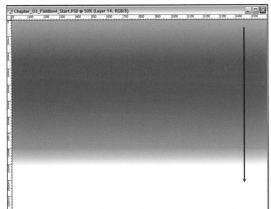

Great, now let's create the shape for the fishbowl. You can create this shape in several ways. Since paths and the Pen tool offer a great deal of flexibility, you're going to use them for this task.

5. Choose white as your foreground color and select the Ellipse tool (*U*). It may be hidden by one of the other shape tools or the Line tool.

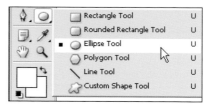

6. In the tool options bar, select the Shape layers button.

7. Create an ellipse that is 675 × 700 pixels in size. You can eyeball the size by using the Info palette as you draw, or you can click the Geometry Options drop-down arrow in the tool options bar and directly enter the width and height settings for the Fixed Size option.

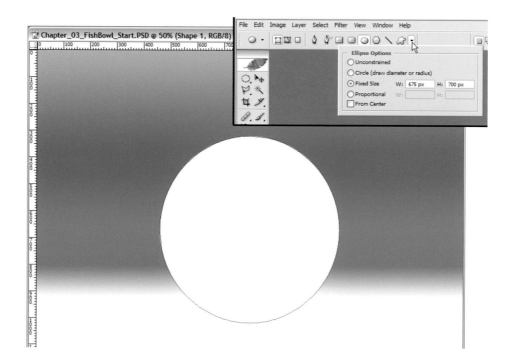

Many professionals always have their Info palette (F8) open and handy. Doing so allows them to quickly see the dimensions of whatever they're drawing or have selected at the time.

Next, you're going to do something somewhat radical. You may not have done this in Photoshop before, but it's a feature that Illustrator users have had available to them for a while. You're going to create another shape on top of your circle shape but, instead of creating an entirely new shape layer, you're going to intersect the two shapes so that only one appears. When you're done, your shape layer will go from containing a simple circle to holding a more complex shape.

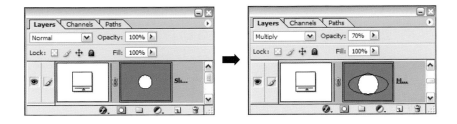

8. Before you can proceed to implement the new technique, you need to do a few things. First, make sure your circle shape layer is active by clicking it once.

9. Make sure the Ellipse tool is selected. Then, in the tool options bar, select the Intersect Shape Areas button.

The previous step can often be confusing. If the Intersect Shape Areas *button is grayed out or isn't visible, it can mean one of two things: either the circle shape layer isn't active or the Ellipse tool isn't selected. If you don't see any of the buttons in the previous screenshot, just select the Ellipse tool and they'll become visible. However, if the circle shape layer isn't active (indicated by a small paintbrush next to the eyeball in the Layers palette), the* Intersect Shape Areas *button will appear grayed out. If you create another shape, it will be created on a new layer, and that's not what you want. Clicking the circle shape layer once to make it active will help solve this problem.*

10. Now draw another oval (don't forget to choose Unconstrained if you used a fixed size in step 7). This time make it very wide. If you'd like to be exact, you can make it 1300 × 600. Otherwise, you can eyeball the size while looking at the accompanying image. Don't forget that as you're drawing the oval, you can use the spacebar to reposition it before you release the mouse. However, you need not worry about placing it in exactly the correct position yet. I've placed mine accurately only to give you a general area about how to create this oval shape. You can take care of repositioning it accurately in the next step.

When you release the mouse button, you'll notice that you didn't create another shape layer. Instead, you removed the area from the first shape that didn't intersect with the second shape. This is because in step 9 you clicked the Intersect Shape Areas button in the tool options bar.

In the end, you're left with only one shape layer to contend with. Better yet, since it's a shape layer, you can scale it up or down to your heart's content and never lose any image quality. Take that, Illustrator users!

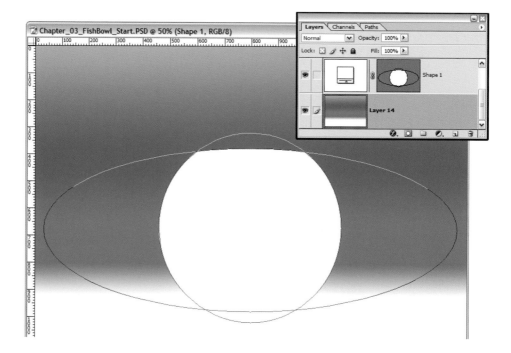

I mentioned that it doesn't matter if the second oval isn't placed perfectly in line with the original circle shape. That's another advantage of shape layers. In essence, they're paths, and you can manipulate them as such. Follow along to see how:

11. Select the Path Selection tool (*A*) in the toolbar. It's the black arrow tool located just to the left of the Type tool and directly above the Pen tool.

12. Click the shape layer once to make it active. Then click the wide oval shape with the Path Selection tool. Notice how it selects only the wide oval and not the circle. This is evident by the bounding box that surrounds the shape. (If you don't see the bounding box, choose Show Bounding Box in the tool options bar.) You can now move this shape anywhere you'd like. It will still retain its intersection properties with the circle shape you drew with it.

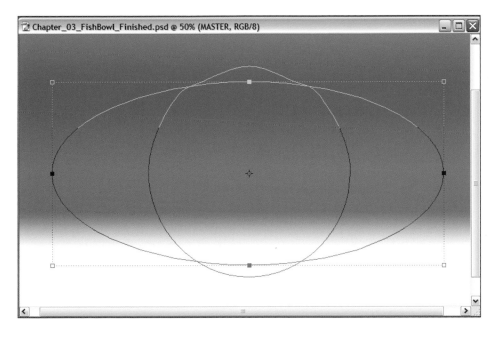

As if that weren't enough stress for one exercise, now you have to modify the shape a bit with the Pen tool to flatten out what will be the top of the fishbowl.

13. Select the Add Anchor Point tool (*P*) from the toolbox. It may be hidden by the Pen tool.

14. Zoom in on the top of the fishbowl and click once where the two shapes intersect to add an anchor point. Repeat this process for the other side of the fishbowl.

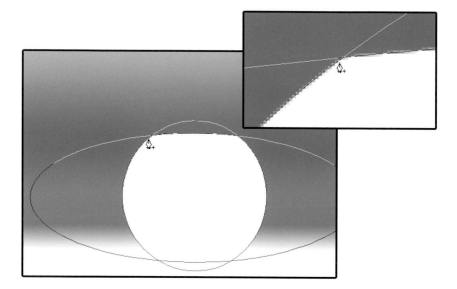

15. Now select the Direct Selection tool (*A*). (Note that it may be hidden by the Path Selection tool in the toolbox.) Click the newly created anchor point once on the left side of the fishbowl. Note the handle that appears to the bottom left of the point. If you don't see a handle appear, you may need to click that area again to reselect the anchor point.

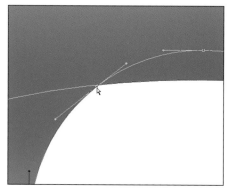

16. Drag this handle upward and out to the left until you almost reach the origin of the anchor point. This will round out the corner a bit and flatten the top of the bowl.

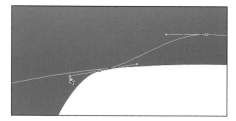

17. Repeat this process for the other side of the bowl.

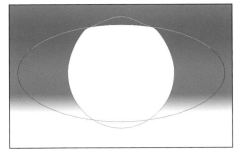

18. Repeat steps 10 through 13 for the bottom of the fishbowl. This time, though, don't make it quite as round as the top. You don't want the bowl to tip over!

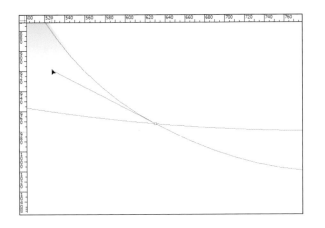

19. Finally, name this layer MASTER, as it will serve as the master shape for the remaining bowl shapes you'll create.

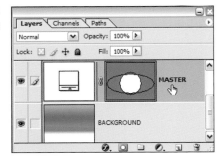

Great! Now let's begin to make the bowl to more realistic. The next few steps will add some depth to the fishbowl. If you study rounded glass surfaces, you'll notice that they're less transparent at the edges. Try it. Find a glass in your cabinet and set it down in front of a defined background. Note that the transparency of the glass becomes less noticeable as the curvature becomes more pronounced toward the edges of the glass. To re-create this effect in Photoshop, you'll use an Inner Shadow layer style to give the bowl some volume. You'll also learn how to use a clipping group to further enhance the effect.

20. Double-click the shape thumbnail on the MASTER layer to display the Layer Style dialog box. Click Inner Shadow and change the settings to match the following reference image. Click OK to apply the layer style.

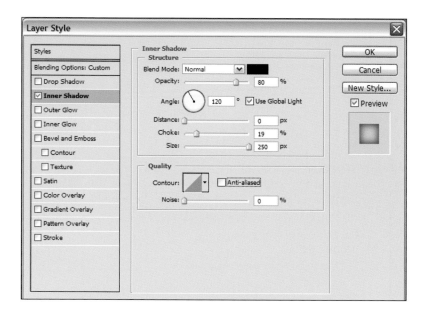

21. Change the blending mode of the MASTER layer to Multiply.

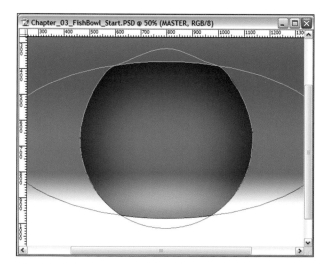

This shadow really helps to add some depth to the bowl. However, notice how the shadow affects all the edges of the bowl. This isn't quite what you want, as the top and bottom won't be affected in the same way as the far left and right edges. To fix this, you'll use an old trick with a clipping group.

22. Duplicate the MASTER layer by pressing *CTRL/⌘+J*. Rename the top duplicate MASTER CLIP. You may need to widen your Layers palette to click the layer name to rename it.

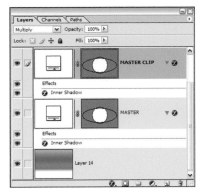

23. Delete the Inner Shadow layer style from the MASTER layer by dragging it over the trash can icon at the bottom of the Layers palette.

24. Now for the trick. With the MASTER CLIP layer active, press *CTRL/⌘+T* to bring up the Free Transform bounding box.

25. Drag the top-center handle up slightly and drag the bottom-center handle down slightly. Alternatively, you can hold the *ALT/OPTION* key down while dragging either the top or bottom handles to drag both of them at once. Press *ENTER* to confirm the changes when you're done.

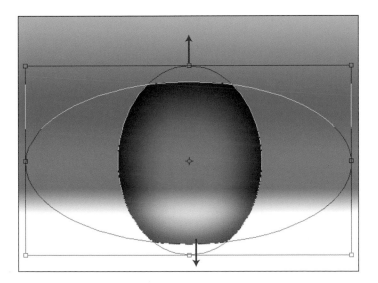

I can hear you saying to yourself that the bowl isn't looking very realistic. Here's the good part.

26. With the MASTER CLIP layer active, choose Layer ➤ Create Clipping Mask (*CTRL/⌘+G*). Voila! The shadow now barely shows through at the top and bottom, but the sides remain less transparent.

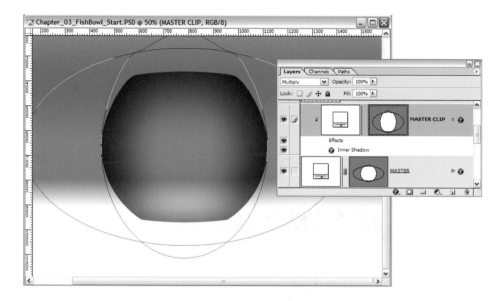

27. Change the blending mode of the MASTER CLIP layer to Overlay and drop the opacity down to 70%.

Next, let's create the water layer.

28. Select the Pen tool (*P*) and click the Paths button in the tool options bar.

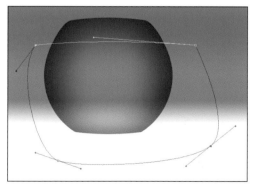

29. Draw a slightly rounded path toward the top of the bowl where you'd like the waterline to start. Continue around the bowl, not worrying about the shape of the path once you've completed the top segment. (Use the following image as a reference.)

30. Switch over to the Paths palette. You should now see a Work Path layer inside it. With this layer active, click the Load path as selection button at the bottom of the palette to turn the path into a selection.

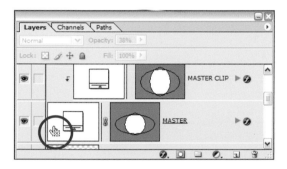

31. Now switch back to the Layers palette. *CTRL/⌘+ALT/OPTION+SHIFT*-click the MASTER layer. As you hold down these shortcut keys, you'll notice a small *x* appear within the cursor to let you know that you're about to intersect the active selection with the selection of the layer you're clicking. This is a great little trick that's worth remembering.

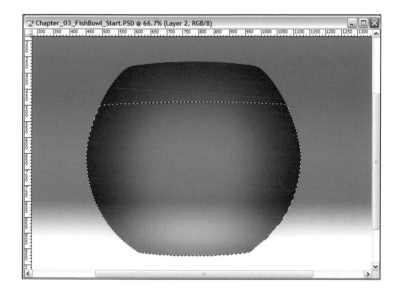

You should be left with a selection of the bottom two-thirds of the fishbowl.

32. Create a new layer named WATER, and fill this selection with white.

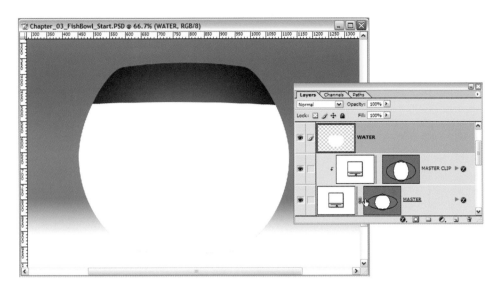

33. Change the blending mode of the WATER layer to Overlay and drop the opacity to 40%.

Next, you need to add reflections. Reflections are great on glass, because you have so much flexibility when you create them. Many times, the reflections take the form of random and odd shapes. The best way to become familiar with adding them is to examine objects in the real world. Look around your house or apartment and see how light interacts with transparent objects. Also, Google (www.google.com) is a great place to start your search when you're looking for inspiration.

There's a particular concept known as the **Fresnel Effect** (pronounced "fre-nel"; the *s* is silent) that you should keep in mind when creating reflections for transparent objects such as the glass fishbowl. The Fresnel Effect is the variation in the amount of reflection you see on a surface depending on the viewing angle. As shown in the following picture of a fishbowl, you don't see very much reflected light from the front of the bowl since you're looking straight at it.

Notice that you can see the fish fairly clearly. In this exercise, the reflected forms correspond to the shape of the reflective object. This also holds true for the wine glass picture used to demonstrate refraction.

You'll notice that as the shape of the object changes, and thus your viewing angle changes, the more skewed the reflection becomes. You can see this effect on the outer edges of the glass bowl and the wine glass. In fact, the reflections and refractions become so intense on the outer edges (the steepest viewing angles from your vantage point) that the effect is a reduction in the transparency of the glass. Keep this concept in mind when you create the reflections for the bowl.

The first reflection you're going to add is a bit odd, but it works great for this exercise. It's called a **pixel stretch**.

34. Create a new layer above WATER named PIXEL STRETCH. Using a 10- to 15-pixel hard-edged brush, paint some dots and lines in a small grouping.

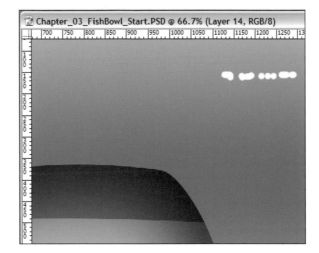

35. Zoom in on the area to which you just added the brush strokes. Select the Rectangular Marquee tool (*M*) and create a small, thin selection over the white brush strokes, as shown in the following image.

36. Zoom back out. Press *CTRL/⌘+T* to transform the selection and drag the bounding box downward. When the height of the white area is close to the height of the bowl, press *ENTER* to accept the transformation. Also, position the white lines to the right side of the bowl. Essentially, you have just stretched the pixels. This produces an effect that works nicely for this purpose. Keep in mind that your results may not look exactly like mine—the effect is meant to be random, and your results may vary.

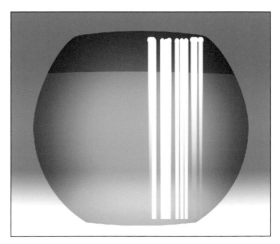

37. Now, using the Elliptical Marquee tool (*M*), draw a circle around the stretched lines and the bowl shape.

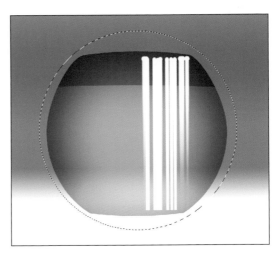

3

38. Choose Filter ➤ Distort ➤ Spherize and enter the settings shown in the following screenshot. Click OK to apply the filter.

39. Press *CTRL*/⌘+*F* two more times to reapply the filter, for a total of three times.

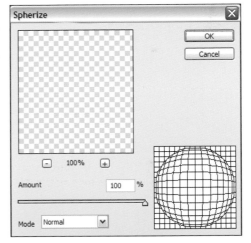

40. Position the lines toward the edge of the bowl. You may need to scale them down using the Free Transform tool (*CTRL*/⌘+*T*).

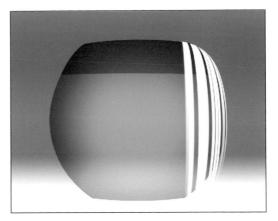

41. Now *Ctrl/⌘*-click the MASTER layer to activate the selection of the fishbowl. Then choose Select ➤ Inverse (*Ctrl/⌘+Shift+I*) to select everything but the bowl shape. Finally, with the PIXEL STRETCH layer active, press the *Delete* key to remove any excess area around the bowl.

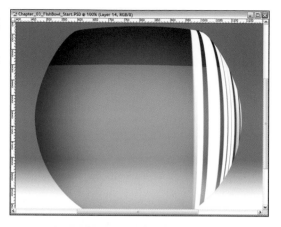

42. Drop the opacity of this layer to approximately 15%.

43. Add a layer mask to this layer by clicking the Add Layer Mask button at the bottom of the Layers palette.

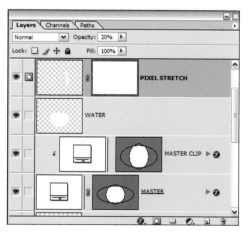

44. Using a linear gradient, drag a black-to-white gradient across the reflection to soften the center area slightly. Remember, the edges aren't as transparent as the rest of the bowl, and the reflections will be stronger there.

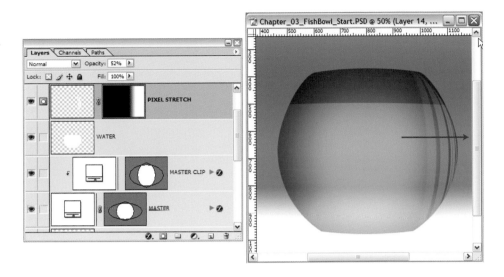

Let's add another reflection using a different method.

45. Select the Pen tool. Be sure to click the Paths button in the tool options bar, and draw a shape similar to the one shown in the following image. Note that this doesn't create a layer in the Layers palette; rather, it creates a new work path in the Paths palette.

46. Convert this path into a selection using the same process as in step 30.

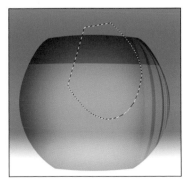

47. Now remove the excess selection area around the fishbowl.

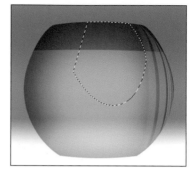

48. Create a new layer. Set your foreground color to white. Select the Gradient tool (*G*) and choose the Radial Gradient option. Pick the white-to-transparent radial gradient and drag from the top right to the bottom left of the selection.

49. Adjust the opacity of this layer to around 85%. The opacity setting you choose will depend on how soft you'd like the reflection to be and how you dragged the gradient in the previous step.

I've added a couple more reflections to enhance the shininess of the glass bowl, as shown in the following image. I added one of them following the previously described steps. I created the windowlike square reflection by making four squares on the same layer and filling them with white. I then drew a circular selection around them with the Elliptical Marquee tool and applied the Spherize filter to bulge it out a bit. You can review these reflections in the final PSD file (Chapter_03_FishBowl_Finished.psd) in the download files if you'd like to examine them more closely.

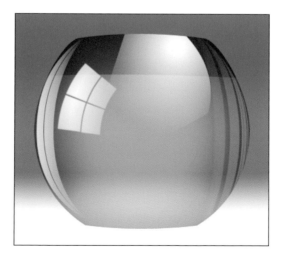

Notice the square, windowlike reflection on the bowl? This is a common technique you can use when adding reflections to surfaces. Since reflections are caused by light, and light often shines through windows, this shape is a great reflection to place on any object that's supposed to be indoors. It's worth creating a library of these types of reflections so you can apply them to other designs quickly and easily.

Exercise: Adding a reflection map

Next, you'll add a reflection map. If you recall from earlier in this chapter, a reflection map is an image used on a shiny or glossy surface to simulate a reflection. In Photoshop, it's common to use outdoor scenery for this purpose. Pictures of clouds, beaches, or people work well. The key to the reflection map and a glass surface like this is that you usually don't notice what the reflection actually is. It's distorted and mostly transparent, so you shouldn't be able to tell that it was a picture of some clouds. This works great for highly reflective surfaces such as chrome, too. However, depending on the type of surface and the lighting, the reflection map may be more pronounced and noticeable.

1. To add a reflection map, open Chapter_03_ReflectionMap.psd from this chapter's source files. Alternatively, you can use an image of your own if you prefer. Just be sure the image is large enough to cover the area in which you're working.

This is a good time to save your original fishbowl file.

2. Using the Elliptical Marquee tool (*M*), draw a circle around an area within the image. Press *Ctrl*/⌘+*Shift*+*I* to select the inverse, and press the *Delete* key to remove the area around the circular selection. Don't deselect yet, though.

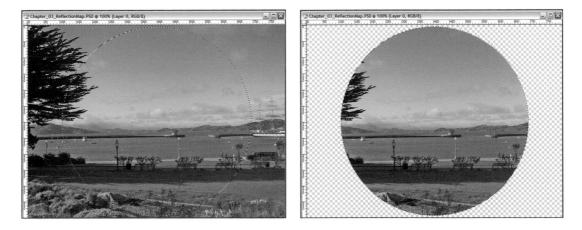

3. Deselect by choosing Select ➤ Deselect (*CTRL*/⌘*+D*).

4. Choose Filter ➤ Distort ➤ Spherize and use the settings shown in the following screenshot.

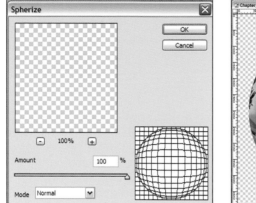 

5. Reapply this filter once more by pressing *CTRL*/⌘*+F*.

6. Choose Filter ➤ Distort ➤ ZigZag and use the settings shown in the following screenshot. Click OK to apply the filter.

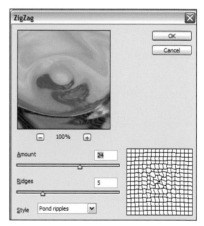

7. Drag this layer into your fishbowl file and position it below all the reflection layers. Name it REFLECTION MAP.

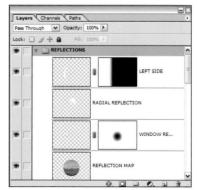

8. Remove the area of the reflection map that's outside the bowl using the same select and select inverse commands you've used several times before.

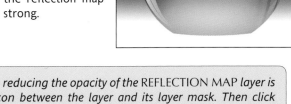

9. Add a layer mask to the REFLECTION MAP layer and drag a black-to-white linear gradient across the mask. Again, this simulates reality in that the edges of the bowl are less transparent, therefore the reflection will be stronger in that area.

10. Reduce the opacity of the reflection map layer if you find it's too strong.

An alternative method to reducing the opacity of the REFLECTION MAP *layer is to click the small link icon between the layer and its layer mask. Then click the layer mask you use the Move tool to drag the gradient around to reposition it to your liking. When you're done, just click between the two layers to link them again.*

11. Next, you need to work on the top of the bowl. Create a new layer above WATER named TOP.

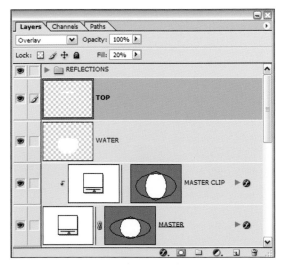

12. Zoom in on the top of the bowl and use the Elliptical Marquee tool to create a wide oval selection around the top area of the bowl. Since you're zoomed in, you should be able to get pretty close to the edges of the actual bowl. Fill this selection with white.

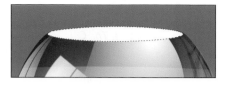

13. Double-click the TOP layer and add an Inner Shadow layer style using the settings shown here:

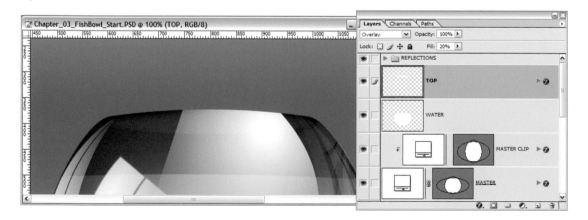

14. Change the blending mode of the layer to Overlay and reduce the Fill opacity to 20%. This removes nearly all of the white area, so only the small shadow is visible.

The difference between the Opacity *setting and the* Fill *opacity setting for a layer is simple. The* Opacity *setting affects the entire layer, including the actual pixel content on the layer as well as layer effects.* Fill *opacity, on the other hand, affects only the layer contents (or pixels). In the previous step, when you reduce the* Fill *opacity, you're essential telling Photoshop to get rid of the white area but keep all of the characteristics of the* Inner Shadow *layer style.*

3

15. Next, you're going to add a waterline at the top of the water. Create a new layer named WATER LINE above WATER.

16. *CTRL/⌘*-click the WATER layer to put a selection around the water.

17. Hold down the *ALT/OPTION* key to subtract a selection and drag a rectangular marquee from the bottom of the water up. Leave just a few pixels unselected, though, so you're left with a thin rectangular selection. Fill this selection with white.

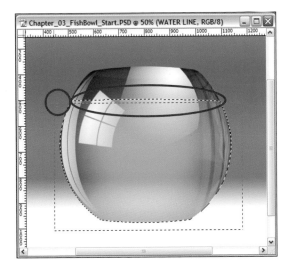

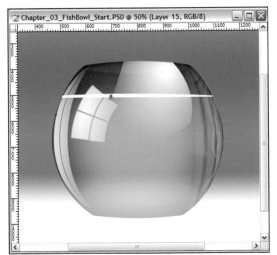

18. Add the following settings for a Bevel and Emboss layer style. Then drop the opacity of this layer to 50%.

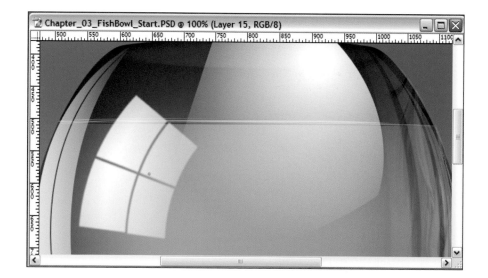

OK, you're almost done. Now your fishbowl needs some shadows. One key point to keep in mind is that, in real life, shadows aren't only shades of gray. Many times, shadows take on the color characteristics of the object casting them. This is especially true of transparent objects. When light hits a transparent object, it will not only cause a shadow to be cast on the opposite side of the object, but also some of the light will pass through the object and cause any colors within the transparent object to be cast with the shadow as well.

19. Create a new layer named SHADOW below MASTER.

20. Use the Elliptical Marquee tool to create an oval selection at the base of the bowl. Fill this selection with black.

21. Create a smaller selection on the same layer within the black oval and fill it with R:90 G:159 B:197. When you've finished, deselect everything (*CTRL*/⌘+*D*).

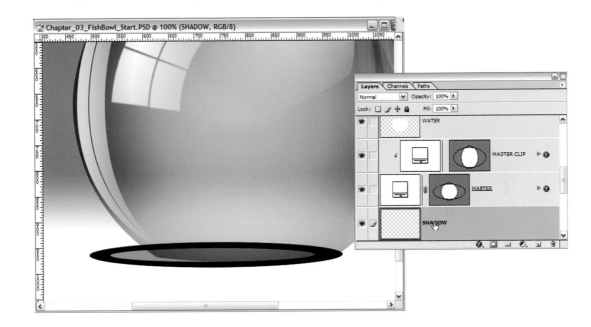

22. Next, choose Filter ➤ Blur ➤ Gaussian Blur and enter a Radius setting of 15 pixels.

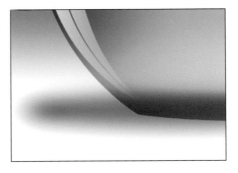

23. If necessary, reduce the opacity of the SHADOW layer. I reduced this one to about 75%. Instant shadow! Notice how it's not all gray, though. The shadow is slightly illuminated by the light shining through the water and the blue color of the bowl reflecting off the surface. It's details like these that bring your 3D and realistic illustrations to life.

Lastly, you could always add something to line the bottom of the fishbowl. Often, people use marbles or rocks.

24. Find a suitable picture of a marble or rock. Alternatively, you can open `Chapter_03_Marble.psd` from the source files.

25. Create a new layer above SHADOW and drag the marble into your fishbowl file. Duplicate it many times and position the duplicates randomly throughout the bottom of the fishbowl. Merge all the marble layers together into one and name this layer MARBLES.

26. Draw a circular selection around the fishbowl, as you've done several times throughout this exercise, and apply the Spherize filter to warp them.

27. *CTRL*/⌘-click the MASTER layer to activate the bowl selection.

28. Select the inverse (*SHIFT*+*CTRL*/⌘+*I*) and press *DELETE* to remove the excess marbles from beyond the shape of the bowl.

29. Now add an Inner Shadow layer style to the marbles to add some depth. This also helps take into account the increased effect of refraction as the bowl begins a more pronounced curvature at the bottom.

Layer Style

Styles	**Inner Shadow**
Blending Options: Custom	Structure
☐ Drop Shadow	Blend Mode: Multiply
☑ **Inner Shadow**	Opacity: — 75 %
☐ Outer Glow	
☐ Inner Glow	Angle: 120 ° ☑ Use Global Light
☐ Bevel and Emboss	Distance: 7 px
☐ Contour	Choke: 0 %
☐ Texture	Size: 84 px
☐ Satin	Quality
☐ Color Overlay	Contour: ☐ Anti-aliased
☐ Gradient Overlay	Noise: 0 %
☐ Pattern Overlay	
☐ Stroke	

OK
Cancel
New Style...
☑ Preview

3

30. OK, you're just about done. *CTRL/*⌘-click the MASTER layer to activate the fishbowl selection. Then click the BACKGROUND layer to make it active.

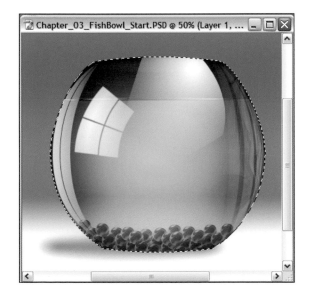

Chapter_03_FishBowl_Start.PSD @ 50% (Layer 1, ...

31. Choose Filter ➤ Liquify. Using the Warp tool (*W*) with a brush size of 300 and a pressure of about 50, warp the blue-to-white transition area of the background slightly to simulate the refraction effect I spoke about earlier. Brush the center area down slightly, and brush the far edges up a little.

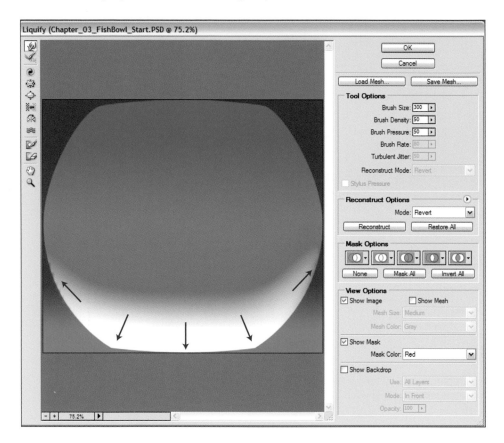

That's it! Your fishbowl is complete.

3

Summary

This chapter has given you some professional-grade techniques and ideas with which to create 3D illustrations in Photoshop. As I mentioned at the beginning of the chapter, those who truly master Photoshop learn its intended capabilities and then push them beyond their normal, everyday use. 3D is one of those areas that allows you to push Photoshop to the extreme limits of what the program can and should do. As a result, you'll learn the tools better because you've used them for many different types of applications. Even better, you'll also become a well-rounded professional designer able to tackle a multitude of projects because you feel confident that you control the tools in Photoshop and are able to make them work for you.

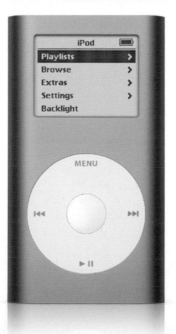

Up until now, the techniques I've covered in this book have dealt primarily with adding realism to your designs or illustrations using Photoshop. You've learned many techniques and concepts that can help entice people to look more closely at your work and allow them to feel comfortable with the level of realism that's portrayed.

In this chapter, you're going to take a different approach. The art of photorealism implies that viewers can't tell the difference between the photograph and the actual artwork itself. As I mentioned in Chapter 1, not all realism-based designs need to be photorealistic. You've seen in the last couple of chapters that you can often make use of many realism concepts to draw viewers into an illustration and allow them to forget that they're looking at a computer-generated design. However, in those chapters your aim wasn't to try to fool viewers into thinking that what they're looking at is the real thing. With photorealism, though, that's exactly the idea.

Why photorealism?

If you're the logical type, then your next question may naturally be "Why photorealism?" (If you're not necessarily the logical type, and the beauty, challenge, and end results of photorealism are enough for you, then feel free to skip this section.) You're probably thinking to yourself, "Why not just take a picture and be done with it?" The following sections offer a few reasons that will appeal to your creative, professional, and financial sides.

Product shoot modifications

Product shoots can be expensive. Sometimes after a product shoot is finished, a client may realize that something is missing or something needs to be removed from the photos. Colors can change, for example, or backgrounds may need to be deleted. As you'll see, you can achieve these effects through photorealism techniques.

Accessory additions

Perhaps you have a good photograph of your product, but you want to add accessories. Photorealism lends itself perfectly to this application, as the accessories you want to add may not be available in a photograph. In this case, you need to add the accessories but maintain the believable characteristics of the original photograph and not compromise the reality of the overall piece.

Photo quality

An available photograph may not be of a high enough quality—a common scenario in today's world. Often, the Web may have been the only medium considered for output when a particular photograph was taken. As a result, you may be given a 400 × 300-pixel 72 dpi file of an image that doesn't lend itself to printing very well. If you were to try to enlarge the image to make it suitable for print, you would most likely get undesirable results.

For example, the image on the left was a 72 dpi photograph taken for a website. If you attempt to enlarge this photograph (to 300 dpi, for instance) to make it suitable for printing, you'll begin to see fuzzy edges (or pixelation) occur. A larger version of this photograph—the image on the right—is also available at 300 dpi for comparison purposes. You can immediately see how much clearer and crisper the high-quality photograph is.

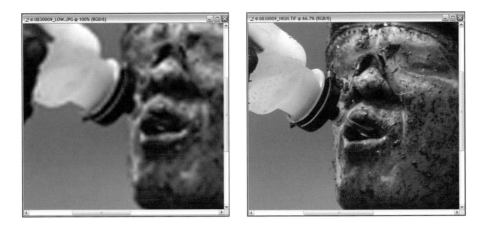

This problem occurs because the process of enlarging a photograph requires the imaging application to interpolate, or guess, what each pixel should look like at a larger size. Since there is often not enough information within the original photograph to determine what it should look like at a larger size, the application will guess and add its own pixels. This results in the clarity and integrity of the original photograph being compromised as it is enlarged, hence the appearance of fuzzy, noncrisp edges throughout the enlarged version.

The only way to make this image suitable for printing would be to reduce the overall size while increasing the resolution. However, this would result in the new image being very small in comparison to the original.

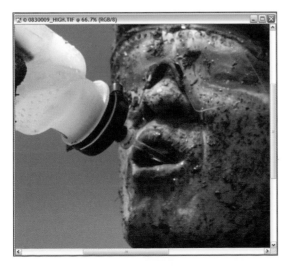

You can see in the preceding images the relative size of a photograph taken for display on the Web and the size at which it will print relative to its original size. The left image shows the image at full size, and the right image displays the size that the original would need to be scaled down to in order to remain sharp for print. Often, this scaled-down size is nearly 25% the size of the original.

The moral of this story is that if you can't retake the photograph, then re-creating it at a very large size in Photoshop may be a great alternative.

A photograph doesn't exist

This is another common scenario. Perhaps the photo was lost and all you're left with is a file that was used on a website. This is similar to the situation described in the previous section. In addition, maybe a photograph can't be taken because the cost of traveling to the location is prohibitively expensive. In this case, you need to pore through books, the Web, magazines, and any other resources you can use to create "reality" from scratch.

It's just plain cool

If none of the other reasons excites you when it comes to justifying photorealistic designs in Photoshop, then consider this one: photorealism is just plain cool.

This book is about pushing Photoshop to the extremes. What better way to accomplish this than to use the large percentage of tools that it requires to re-create reality? When you're finished with a photorealistic illustration and someone asks you if it's a photograph, the feeling of accomplishment is outstanding. The art form is amazing to look at, and it can produce illustrations that add a powerful punch in your portfolio. Sometimes this is reason enough to embrace this type of artwork.

Reference images

Reference images are just what their name implies: images for a designer to refer to when creating artwork. Nearly all artists use them. If you're working in a professional environment, then it's imperative that you become familiar with reference images. They'll make your life much easier, and allow you to work quickly and achieve high-quality results for your client.

Artists use reference images to help them re-create something they want to incorporate into their artwork. In some circumstances, an artist is re-creating the exact scene depicted in the reference image. In other cases, an artist is combining elements of various reference images to create unique artwork. A great example of this is when an artist is creating a beach scene. Perhaps he has the scene completed but decides he'd like to add a palm tree. The artist may then take a picture of a palm tree or find one in a book and use it as a reference with which to create his own. This is a perfectly acceptable practice. Very few artists and designers can look at an object or scene and remember the exact characteristics of it right away. Or, if the object or scene is something the artist has never seen before, he will, of course, need to refer to pictures to create it.

You can find reference images anywhere, and they can consist of anything. Books, magazines, the Web, and photographs are a few examples of places to look for them.

Exercise: Re-creating an iPod mini

In the following exercise, you're going to simulate a potential real-world project. Say you work for Apple Computer, Inc., and your manager comes to you with some bad news. She says that the source files of photos taken of an iPod mini can't be found. All that remains are the images that were used on the website (a highly unlikely scenario at Apple, by the way). She points you to the website's product page (www.apple.com/ipodmini) and shows you exactly what's left. She then informs you that she needs to put this product in a full-page magazine ad. This means that it needs to be at a much higher quality than the 600 × 800 72 dpi image you can get off the website.

With the stage set, this exercise will walk you through the steps you can take to get this job done. Along the way, you'll not only see how to re-create a photograph in Photoshop, but also develop an appreciation for photorealistic artwork and the techniques involved in creating it.

1. Open `Chapter_04_iPod_Start.psd`. This file contains the iPod image from the Apple website. The quality and size of this image aren't high enough for print standards.

First off, you'll need the general shape of the iPod as an outline. Since you have a reference image, you'll use it by tracing the outline of the blue area. There are many opinions on tracing and whether or not it's "cheating." Here's a good rule of thumb. If you're tracing something and claiming it's your own, then you're probably cheating. If you're working with fine art, I suggest that you don't trace. In this case, though, you're not cheating. You're working under the assumption that this is a professional, work-related task. In the business world, time is money. If your boss hands you this file and says she needs it re-created digitally in an hour, why not use the reference image as just that: a reference? Use the fact that you have this image. There's no shame in tracing the general outline and using the reference to get a feel for the various dimensions of the iPod. Also, make extensive use of the Eyedropper tool to sample colors and tones throughout the image. There's no reason to attempt to eyeball the image and spend extra time trying to get it just right. Again, time is money, and these techniques will save you time and get the job done quickly. That said, let's trace.

2. Select the Pen tool (*P*) and make sure the Shape layers button is selected in the tool options bar.

3. Select the Eyedropper tool (I) and click once in the center of the original iPod image. This will set your foreground color to the exact blue (R:140 G:193 B:224) that you're going to use for the iPod.

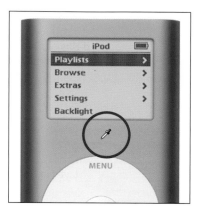

It's good to get into the habit of using not only the shape of an object in a reference image, but its colors as well. This works much better than trying to match the exact color by sight.

4. Now trace around the iPod. Note that I've reduced the opacity of the iPod to make the path easier to see. This is a fairly simple object to trace, and it shouldn't require too many anchor points. When you're done, name the new shape layer that was created BASE.

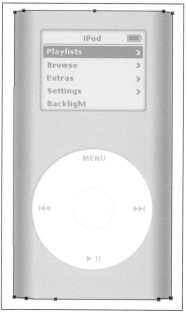

Next, let's work on the screen. Again, use the reference picture available to you.

5. Set your foreground color to R:209 G:211 B:229 or use the Eyedropper tool to sample the screen color from the original.

6. Select the Rounded Rectangle tool (*U*) and ensure that the Shape layers button is selected in the tool options bar. Also note the Radius setting in the tool options bar. I adjusted this size several times to try to re-create the exact curvature of each corner. For this example, I found that a Radius setting of 5 px works well.

7. Drag a rounded rectangle around the original until you're happy with the size in reference to the actual picture. Name this shape layer SCREEN. You may need to hide the BASE layer to see the original screen.

4

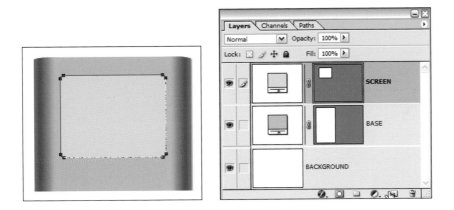

8. Create two inner circles that serve as the iPod's controls, but use the Ellipse tool (*U*) instead. Again, be sure that the Shape layers button is selected in the tool options bar. Fill these two circles with white.

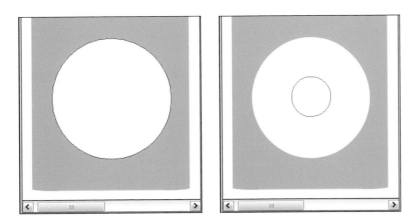

9. Rename the large circle shape layer as OUTER CIRCLE and the smaller inside circle layer as INNER CIRCLE.

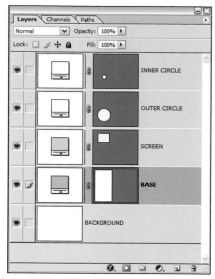

OK, now that you have the basic shapes in place, you can scale up. Since you've used shape layers for everything, this shouldn't be a problem, as you can scale them up and down without losing any image quality.

10. Choose Image ➤ Image Size. Enter 1600 for the width and 1200 for the height, and click OK.

Great! Now you've doubled the size of the original file, and you haven't lost any image quality. At this point, you're done tracing, so you can move the original iPod off to the side if you'd like to make it easier to see.

The next steps entail adding detail to make this iPod look real. First off, you need to make it appear rounded on the left and right sides. You have several ways to achieve this. You can use the Dodge and Burn tools, and brush in the shadows and highlights that give the iPod some depth, or you can create a gradient. I prefer the gradient method because it makes it easier to consistently re-create the same results.

11. Create a new gradient by sampling colors from the rounded edges on one of the sides of the iPod. When you've finished, the gradient should look something like the gradient in the picture on the right.

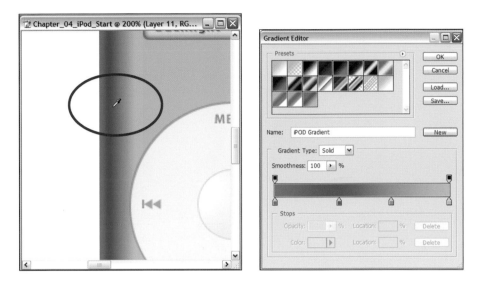

12. Create a new layer named ROUNDED SIDES above the BASE layer.

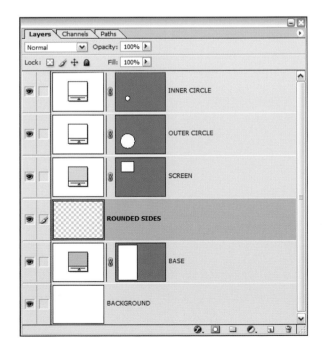

13. Using the Rectangular Marquee tool (*M*), draw a long rectangle along one of the sides of the iPod. It's OK if the selection overlaps the white background slightly.

14. With the ROUNDED SIDES layer active, drag your new gradient from left to right.

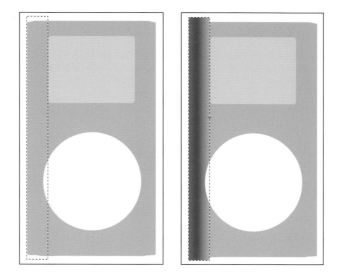

15. Press *CTRL/⌘+D* to deselect the current selection. You'll then notice that the transition isn't quite as smooth as it should be. To fix this, create a thin rectangular selection that encompasses the right edge of the ROUNDED SIDES layer and part of the base iPod shape.

16. Again, with the ROUNDED SIDES layer active, choose Filter ➤ Blur ➤ Gaussian Blur. Enter an amount of 5 px for the Radius setting.

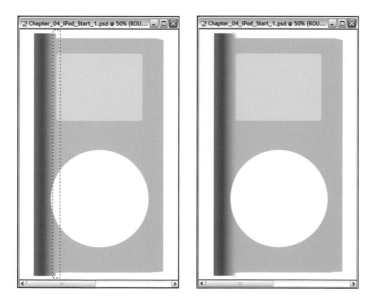

17. If you find the transition is still too sharp, press *CTRL*/⌘+*F* to reapply the filter once or twice more.

18. Once you're happy with the results, duplicate this layer (*CTRL*/⌘+*J*).

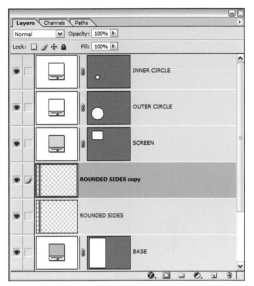

19. Choose Edit ➤ Transform ➤ Flip Horizontal and position this duplicate on the right side of the iPod.

20. With the duplicate layer selected, press *CTRL*/⌘+*E* to merge this layer with the ROUNDED SIDES layer.

21. Finally, to get rid of the overlap area, be sure the ROUNDED SIDES layer is active and group it with the BASE layer by pressing *CTRL/⌘+G*.

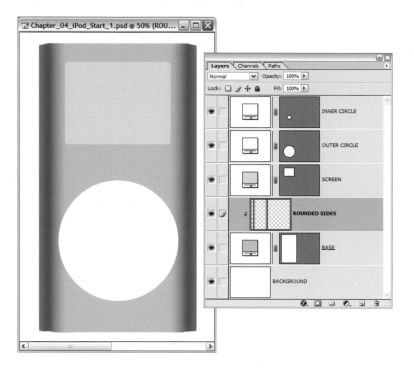

Next, you're going to use layer styles to add some depth to the screen and iPod controls.

22. Double-click the SCREEN layer to display the Layer Style dialog box. Click Inner Glow and enter the following settings:

23. For the OUTER CIRCLE layer, add an Inner Shadow and a Stroke layer style with the following settings:

24. Add Gradient Overlay and Stroke layer styles to the INNER CIRCLE layer.

Much better! Now the iPod should be starting to look real.

Next, you're going to add some text. It can often be a difficult process to match the font on a product. With this one, I got lucky and quickly discovered that Verdana was the font used on the iPod. However, there's a small trick to this process. Since the text is on an LCD screen, it isn't anti-aliased. Follow along and see how to re-create this effect.

25. Select the Horizontal Type tool (*T*). Set the font type to Verdana and the font style to Bold. Set the foreground color to R:89 G:91 B:140.

26. Create five new type layers for the words Playlists, Browse, Extras, Settings, and Backlight.

27. To keep things tidy, click the Playlists type layer to make it active and link the other four text layers to it.

28. Choose New Set From Linked from the Layers palette options menu to create a layer set from these layers. Name this layer set SCREEN TEXT.

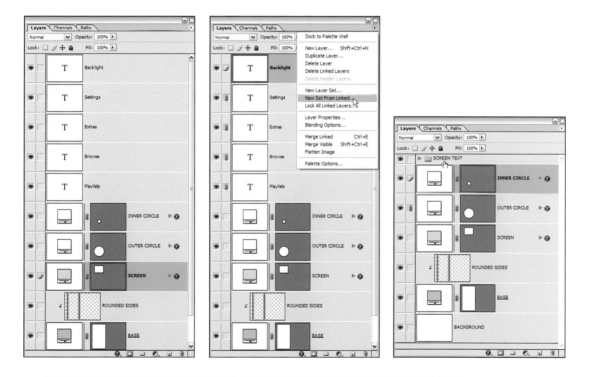

> *If you're not familiar with layer sets, they're an invaluable way to maintain organization in multiple layered Photoshop files. It's a similar concept to placing files into different folders on your computer system. If you didn't have folders, it might be difficult to try to find a file. The same holds true for layer sets in your PSD files.*

Now you're going to change all the type layers at once.

29. Click one of the type layers. They should all still be linked. Also, be sure the Type tool is selected in the toolbox.

30. Hold down the *SHIFT* key and set the anti-aliasing method to None. All of the linked layers should change at the same time.

31. Double-click the Playlists layer to display the Layer Style dialog box. Add a Drop Shadow layer style with the following settings:

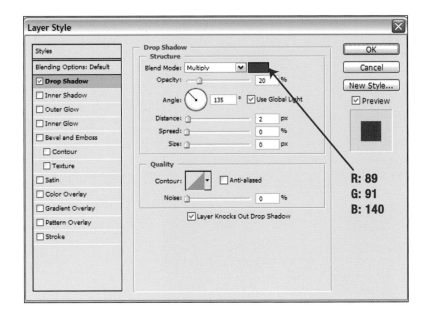

32. Right/*CTRL*-click the Playlists type layer and choose Copy Layer Style. Then right/*CTRL*-click any of the other type layers and choose Paste Style To Linked.

33. Repeat the previous steps for the iPod text at the top.

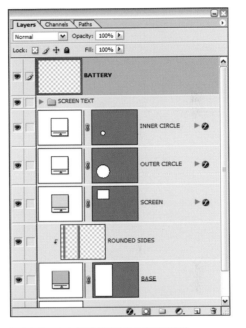

34. To create the battery and divider line, begin by zooming in on the screen.

35. Create a new layer named BATTERY above the SCREEN TEXT layer set.

4

36. Select the Pencil tool (probably hidden by the Brush tool) and set its diameter to 1 pixel. Draw the battery shape as displayed in this image.

119

37. Right/*CTRL*-click one of the type layers you created previously and select Copy Layer Style. Then right/*CTRL*-click the BATTERY layer and select Paste Layer Style to paste the same Drop Shadow layer style.

38. Paste the same layer style to the divider line layer, and add the battery layers and divider line to a layer set named BATTERY.

39. Create the arrows on the left in a similar way. First, create a new layer above BATTERY named ARROW.

40. Zoom in and use the Pencil tool to draw the arrow as displayed in this image. Your layer style should still be copied to the clipboard, so you should be able to right/*CTRL*-click the ARROW layer and select Paste Layer Style to add the drop shadow.

41. Duplicate the ARROW layer four more times and add them to a layer set named ARROWS to keep things organized.

Notice that the Playlists text is actually the selected item from the menu. The text is a different color, and it has a blue bar behind it to signify that it is selected.

42. To fix this, create a new layer named BAR below the SCREEN TEXT layer set.

43. Use the Rectangular Marquee tool to draw a rectangle for the bar. Fill it with R:89 G:91 B:140 (as shown in the leftmost image).

44. Change the color of the Playlists type to R:209 G:211 B:229, the same color as the screen (as in the center image).

45. The arrow will need to be changed too. Since this isn't a type layer, you'll have to *CTRL/*⌘*-*click the appropriate ARROW layer and fill it with R:209 G:211 B:229 (as in the rightmost image).

46. Change your foreground color to R:149 G:149 B:149. Create a new type layer and type the word Menu at the top of the OUTER CIRCLE layer. Set the font to Myriad, and set the anti-aliasing method back to Smooth.

I used custom shapes for the reverse, forward, and play/pause controls. Photoshop includes a triangle custom shape that works perfectly for this task. You can find it by clicking the Shapes options in the Custom Shapes palette options menu.

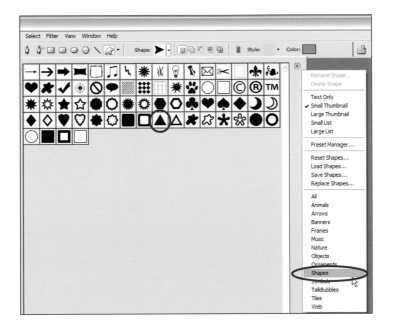

47. Select the Custom Shape tool (*U*) and press the small drop-down arrow to display all available shapes. Select the triangle shape. Also be sure that the Shape layers button is selected in the tool options bar.

48. Set your foreground color to R:168 G:168 B:168. Zoom in on the iPod control area and drag out a small triangle shape at the bottom for the play function.

49. Choose Edit ➤ Transform ➤ Rotate 90 degrees CW to rotate the triangle so it appears to be a small arrow.

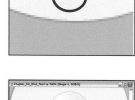

50. Create four copies of this arrow for the forward and reverse functions. You can quickly accomplish this by first making sure the small triangle you just created is the active layer. Then select the Move tool (*V*), and hold the *ALT/OPTION* key down and drag. You'll notice that a double arrow will appear when you hold the *ALT/OPTION* key down. This means that you're going to create a duplicate layer.

51. Position the four copies in the appropriate places on the control wheel. Don't forget to use the Edit ➤ Transform functions to flip the two arrows horizontally for the reverse function.

52. Select the Rectangle tool (*U*) and create a small rectangle. Duplicate this shape and place it accordingly.

53. Now create three layer sets named FORWARD, REVERSE, and PLAY. Place the corresponding layers in these sets to keep the Layers palette organized.

You're almost done! Your iPod should look almost identical to the photo. However, there's one thing missing: the reflection. Adding it is very simple.

54. Hide your Background layer so you can see the transparency grid behind the iPod. Using the Rectangular Marquee tool, place a rectangular selection around the iPod.

> *You need the transparency grid to be visible because the next command (Copy Merged) copies all visible contents on **all** layers to the clipboard. You don't want the white background included in this copy, so you must hide it.*

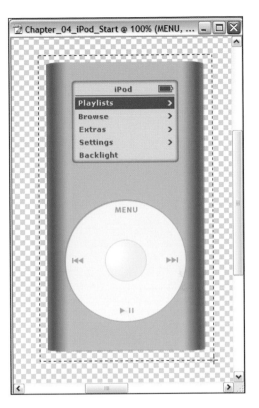

55. Choose Edit ➤ Copy Merged (*SHIFT+CTRL/⌘+C*). Create a new layer named REFLECTION below BASE, and paste (*CTRL/⌘+V*) the copied iPod into this layer.

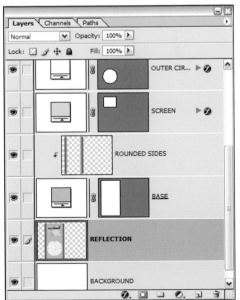

56. Choose Edit ➤ Transform ➤ Flip Vertical. Position the flipped iPod so the top of it matches with the bottom of the BASE layer's iPod. Also note that you can now unhide the white background.

57. Add a layer mask to the REFLECTION layer by clicking the Add Layer Mask button at the bottom of the Layers palette.

58. Using a linear gradient, drag a white-to-black gradient from the top down to simulate a fading reflection, and you're done. Remember that you can unlink the mask from its layer and reposition it to try to get the gradient just right. This may take a few attempts, so don't be discouraged if you don't get it perfect on the first try.

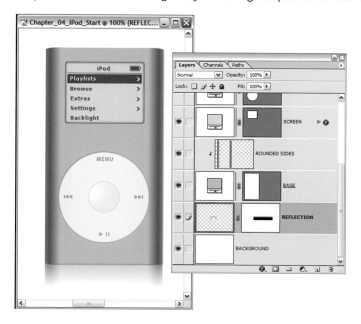

59. A final touchup would be to add small drop shadow to the entire iPod. To do this, select the BASE layer and add a Drop Shadow layer style with the following settings:

60. Save your file as Chapter_04_iPod_Finished.psd.

Layer comps

Now that you've completed your iPod illustration, it seems only natural that your manager may wait until now to ask you to change the iPod's color to green. You have a few ways to complete this task. You can duplicate the source PSD file, saving one file as the blue version and one as green, but that leaves you with two separate files. If you do this enough, you'll double the number of files on your system, and we all know how difficult it can be to manage source files.

Another option is to create two separate layers within the PSD file, with one containing the green iPod. You can then turn the layers on and off depending on which version you need at the time you're showing the client or working on the file. This method gets you slightly closer to a good solution, but what happens when your boss is standing behind you asking you to show her the different options? You'll need to quickly remember what layers need to be hidden or unhidden for the various options. Even worse, what happens one or two years later when you need to reopen the file? You need to remember just what layers need to be hidden and unhidden. I don't know about you, but I can't remember what layers I've hidden in a file or why I've done so even a week after I've created it.

As you may have guessed, this is indeed leading somewhere. With the introduction of Photoshop CS, Adobe has given us a great new tool called **layer comps**. These are snapshots of the current state of the Layers palette.

In short, layer comps allow you to save your Layers palette in a certain state (in this case, the blue iPod). Then when you add layers to make the green iPod, you can create another layer comp. When you switch back and forth between the two layer comps, Photoshop will automatically take care of hiding and showing the appropriate layers for you.

Let's go through a quick layer comps exercise to help make the use of this great feature clearer.

Exercise: Using layer comps

1. Open the file you created in the previous exercise (or you can use Chapter_04_iPod_Finished.psd from the download files).

2. Make the Layer Comps palette visible by choosing Window ➤ Layer Comps. The layers in this file are now in a state that displays the blue iPod. Go ahead and create a layer comp to take a snapshot of this version.

3. Choose New Layer Comp from the Layer Comps palette options menu or click the Create New Layer Comp button at the bottom of the palette. When the New Layer Comp dialog box appears, give the layer comp a meaningful name and be sure Visibility is checked.

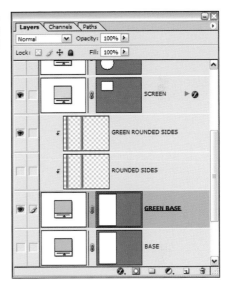

You now have a layer comp of the blue iPod. Next, you're going to make a green version of the iPod and save that as a layer comp.

4. Duplicate the BASE and ROUNDED SIDES layers. Hide the originals and rename the duplicates descriptive like GREEN BASE and GREEN ROUNDED SIDES.

5. Make the GREEN BASE layer active and choose Image ➤ Adjustments ➤ Hue/Saturation. Check Colorize and enter the settings shown here:

You'll notice that the rounded sides don't match up very well. They need to be blended into the new green color of the iPod.

6. To fix this, choose the GREEN ROUNDED SIDES layer and place two rectangular selections around the inner edges of the shadows. Include a good sampling of the area that needs blending as well as the original base layer area. Hold down the *SHIFT* key when you draw the second selection to add it to the first.

7. Choose Filter ➤ Blur ➤ Gaussian Blur and enter 4 px for the Radius setting. Note that this setting may vary for you, so you should experiment with the Radius values.

This procedure takes care of creating a smooth blend between the rounded sides of the iPod and the front. Now all that remains for you to do before creating the layer comp is to replace the blue reflection with a green one.

8. Hide the original REFLECTION layer and create a new reflection by using the process outlined in the previous exercise. You could also attempt to use a Hue/Saturation adjustment on the reflection layer just as you did in step 5. However, it's sometimes difficult to get the colors to match up well.

You now have a green iPod. All that is left to do is make a layer comp out of it.

9. Choose New Layer Comp from the Layer Comps palette options menu once again. Enter a descriptive name (e.g., Green iPod) and click OK.

New Layer Comp

Name: Green iPod

Apply To Layers: ☑ Visibility

☐ Position

☐ Appearance (Layer Style)

Comment:

OK

Cancel

10. Now you can switch back and forth between the two comps by clicking the small area to the left of the layer comp name. Notice how Photoshop takes care of hiding and showing the appropriate layers for you. There's no need for you to remember what layers are associated with a certain comp.

Layer Comps

Last Document State

Blue iPod

Green iPod

As you can see, layer comps are a welcome addition to Photoshop CS. The feature may not have seemed like much in this exercise, as you had only two layers that needed to be hidden or shown. But you can imagine the time savings layer comps can provide to a professional designer working with multiple files and many more layers. Remember that in the design industry (like most others) time is money. Any feature that can save you time now or in the future is well worth learning.

Summary

To wrap up this chapter and, for that matter, this section of the book on realism and photorealistic techniques in Photoshop, the suggestion I'd like to leave you with concerning where to go from here is to build your portfolio. A good portfolio is the best way to move forward with this type of work in the professional world. The good part about this suggestion is that, because of the technology available today, inspiration is all around you. With digital cameras and scanners as inexpensive as they are, you can capture a scene from real life and use that reference to begin building your portfolio in Photoshop. Also, inspiration and knowledge for realism-based work is all around you. As you sit at your desk, on an airplane, or in a car, just look around you. Study the environment and try to imagine how you can apply what you see to your work in Photoshop. Light, shadows, depth, perspective, and volume are properties of everything you see. The more you study them in real life, the closer you'll be able to imitate these aspects of realism in Photoshop, and the better your work will be.

PART TWO CARTOONING IN PHOTOSHOP

What can I say about pixel art other than that the designers who create it have way too much time on their hands? All joking aside, pixel art has taken on a life of its own in recent years. Once at center stage in the gaming revolution, pixel art has been forced into the background, mostly as the result of advances in processing power and the popularity of 3D. However, pixel art still has a place in today's graphic design market. Mobile phones, PDAs, and other small, handheld devices use this very compact graphic design medium as their primary graphic display. This coupled with the fact that pixel art employs the most fundamental graphic design principals and is the very heart of all graphics displayed on the computer screen assures us that this art form will be here for many years to come.

In this chapter, we will examine the basics of pixel art. You'll learn how isometric systems are involved in pixel art, and how simple lighting and shading techniques make this art form come to life. In addition, you'll discover how to deconstruct simple shapes and develop the framework for creating more complex illustrations. Finally, you'll learn how to create professional-grade pixel art illustrations.

Setting up

Setting up for pixel art is a fairly easy process. Since the very basis of pixel art is so simple, it requires few Photoshop tools. Before delving into any exercises, let's explore the basic tools you'll use and discuss how to set Photoshop up to make your life simpler.

Pencil tool

First and foremost is the Pencil tool. It's a seldom-used tool in Photoshop. Heck, you may not have used it before if you've never worked with pixel art. While working through this chapter, you'll get to know this tool well. In fact, why don't you repeat after me: "The Pencil tool is my friend." Great! Now that we've got that covered, let's see where this tool resides.

As you can see from this reference image, the Pencil tool is located next to the Brush tool. You can access it by clicking the Brush tool icon in the toolbar and holding down your mouse button to reveal the flyout menu. Alternatively, you can press the *B* key (*SHIFT+B* if you haven't changed your preferences as discussed in Chapter 1) until you notice the Pencil tool move to the front.

Once you've selected the Pencil tool, you'll see a brush size setting in the tool options bar similar to the brush-based tools in Photoshop.

The first thing you'll need to do is set this size to 1 pixel. Every image you see on your computer screen is formed from pixels. The pixel is the building block of digital art and the most basic shape in Photoshop.

Marquee tools

The Rectangular and Elliptical Marquee tools will also come in handy when you create pixel art illustrations. You should already be familiar with these tools, but there's one trick to using them that you might not know. When you work with

the Elliptical Marquee tool, you need to turn off the anti-aliasing function. For most digital artwork this function is necessary, but in the pixel art world it's a bad thing. To turn this function off, just uncheck the Anti-aliased check box in the tool options bar when the Elliptical Marquee tool is selected.

5

> *Be sure to recheck the* Anti-aliased *box when you've finished working on your pixel art project. It can wreak havoc on your patience when you're trying to create something in Photoshop that requires anti-aliasing to be turned on.*
>
> *On a positive note, unchecking the* Anti-aliased *box is a great prank to play on a fellow designer when he isn't looking. It's rather amusing to watch him look at Photoshop and know something just isn't right, but not being able to figure it out!*

Magic Wand tool

The Magic Wand tool will often be your savior when working with pixel art. It allows you to quickly select large areas to color. The Magic Wand tool resides directly below the Move tool.

When you use the Magic Wand tool, it's important to remember that you need to click the layer that contains the area you would like to select. In most of the exercises in this book, you'll use layers to keep things organized. In the pixel art exercises in this chapter, you'll use one layer for outlines and one for fill colors. The outline layers will provide you with the selection needed for your fill layers. Just remember to have the outline layer active when you click inside it with the Magic Wand tool.

An important setting in the Magic Wand tool is the Contiguous option. You can find this setting in the tool options bar when the Magic Wand tool is selected.

Checking the Contiguous check box forces the resulting selection to be constrained to adjacent areas of the same color. Without it, you may inadvertently select unwanted areas in your illustration to fill.

One final note about the Magic Wand tool is that it also has an Anti-aliased option, much like the Elliptical Marquee tool. While not always necessary, it's a good idea to ensure that anti-aliasing is turned off when you work with pixel art.

Zooming and navigating

Zooming is a fairly simple process in Photoshop, and you've likely done it a million times. However, there's one trick that you might not be aware of. It comes in handy with pixel art especially, but it's good to keep this technique in mind for other types of work as well. There's an option within the Window ➤ Arrange menu called New Window For (*your current document title*). If you've used this feature in previous versions of Photoshop, you may recall accessing it by choosing View ➤ New View.

When you choose Window ➤ Arrange ➤ New Window For (*your current document title*), Photoshop will open a new window to display the same document you're currently working on.

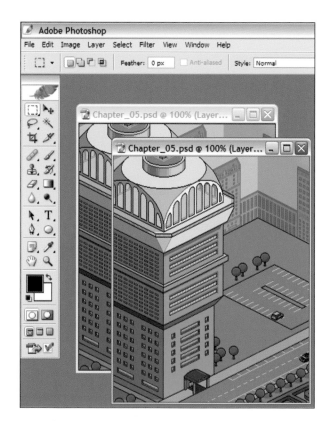

Note that this function is different from choosing the Duplicate option under the Image menu. Instead of creating a new file, which is what Image ➤ Duplicate does, this function creates a new view of your existing file. Since you'll often work in a zoomed-in state with pixel art, you can keep one window zoomed in at all times and the other set at 100% view.

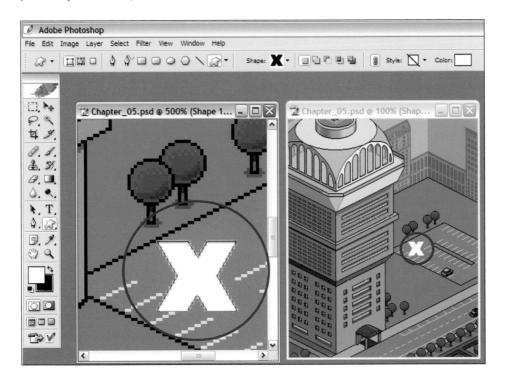

As you can see from the preceding image, when a white *X* is added to one window, it's also displayed in the other window, since both windows refer to the same file. This technique enables you to always see what your actual image will look like without continuously zooming in and out.

The process of navigating around the image is also important when you're working with pixel art. Since dragging the horizontal and vertical scrollbars in a window can be time consuming, Photoshop provides several other methods of navigating to different areas of your image. The first is the Navigator palette.

This palette allows you to scroll through your current image visually by providing a small thumbnail of the entire canvas. This thumbnail displays the area of the image that is currently in view by displaying a red square around it.

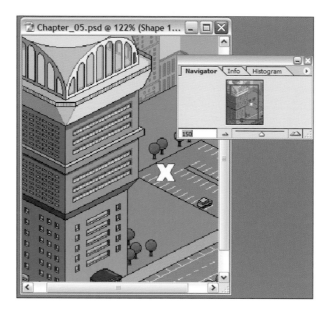

When you hover your mouse pointer over an area in this palette, it will change to a small, pointed-finger icon. This lets you know that if you click this point, your window view will jump to the area clicked in the Navigator palette.

If you hover your mouse pointer over the red rectangle, it will change to an open-hand icon. This lets you know that you can drag the red rectangle (your current view) around the thumbnail.

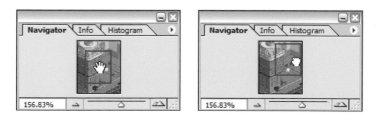

Here are a few more helpful shortcuts for zooming and navigating:

- Hold down the spacebar to temporarily access the Hand tool when you work on your images. This allows you to navigate around your image with the ease and speed of the Hand tool (*H*), while keeping whatever tool you're working with active.

- The *CTRL*/⌘ + (plus) and *CTRL*/⌘ – (minus) shortcuts provide quick access to the zoom feature in Photoshop. Much like the spacebar shortcut, they allow you to quickly zoom in or out of your image without switching tools.

Navigating and zooming are indeed important aspects of your workflow in Photoshop. You'll find that by taking advantage of the tools and shortcuts offered to make these tasks easier, you'll significantly increase the efficiency and speed of your work within the application.

ImageReady

ImageReady is the last area of pixel art setup that I'll discuss. If you're not familiar with ImageReady, it's a complementary software program, included with Photoshop, that is mainly geared toward web graphic creation and animation. Many designers create their graphics in Photoshop and jump over to ImageReady to slice up the graphics for the Web or to create animations bound for a website. Although ImageReady is similar to Photoshop, there are some significant differences between the programs that make it an appealing choice for creating pixel art. One difference is that when you move the contents of a layer in ImageReady, the graphics actually appear less opaque. This allows you to see through and place your graphics more accurately.

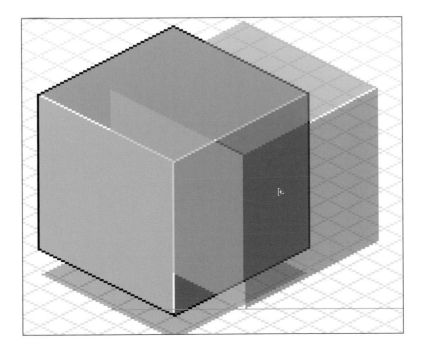

In pixel art, this capability can be a great advantage because you may often tile objects together. A good example of this feature's usefulness is a simple pixel art box.

In Photoshop, you can duplicate this box and use the arrow keys to nudge it into place next to the original, which can be a time-consuming process. In ImageReady, you can just select the Move tool (*V*), click the layer that you'd like to tile, and position the box in place visually because you're able to see through it to the layer below.

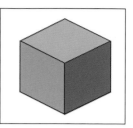

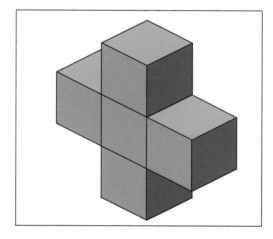

That said, the choice of using Photoshop or ImageReady for pixel art is yours. You can complete this chapter's exercises in either program, and the tools are the same. I'll use Photoshop throughout the chapter, but I wanted to draw this little-known feature of ImageReady to your attention. It may prove to be a real time-saver one day.

The mathematics of pixel art

First off, please don't run for the hills because "mathematics" appears in this section's title. I know I may be bringing back horrible memories from high school or college, but please keep the mental anguish accusations to a minimum. I promise to be brief.

Isometric perspective

Pixel art is based on an isometric view of objects. In short, **isometric** scenes, views, and objects contain no vanishing point and have no perspective. This means that all measurements in pixel art are to scale, no matter how close or how far away they are from the viewer's perspective. Conversely, when you view objects in true perspective, they appear reduced in size as they recede toward the horizon.

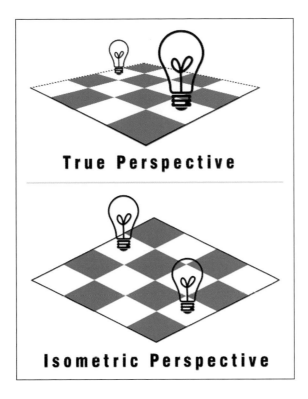

True Perspective

Isometric Perspective

Isometric perspective was commonly used in games and technical illustrations many years ago, and to a large extent it's still used today. Although 3D has replaced many instances where an isometric view would have been used, this concept is still very important in graphic design and is worth knowing more about.

To keep this brief, isometric views are typically based on angles of 30 degrees. However, in pixel art, angles of 30 degrees will produce a jagged line.

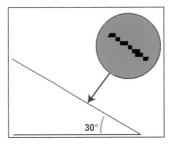

Instead, pixel art uses an angle of 26.565 degrees. It sounds crazy that the number makes such a difference, but consider the quality of the line in the following image drawn at that angle:

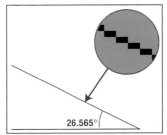

By now, you're probably thinking that I lied when I said there wouldn't be much math involved—this angle and degree stuff sure sounds like math. Actually, you rarely need to remember the 26.565-degree angle because, in Photoshop, this translates to a simple process with the Pencil tool. To see this in action, place 2 pixels next to each other, then move the cursor up, and insert 2 more pixels. The following image shows this process repeated six times each to the right and left, creating a stair-step effect.

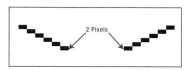

There are times when you'll type the angle setting directly into a text box, but this will only speed up the pixel art creation process, and that one angle is all you'll need to know. For now, just remember the pixel art motto: "Two across, one up."

If you'd like to verify the 26.565-degree angle mentioned previously, the process is simple. Zoom in on your stepped pixel art image. Select the Measure tool (located under the Eyedropper tool). Now click the bottom and drag it toward the top-right corner. As you drag, you'll notice several numbers changing in the tool options bar. The number you're concerned about here is the angle setting, which is displayed as an A in the tool options bar.

Breaking the rules

As you most likely already know, there are exceptions to every rule, and sometimes you must break the rules altogether. I made a habit of this in grade school and high school, and that practice has served me well in my adult years when using various software programs.

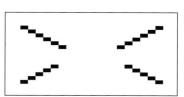

One of the rules to break relates to the stepped approach I described in the previous section. If take the process at face value, the only pixel art lines you would create would be the "Two across, one up" kind.

Who says you need to always move up? Perhaps you need to move down. The same rule applies.

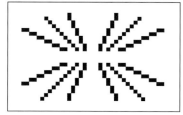

In addition, you may find that you need a steeper angle to complete certain objects. In those situations, you can take a patterned step approach, even though it doesn't conform to the "Two across, one up (or down)" rule.

Finally, you'll often need horizontal and vertical lines. Remember from Chapter 1 that vertical lines in the real world are always vertical in art as well. This holds true for pixel art. In fact, the height of any vertical structure in pixel art will be built with a vertical line. In general, you use the stepped approach to add depth to an object. With that said, here is the final pixel art matrix of acceptable lines:

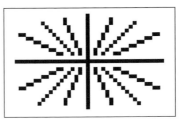

Again, the stepped approach may not always work, and you may need to resort to another approach for more complex objects. This is especially true for rounded forms. But this approach offers more flexibility and options to you when you're faced with various pixel art tasks.

Exercise: Setting up the isometric grid

Setting up an isometric grid can be a great time-saver when you're working with pixel art. Positioning this grid below your pixel art illustration can help make your pixel work more accurate and less time consuming. In addition, you need to create this grid only once. After you save it, the grid will be available for any pixel artwork that you face in the future.

1. Create a new RGB Photoshop canvas that is 40 X 40 pixels. Zoom in to 1600% view on this small document. Create a new layer above the Background layer.

> It's helpful to remember that 1600% is the maximum zoom level in Photoshop.

2. Select black as your foreground color, and then select the Pencil tool. Be sure the brush size is set to 1 pixel.

3. On the new layer, starting in the top-left corner, draw 2 pixels from left to right.

4. Move down 1 pixel and draw 2 more pixels to the right of the original 2 pixels.

5. Repeat the previous step twice.

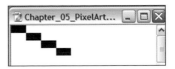

6. Next, press *CTRL/⌘+J* to duplicate the layer.

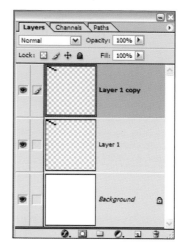

7. Drag the pixels in the new layer down and to the right of the original to continue the stepped approach.

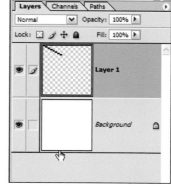

8. Merge the two pixel layers together (*CTRL/⌘+E*) so there is only one layer above the Background layer.

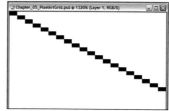

9. Repeat this process until the pixels run off the canvas. Also, be sure that you've merged all pixel layers so only one pixel layer exists above the Background layer.

10. Duplicate this layer (*CTRL/⌘+J*), so you now have two layers above the Background layer.

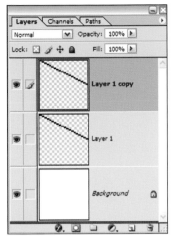

11. With the duplicate layer active, select the Move tool (*V*), hold down the *SHIFT* key, and press the down arrow key once. This will move your pixel line down 10 pixels.

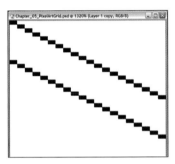

12. Repeat this process three more times: twice to create the two lines below the two you've already created and once more for the line above your original line.

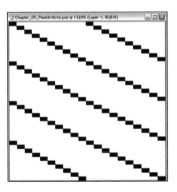

13. Merge all of the pixel layers so that once again you have only one layer above the Background layer.

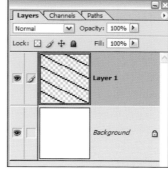

14. Duplicate this layer. Make the duplicate layer active and choose Edit ➤ Transform ➤ Flip Horizontal.

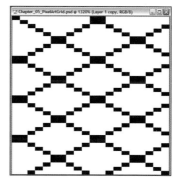

15. OK, you're almost done. All that remains is to nudge the duplicate up one time with the up arrow key. This makes the pattern line up perfectly and allows you to tile it in the future.

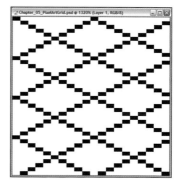

16. Hide the Background layer so the transparency shows through, and choose Select ➤ All (*CTRL*/⌘+*A*). This puts a selection around the entire canvas.

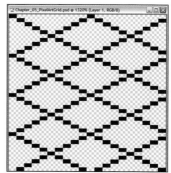

17. With the selection active, choose Edit ➤ Define Pattern. Name your pattern Pixel Grid and click OK.

There you have it: a pixel grid pattern. Now, every time you begin a pixel art illustration, you can open Photoshop and apply this pattern to the background. It will tile perfectly and create a pixel grid to aid you in your pixel art development. Here's how:

18. Create a new 640 × 480-pixel canvas in Photoshop.

19. Create a new layer above the Background layer named GRID.

20. With the new layer active, choose Edit ➤ Fill (*SHIFT+BACKSPACE*). In the Fill dialog box, choose Pattern from the Use drop-down list. Then set Custom Pattern to the pixel grid pattern you just created.

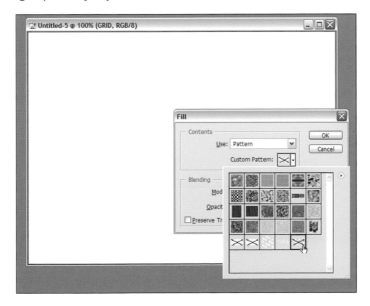

21. Click OK and your pattern will be applied seamlessly to the new layer.

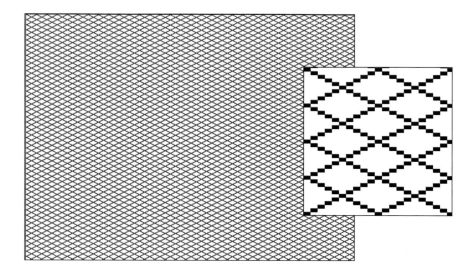

22. You can also reduce the opacity of the GRID layer to make it easier to trace over. In the following image, I've reduced the opacity of the grid to 25%.

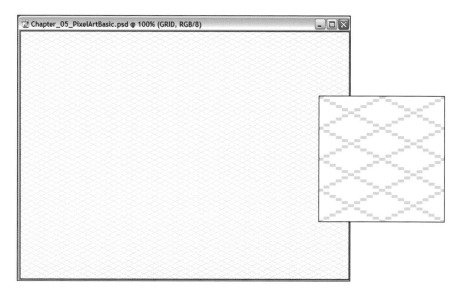

Exercise: Using basic outline, fill, and coloring techniques

1. Create a new 640 × 480 RGB Photoshop canvas. Create a new layer above the Background layer named GRID and fill it with the pixel grid pattern, as described in the previous exercise.

2. Next, create a new layer above GRID named OUTLINE.

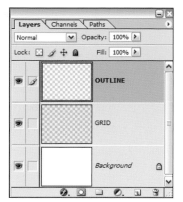

3. Select the Pencil tool and set black as the foreground color. Zoom in as much as needed so you don't go blind trying to see the pixels you're about to paint. (Somewhere between 500% and 800% usually works well for me. Then again, I wear glasses with "Coke-bottle" lenses, so you may need to find your own personal preferences.)

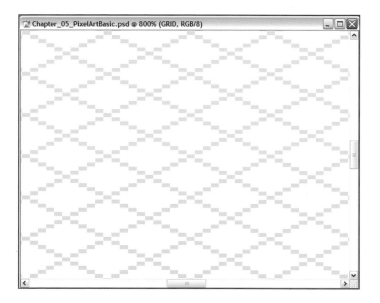

4. Use the Pencil tool to paint pixels along seven grid boxes just as you did when building the grid. Feel free to use the duplicate and merge process you used earlier, so you don't have to paint the entire line.

> *Photoshop often has the* Snap *feature turned on by default. While* Snap *may be useful in many circumstances, pixel art is typically not one of them. If you find snapping gets in your way, you can choose* View ➤ Snap *to turn off the feature.*

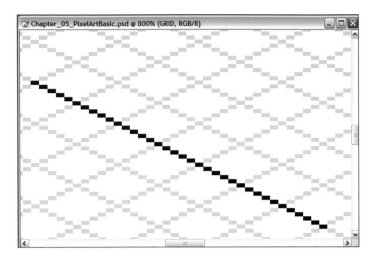

For duplicating pixel art, selecting the Move tool and holding the ALT/OPTION key provides a great shortcut.

5. Now duplicate the layer containing this line. Choose Edit ➤ Transform ➤ Flip Vertical. Then position the new line in place, so the bottom-left 2 pixels of the duplicate overlap the top-left 2 pixels of the original.

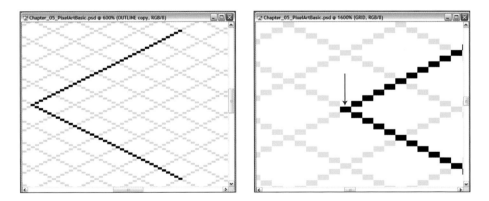

The alternative to using the menu to transform is to press CTRL/⌘+T to display the Free Transform bounding box. Right-click and you'll see a context menu appear with the same options you see when you choose Edit ➤ Transform through the menu.

6. Merge these two layers together (*Ctrl/⌘+E*).

7. Duplicate the layer once again. Flip this layer horizontally and position it in place so the top-left and bottom-left 2 pixels overlap the original layer's top-right and bottom-right 2 pixels.

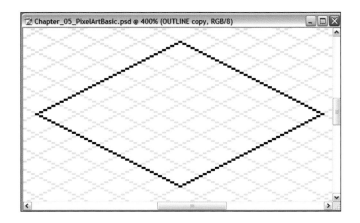

8. Merge these two layers together as well (*Ctrl/⌘+E*).

The basic outline is in place. Now you need to color it.

9. Select the Magic Wand tool (*W*). Ensure that the Contiguous option is checked in the tool options bar.

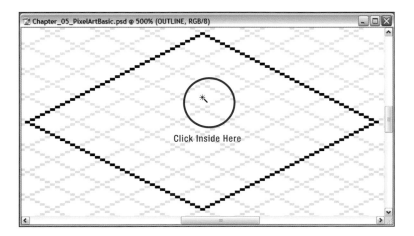

10. With the OUTLINE layer active, click once inside the outline. This will put a selection around the inside of the outline.

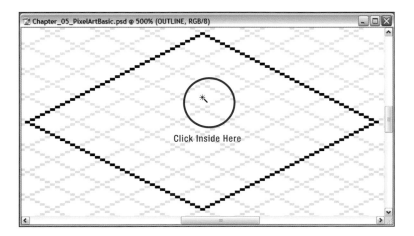

11. Create a new layer above OUTLINE named FILL. Do not deselect yet, though.

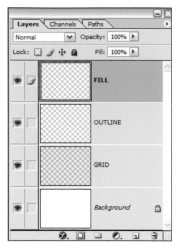

12. Set your foreground color to R:0 G:174 B:239. On the FILL layer, fill the selection with the foreground color (*ALT/OPTION+BACKSPACE*).

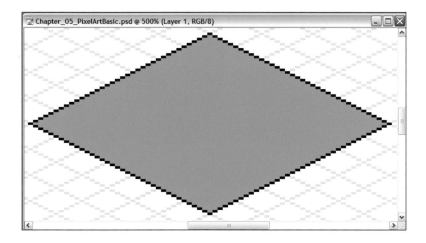

Now that wasn't too difficult, was it? This exercise forms the basis of pixel art. Everything from here builds on these steps, but the basic creation of objects in pixel art will usually follow the same processes.

Lighting

Lighting is a very important aspect of pixel art. Without it, this pixel art cube appears very flat:

Lighting in the pixel art world is similar to lighting in the real world. A light source exists at some point in your image. That light source shines on an object and produces highlights, shadows, light tones, and dark tones. For simplicity's sake in this chapter, you'll assume that the light source is always positioned at the top left. In fact, whenever you produce pixel art, this is generally a safe assumption.

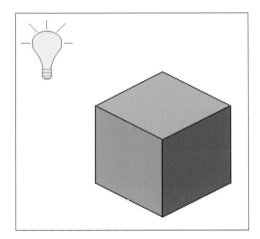

As you can see from this image, the pixel art cube reacts to light in a similar way to an object in the real world.

Shading

Shading works in a similar way to lighting. Whatever surfaces aren't facing the light source are darker. However, varying degrees of shading make pixel art look more professional. The following image displays the same cube as before, with only two shades of purple used: a light shade for the sides facing the light source, and a darker shade for all other sides.

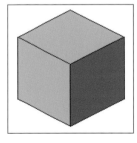

As you can see, the preceding image doesn't look quite right. The image doesn't take into account the fact that even if a side of the cube isn't facing the light source directly, it may still be indirectly picking up some of the light. This will cause those sides to be shaded darker than the most lit side, but lighter than the side that isn't facing the light source at all.

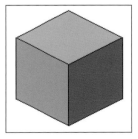

The important thing to take away from this discussion is that you need only three basic colors for an object in the pixel art world: a light tone, a mid tone, and a dark tone. Nearly all pixel art objects follow this pattern. There are, of course, exceptions to this rule, and as your pixel art becomes more complex, you may notice that you're breaking this rule more often. But even then, the basic principles of lighting and shading still apply.

Exercise: Creating a cube

1. Create a new 800 × 600 RGB Photoshop canvas. Start by adding the pixel art grid as you did in the previous exercise. Also, create a new layer named CUBE OUTLINE above the GRID layer. Either reuse the outline from the previous exercise or create a new one here. Either way, you should have an image like the following when you begin:

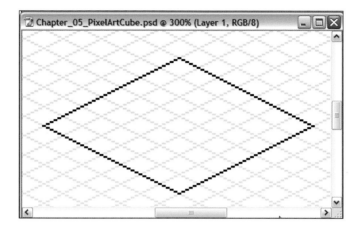

2. Duplicate the CUBE OUTLINE layer. Using the Move tool, drag this layer up seven grid squares.

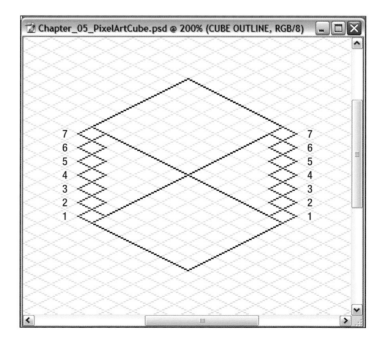

3. Merge the two layers together.

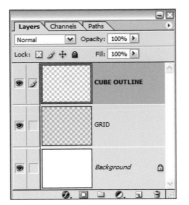

4. Use the Pencil tool to connect the top outline to the bottom outline. You can do this by clicking the top leftmost pixel once to place a starting pixel. Then, hold down the *SHIFT* key and click the bottom leftmost point. This produces a straight line with just two clicks.

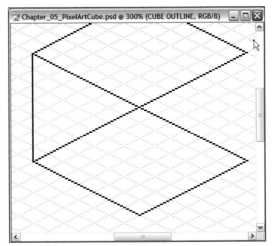

5. Duplicate this line for the center and the right side of the cube. Merge them all together once when you're done.

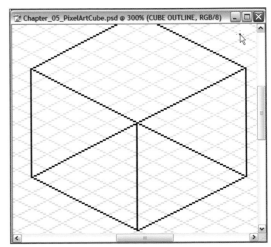

6. Now erase the unwanted lines inside the cube surfaces with the Eraser tool (*E*). Be sure to change the Mode setting of the Eraser tool from Brush to Pencil. Alternatively, you can use any of the selection tools and press the *DELETE* key to clear the areas.

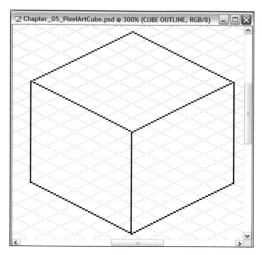

7. Now let's add some color. This time, instead of using just one color, you're going to take lighting and shading into consideration. I've included a small light source icon at the top left to remind you.

8. Create a new layer named CUBE FILL above CUBE OUTLINE.

9. Just as before, select the Magic Wand tool and be sure Contiguous is selected in the tool options bar.

10. With the CUBE OUTLINE layer active, click once inside the left side of the outline. This puts a selection around the inside of the outline.

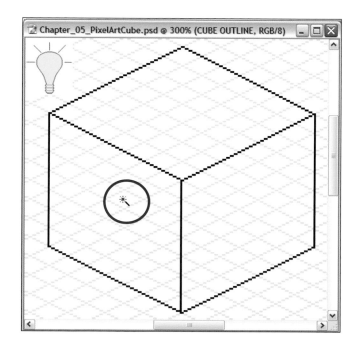

11. Set your foreground color to R:204 G:154 B:204. On the CUBE FILL layer, fill the selection with the foreground color (*ALT/OPTION+BACKSPACE*).

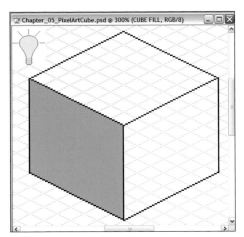

12. Click the CUBE OUTLINE layer to make it active. Use the Magic Wand tool to select the far-right side. Then click the CUBE FILL layer once and fill that selection with R:153 G:102 B:153. Notice that the color is darker than the first color you used. This side is the furthest away from the light source, so it will be the darkest.

> Note that in order for the Magic Wand tool to work properly, the layer in which you want to select an area from must be the active layer.

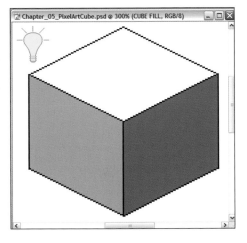

13. Repeat this process for the top side of the cube. This time, fill it with R:232 G:174 B:232. The top side receives the most light, so the color will be the brightest.

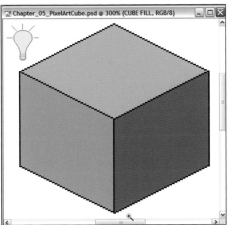

OK, the cube is looking good so far. It's shaded, and you now have a good grasp of how to build and color most objects in pixel art. One last trick that many pixel artists use is to add a highlight outline around the edges of an object.

14. Duplicate the CUBE OUTLINE layer and rename it HIGHLIGHT OUTLINE.

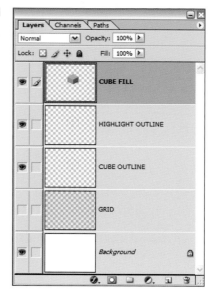

15. Choose Image ➤ Adjustments ➤ Invert (*CTRL*/⌘+*I*) to invert the color of the highlight outline and change it from black to white.

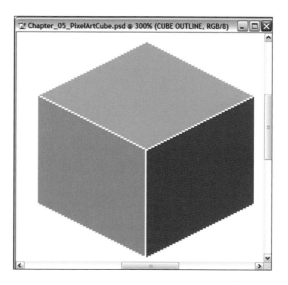

16. Now select the Eraser tool. Set the Mode to Pencil in the tool options bar and change the brush size to 8.

17. With the HIGHLIGHT OUTLINE layer active, erase all but the center line and the top two lines that protrude from it. The larger brush setting you selected in the previous step makes this process easier. However, you may find it necessary to reduce the size of the brush when you get closer to the edges, to ensure accuracy.

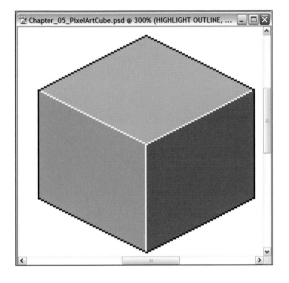

Exercise: Creating a circle

Rounded shapes can be the hardest ones to create from an isometric viewpoint. While a circle can be fairly easy, other rounded shapes become more difficult. This is not only true from a pixel drawing standpoint, but also from a coloring standpoint. Rounded shapes tend to be difficult to shade since most don't contain flat sides, but gradations of color. However, you'll see that with a few simple techniques, you can understand and tackle this process quickly.

Let's start with a circle.

1. Create a new 640 × 480 Photoshop canvas. It's always good to repeat the same grid-creation process from the first exercise (fill the Background layer with the saved grid pattern). Even though this exercise won't directly take advantage of the grid, most other shapes will, so it's always a good idea to have one.

2. Select the Elliptical Marquee tool. As mentioned earlier, be sure that Anti-aliased is unchecked in the tool options bar.

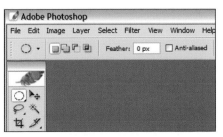

3. Create a new layer named CIRCLE OUTLINE above your grid.

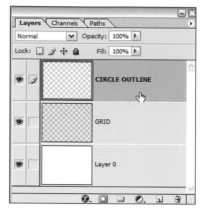

4. Zoom in on the grid. Hold down the *SHIFT* key and use the Marquee tool to create a perfect circle. Mine is seven grid squares wide, but the width really doesn't make a difference here. (See the illustrations below Step 5.)

5. Choose Edit ➤ Stroke. Set the stroke width to 1 pixel, the color to black, and the location setting to Center. Leave the other settings at their defaults and click OK. Don't deselect yet, though. Note that I've hidden the selection in the following reference image so you can see the stroke.

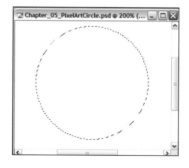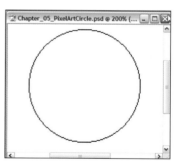

6. Next, create a new layer above CIRCLE OUTLINE and name it CIRCLE FILL.

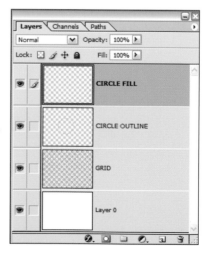

7. Choose Select ➤ Modify ➤ Contract. Enter 1 in the Contract By field and click OK. This will leave the area within the outline selected.

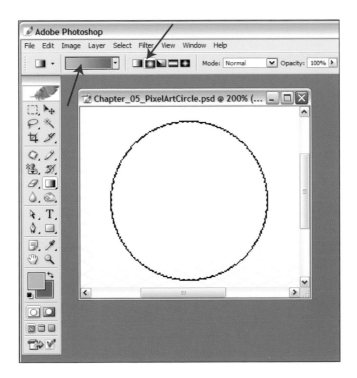

8. Set your foreground color to R:232 G:174 B:232 and your background color to R:153 G:102 B:153. Select the Gradient tool. Click the Radial Gradient button in the tool options bar and be sure that foreground to background is the type of gradient chosen.

9. With the CIRCLE FILL layer active, drag a radial gradient from the top left to the bottom right of the selection.

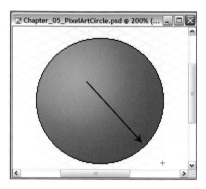

The circle looks good so far, but there's a problem. The piece is supposed to look pixilated, isn't it? The gradient looks way too smooth for pixel art. An alternative to using the Gradient tool is to draw the pixels by hand with the Pencil tool. While this may be necessary for some pixel art objects, it isn't for this example. Here's an easy way to fix it.

10. Be sure the CIRCLE FILL layer is active and choose Image ➤ Adjustments ➤ Posterize. Enter 18 for the Levels setting and click OK. Instant pixelation!

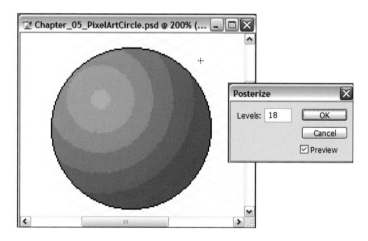

Feel free to experiment with the Levels setting of the Posterize dialog box, as different values may achieve better results for your individual work.

That completes the circle. As you can see, the process is pretty straightforward. Next, let's try a cylinder.

11. Hide or delete the circle layers since you don't need them anymore. Create a new layer named CYLINDER OUTLINE.

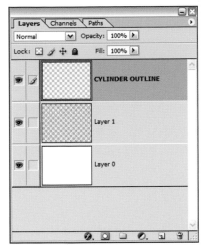

12. Select the Elliptical Marquee tool (again, make sure anti-aliasing is turned off) and draw an oval spanning about six grid squares. Stroke this selection with the same settings you used for the circle.

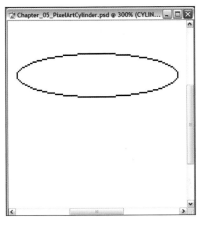

13. Duplicate the CYLINDER OUTLINE layer and drag the copy down on the canvas. Merge (*CTRL*/⌘+*E*) the two layers.

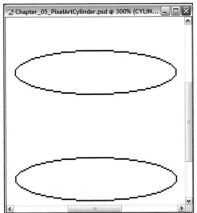

14. Next, select the Pencil tool and draw lines down the sides just as you did with the cube. Again, be sure to merge all outline layers when you're done.

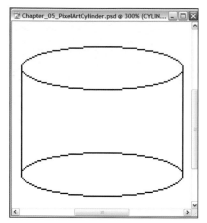

15. Select the Eraser tool and erase the top of the bottommost oval, as this line is hidden from view.

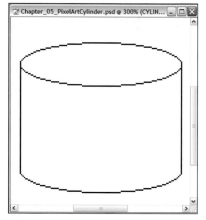

16. Create a new layer named CYLINDER FILL above CYLINDER OUTLINE.

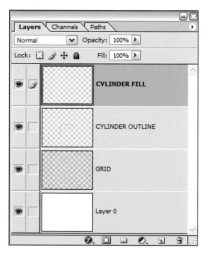

17. Using the Magic Wand tool, select the area within the top of the cylinder. Make the CYLINDER FILL layer active and fill the selection with R:229 G:227 B:102. This is the top of the cylinder, and it's receiving most of the light, so it will be the brightest color.

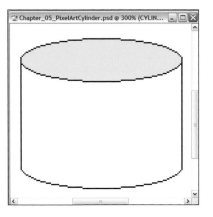

18. Once again, use the Magic Wand tool to select the inside front of the cylinder. Set the foreground color to R:200 G:198 B:89 and the background color to R:151 G:118 B:50.

19. Drag a linear foreground to background gradient from the left to the right of the cylinder. Don't deselect yet, though.

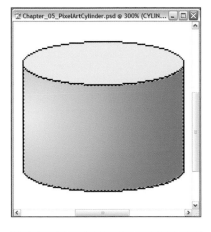

20. Repeat step 10 from the circle exercise to posterize the gradient so it doesn't look too smooth. I used a Levels setting of 18 for the posterize adjustment here.

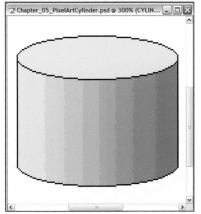

Next, you'll add a highlight to the front of the cylinder outline.

21. Duplicate the CYLINDER OUTLINE layer and name it CYLINDER HIGHLIGHT. Be sure to place the highlight layer above the original outline layer in the Layers palette.

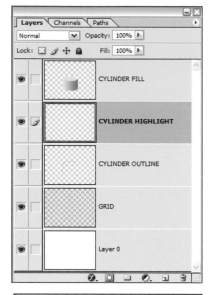

22. With the highlight copy active, invert the colors (*CTRL*/⌘+*I*). You should now see a white highlight instead of a black highlight.

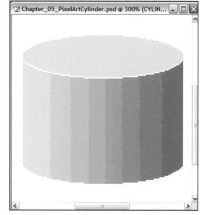

23. Using the Eraser tool, erase all but the bottom of the top oval outline to make it appear as though a highlight is surrounding the front of the cylinder.

Lastly, an essential part of lighting is shadows. Since you have a light shining from the top left, the cylinder should produce a shadow toward the bottom right.

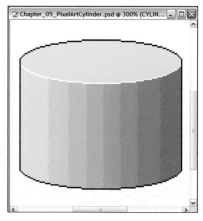

24. Create a new layer named SHADOW below CYLINDER OUTLINE.

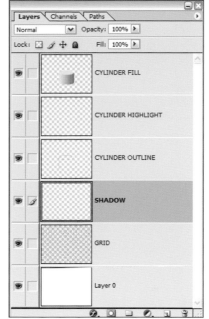

25. Use the Elliptical Marquee tool to create an oval. Position the selection so that part of the oval protrudes from the bottom-right side of the cylinder. Fill this selection with black.

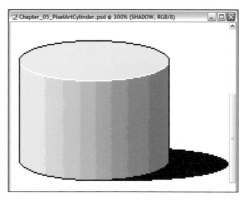

26. Finally, reduce the opacity of the SHADOW layer to around 40%.

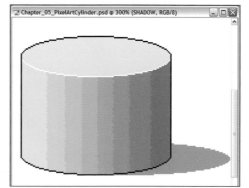

Here's the full, zoomed-out view of the cylinder:

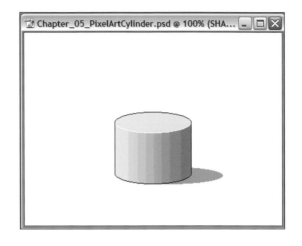

Text

Creating text is another common need in pixel art. Unfortunately, the settings you use to work with type in Photoshop won't work well with pixel art.

Anti-aliasing

The most important of these settings is anti-aliasing. This function lets you produce smooth-edged type by partially filling the edge pixels. The result is edges that appear to blend into the background—a big "no" in pixel art. When anti-aliasing is turned off, this smoothing doesn't occur.

As you can see from the preceding image, the anti-aliased *S* shape breaks all the rules of pixel art. For that reason, it's important to remember to turn anti-aliasing off when you work with type and pixel art. You can do this by setting the anti-aliasing method to None in the tool options bar when you have selected a type tool.

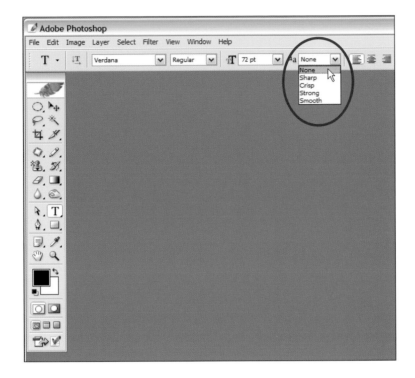

Remember to turn anti-aliasing back on when you're done with your pixel art project. The usual setting for working with type is Smooth.

Pixel fonts

Pixel fonts, commonly known as **bitmap fonts**, are designed so that every part of every character falls on the monitor's pixels. This makes it possible to have crisp and legible fonts at small sizes. Unfortunately, commonly used fonts (e.g., Verdana, Myriad, and Times New Roman) won't work well when converted to pixel art. Pixel fonts, however, are a great alternative to quickly create text for pixel art. Although pixel fonts are designed for small text, you can scale them (usually in increments of 8: 8 pt, 16 pt, 24 pt, etc.) as large as you need them to be. This saves you the time-consuming task of creating each character with the Pencil tool.

Listed here are a few websites that offer free pixels fonts in addition to some very nice fonts available for purchase:

- www.pixelfreak.com
- www.fontsforflash.com
- www.ultrafonts.com

There is one caveat here. Even though using a pixel font makes it easier to create text in pixel art, there is more to the process. By simply creating a character with a pixel font you would get this:

Notice how this font doesn't follow the isometric rules for pixel art? You'll first need to skew the font so it appears at the proper angle:

Then you'll need to add some depth, and some color and outlines just as you did in the previous exercises. This process is fairly simple, and it's faster than creating the text on your own.

Exercise: Creating text

For this next exercise, I downloaded a pixel font, named FFF Forward, from www.fontsforflash.com. This font is free, so you can download it as well to follow along with this exercise.

1. Create a new 640 × 480 Photoshop canvas.

2. Set black as your foreground color. Select the Type tool and make sure that the anti-aliasing method is set to None. Select the FFF Forward font and type the letter E. Most pixel fonts are best suited to multiples of 8 when it comes to font size. For this reason, try to make sure that whatever font size you choose is divisible by 8. For example, I chose a 72 pt size for this letter: 72 / 8 = 9, right? I bet you didn't know you'd get a math lesson here, too!

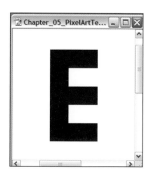

3. With the type layer active, press *CTRL/⌘+T* to display the Free Transform bounding box. Note the settings available in the tool options bar at the top.

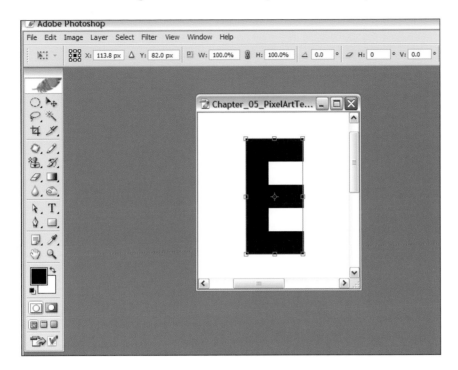

4. Enter −26.565 next to the Vertical Skew (V) setting in the tool options bar. Remember, I mentioned earlier that knowing that angle may help from time to time. This is one of those times. Press *ENTER* to accept the changes.

5. Create a new layer named TYPE OUTLINE above the type layer.

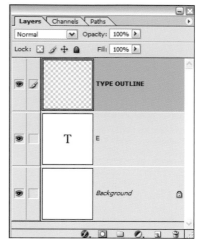

6. *CTRL*/⌘-click the type layer to put a selection around the E. With the TYPE OUTLINE layer active, choose Edit ➤ Stroke. Enter 1 pixel for the width setting, choose black as the color, and set the location setting to Center. Click OK when you're done, and hide the original type layer for now.

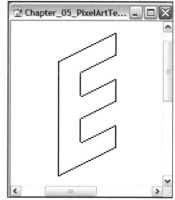

7. Duplicate the TYPE OUTLINE layer. Using the arrow keys, nudge the duplicate back. Remember to use the pixel art "Two across, one up" technique. Repeat this combination four more times.

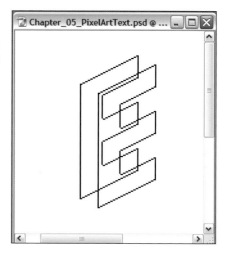

8. Merge the two outline layers. Then use the Pencil tool to join each edge using the "Two across, one up" method.

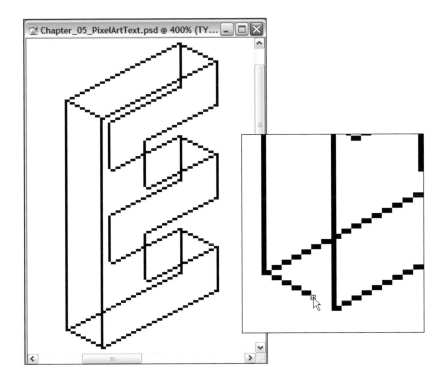

9. Use the Eraser tool to remove any lines that shouldn't be showing from the outline layer.

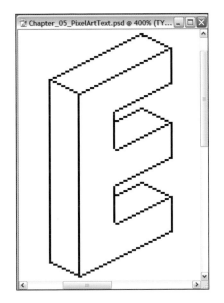

10. Create a new layer named TYPE COLOR above TYPE OUTLINE. Color each side with R:255 G:242 B:0.

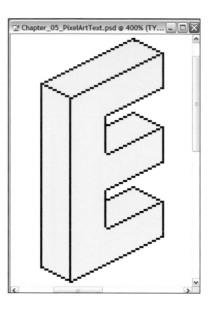

11. Finally, keeping in mind that the light source is shining down from the top left, color each section appropriately. The only trick here is that you're adding a fourth color to the mix. This color is inside the E where it should be extremely dark because not only is it receiving very little light, but also the area above it should be casting a shadow down upon it.

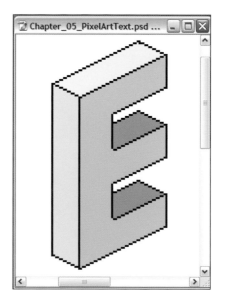

Building your pixel empire

Have you ever heard the phrase "Rome wasn't built in a day"? Well, a pixel art scene was surely not built in that amount of time either. As I mentioned in this chapter's opening paragraph, people who create professional-quality pixel art have some time on their hands (not to mention an incredible amount of patience). I'm not insinuating that they sit around all day creating pixel art, but the process can be slow and tedious. For that reason, as much as I'd like it to, the next exercise won't show you how to create one of the stunning pixel cities, such as the following, that you may have seen on the Web or in magazines:

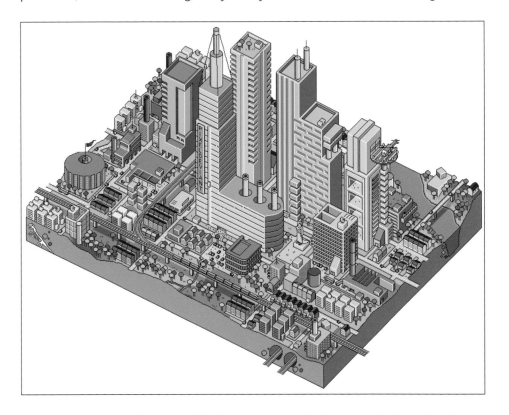

Jared Smith, owner of www.pixeldeviant.com, created this scene. He has created some incredible pixel artwork, and I urge you to stop by his website for inspiration.

In this section, I'll show you the basic techniques for creating pixel buildings and roads. From there, you'll have a strong foundation to continue learning this art form and take it to the next level if you so desire.

Exercise: Creating a pixel art building

1. Create a new 640 × 480 Photoshop canvas. Add a GRID layer on top of the Background layer, and fill it with the grid pattern you made earlier. Reduce the opacity of the GRID layer to around 15%.

2. Using the techniques described earlier, draw a rectangular pixel outline on a layer named BUILDING OUTLINE.

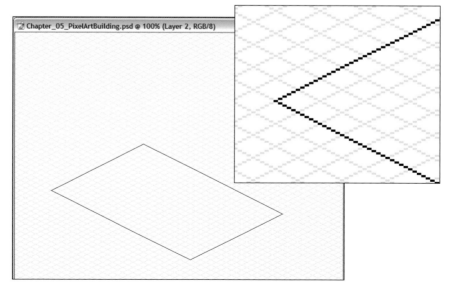

3. Similar to the cube exercise, duplicate the outline layer and move it up. Use the Pencil tool to add lines to connect the two rectangles. Make sure all outline layers are merged when you're done. Also, try to keep your lines along the grid to make things easier as your illustration becomes more complex.

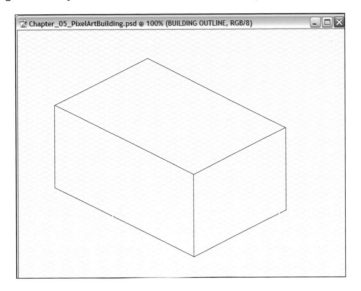

4. Next, you need to color the object. To demonstrate that the rules of pixel art discussed earlier aren't set in stone, you're going to move the light source down a little so the left-front side of the building receives the most light, and thus is the brightest color.

5. Create a new layer named BUILDING FILL above BUILDING OUTLINE. Color each side of the building. Use R:80 G:210 B:255 for the left-front side, R:36 G:157 B:197 for the top, and R:19 G:114 B:145 for the right side.

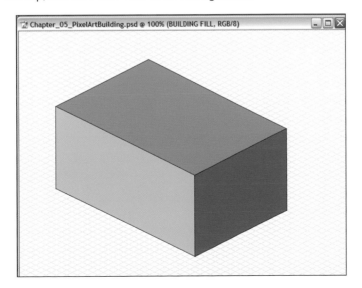

Next, you'll make it appear as if the top of the building has a cutout in it.

6. Create a new layer named CUTOUT OUTLINE above BUILDING FILL. Reduce the opacity of the BUILDING FILL layer so you can trace an outline over the grid within the building outline.

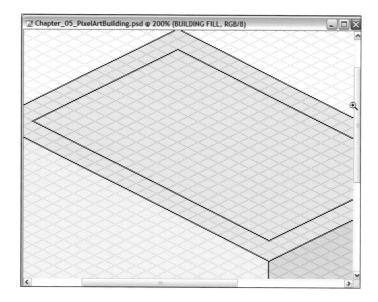

7. Draw two more lines one grid square inside of the top left and right lines on the CUTOUT OUTLINE layer.

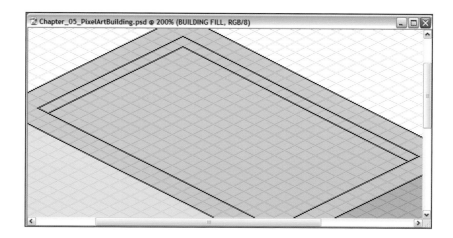

8. Connect the point where the two lines meet with the Pencil tool.

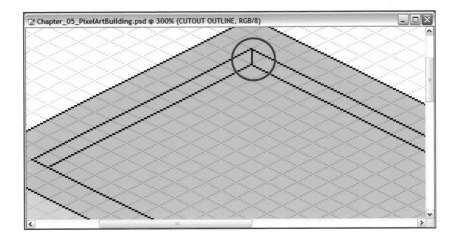

9. Create a new layer named CUTOUT FILL above CUTOUT OUTLINE.

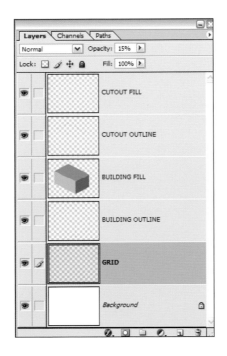

10. Fill the left side of the cutout wall with the same dark color used for the right side of the building. Fill the right side of the cutout wall with the same color used for the left front of the building.

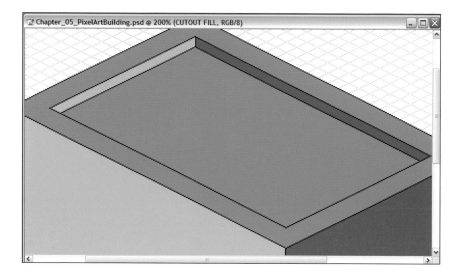

11. Using the same methods described earlier, duplicate the BUILDING OUTLINE layer and name it BUILDING HIGHLIGHT.

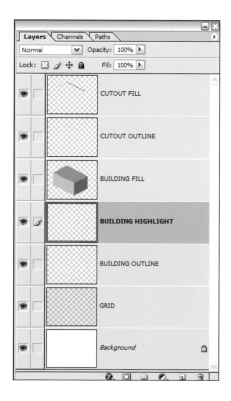

12. Invert (*CTRL*/⌘+*I*) the highlight color so the outline is white, and erase all of the outlines except for three shown here:

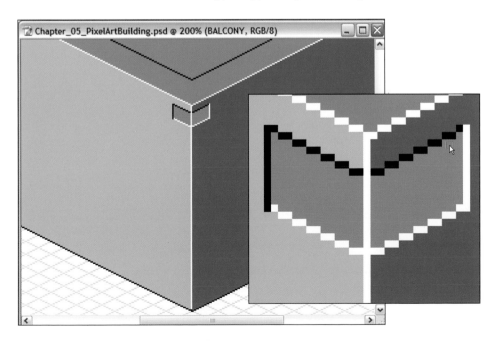

Next, you'll add some decorations to the building.

13. Create a new layer named BALCONY above the CUTOUT FILL layer.

14. Using the Pencil tool, draw a shape similar to the one in the following image. Remember to use the same stepped approach you used in previous exercises.

15. Duplicate this layer seven times and position the layers along the corner of the building.

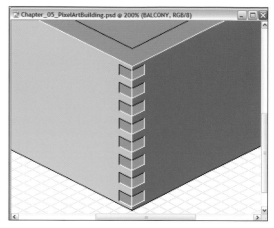

16. Let's add some windows. Create a new layer named WINDOW above BALCONY. Zoom in and draw a square similar to this:

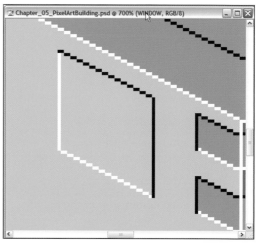

17. Draw a black line that recedes from the bottom left toward the top right to serve as a line between what would be the floor and the wall inside the window. Also, fill the area to the top of the black line with R:36 G:157 B:197. This will be the wall.

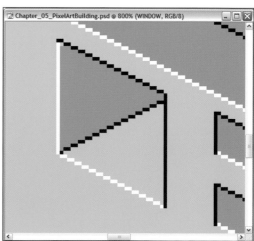

18. To the window, add a light blue (R:200 G:230 B:240) highlight.

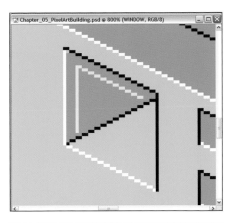

19. Next, add some 3-pixel black lines with a 1-pixel pink top to simulate some people inside.

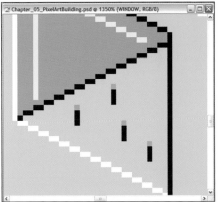

Here's a zoomed-out view of the building:

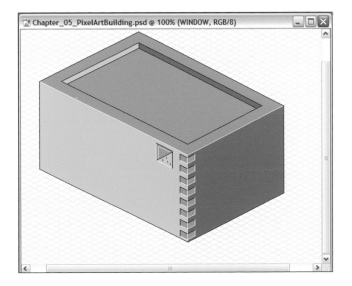

20. Duplicate the window layer twice, and place the copies below the original. Merge all three layers.

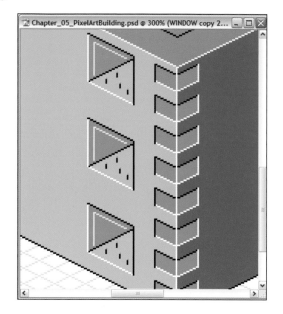

21. Duplicate the new WINDOW layer twice again, and position the two copies across the front of the building.

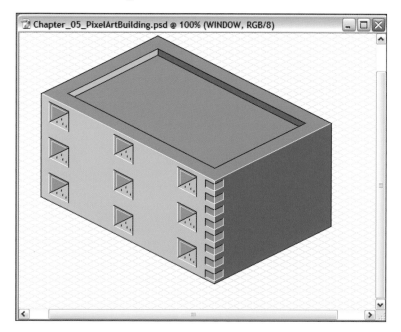

22. Finally, you can add a small bevel to the sides and front of the building for decoration. Do this by creating a straight line colored with R:12 G:75 B:96 from the top to the bottom of the building. Then add a straight white line to the right of each darker colored line.

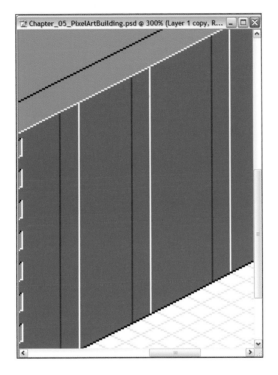

23. Add some lines to the front of the building as well, and you're finished.

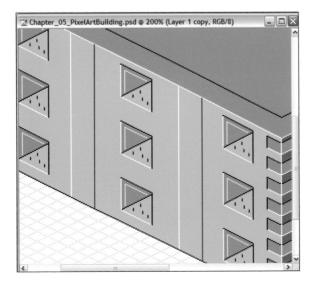

A final effect would be to add a sidewalk and street. This will get you on your way to creating a pixel city.

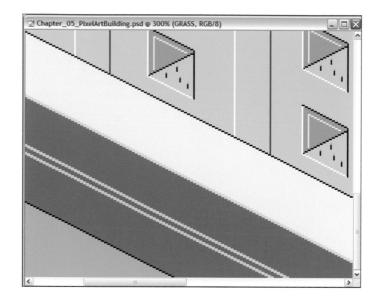

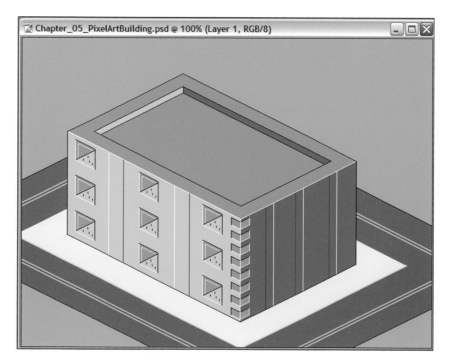

Extending your pixel art illustration

Now that you've built a pixel art building, you'll need to know how to add elements to extend the illustration and form a pixel city. This exercise will walk you through the process of creating some of those elements.

Exercise: Adding foliage

Trees and bushes strategically placed throughout your illustration can add a touch of realism.

1. Earlier in the chapter, I discussed how to create a circle. Choose a light green color (R:0 G:136 B:0) and a darker green color (R:0 G:85 B:0), and create a circle similar to this:

You can now duplicate this circle and cluster a few of them together to simulate a group of bushes. You can also add a small rectangle filled with brown to raise this "bush" up and make it a tree.

2. Using the Pencil tool, draw a black rectangle.

3. Fill the rectangle with R:153 G:102 B:0.

4. To finish off the tree, create a small drop shadow filled with a dark green (R:0 G:119 B:0). Just be sure you don't color over the actual tree trunk.

While the previous steps are a quick way to create trees, there are, of course, more sophisticated methods you can use, should you choose to spend the time on this task.

5. On a new layer, use the Pencil tool to draw a black shape similar to this:

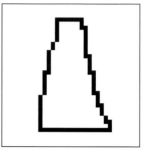

6. Fill this shape with R:204 G:153 B:0.

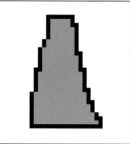

7. Next, on a new layer, draw some palm tree leaf shapes similar to the images here, and fill them with R:51 G:153 B:0. Don't forget to use the Magic Wand tool to select the area inside the leaf shapes to make them easier to fill.

To complete the palm tree, you'll need to add some highlighting to remove the flat appearance.

8. Set your foreground color to R:102 G:204 B:51. Using the Pencil tool, draw some small highlights on the palms.

9. Now switch your foreground color to R:102 G:51 B:0, add some texture to the trunk of the palm tree, and you're done.

Exercise: Creating pixel art from pictures

Finally, I'd like to show you how to create pixel artwork from real pictures. Let's start with a picture of an ordinary basketball.

1. Open `Chapter_05_PixelArtBasketball.psd` from the source files for this chapter.

2. Create a new layer above the BASKETBALL layer. Select the Eyedropper tool (*I*) and click a brighter area of the original basketball. This sets the foreground color to a lighter orange (R:255 G:133 B:77, if you'd like to enter it manually). Then *ALT/OPTION*-click a darker area of the ball to set the background color to a dark orange (R:177 G:55 B:11).

3. Create a circle using the method described earlier in this chapter.

4. Select the Pen tool and make sure the Paths button is selected in the tool options bar. Draw two open paths that follow the shape of the curved lines within the basketball. Note that you'll have to reduce the opacity of the orange circle to see the lines of the original ball below it.

5. Select the Pencil tool and set the diameter to 1 pixel. Set the foreground color to R:153 G:64 B:36.

6. Create a new layer named LINES above the orange circle. Then switch over to the Paths palette and click the Stroke path with brush button at the bottom of the palette.

7. Use the Eraser tool to remove the excess area outside the actual basketball.

8. Repeat this process for the remaining lines on the basketball.

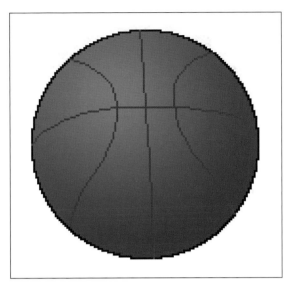

Building a library of reusable pixel art

You've created some great-looking pixel art in this chapter. In fact, you may be so happy with your creations that you'll want to use them over and over again in other projects. As I'm sure you can imagine, you have several ways to go about creating a reusable library. One method is to save your images and reopen them when you begin a new project. At that point, you could hunt around for the layers that make up a tree, for example, and place them into your new illustration. While this does work, it can be time consuming to find exactly the artwork you need and copy it over to a new illustration. Not to mention that the more work you do, the more files you'll have. As the number of files grows, you will likely find it increasingly difficult to access exactly what you need. I'd like to offer a couple of other alternatives in this section.

Let's use the foliage created in the previous exercise as an example. If you open `Chapter_05_PixelArtLibraryStart.psd` from the source files, you can see the exact layers that I used to create the trees and bushes.

Exercise: Reusing the foliage art

The first method is fairly simple and involves a very powerful Photoshop shortcut.

1. Create a new file named `PixelArt_Library_Foliage.psd`. You'll turn to this file whenever you need pixel art trees or bushes.

2. Switch back to the source file. Hide the white Background layer. Then use the Rectangular Marquee tool (*M*) to put a square selection around the palm tree.

3. Now choose Edit ➤ Copy Merged (*CTRL*/⌘+*SHIFT*+*C*). This copies the entire contents of the selection, regardless of what layer the artwork is on. This is different from the ordinary copy command (*CTRL*/⌘+*C*), in that Edit ➤ Copy will copy the contents of only the current layer. By the way, this is one of my favorite and most used Photoshop shortcuts. Remember it, as it will undoubtedly save you time in the future.

Keep in mind a small tip that could save you from pulling your hair out when using the Copy Merged *command. You must have a visible layer active when you copy. If you had the hidden white* Background *layer active in the preceding step, for example, the* Copy Merged *command wouldn't copy anything. This doesn't make much sense, considering the* Copy Merged *command is supposed to copy the contents of all layers. Nonetheless, this is how it works.*

4. Switch back to the PixelArt_Library_Foliage.psd file and paste the copied artwork into it. Give the layer a descriptive name, and you're done. You now have a palm tree ready to use whenever you need it. Even better, since you hid the white Background layer when you copied the original artwork, the area around the tree is transparent, which means you can easily place the tree into any future work without the risk of clashing backgrounds.

Another alternative to this method of creating a reusable library involves layer sets. Since the method just described takes away your ability to edit the original elements that make up the palm tree without resorting back to the source file, you'll need to use another method to work around this restriction.

5. Using the same source file with the palm tree, link together all layers relating to the tree. (See Step 6 illustrations.)

6. Choose New Set From Linked from the Layers palette options menu and name this layer set PALM TREE. Repeat this process for any foliage pixel art you've created, and store the art in the same file.

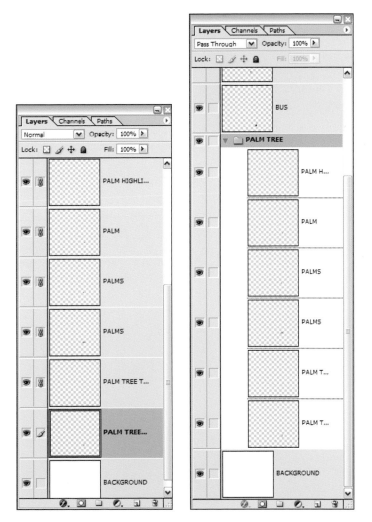

7. Now, whenever you need a pixel art palm tree, you can open this file and drag the layer set into the new illustration. This has the added benefit of leaving all layers that created the palm tree intact, in case you'd like to modify them for a new illustration.

Summary

In closing, I'll say that after you've been creating pixel art for a while, you'll begin to develop a library. This library will dramatically cut down on the production time that I mentioned earlier. Many of the pixel-art pros don't create new windows each time they create a new pixel art scene. They have some "stock" patterns that they've created before, and they simply reapply those patterns to new scenes. Perhaps they change the color, orientation, or other minor detail of the pattern, but the majority of the work has already been done and they can quickly reuse it for other purposes if needed.

If you enjoy this type of artwork, I urge you to go beyond these tutorials. Technology magazines, websites, icons, and PDA devices are all candidates for professional work in this area. Use the Web for inspiration. A quick search on Google (www.google.com) for the phrase "pixel art" will yield many great websites to help you realize the type of artwork that you can create.

In the early 1980s, computers were thought by many to be "intimidating." Apple Computer, Inc., tried to change this perception by commissioning a designer to make its Macintosh icons friendlier. It was then that the smiley-faced computer icon seen on the Macintosh desktop was born. Who knew this icon could stand the test of time so well? In fact, back then, who knew that icons would become such a popular part of today's computer culture?

Every day, millions of people interact with icons of various types. Many of today's new icons barely look like icons anymore. Instead, they resemble small, cartoonlike illustrations. As operating systems become more powerful and processing power continues to increase, the restrictions faced by icon creators several decades ago are no more. Color, transparency, and animation are all qualities of today's icons that designers now have more control over. For this reason, and the fact that the world economy is forcing designers to wear multiple hats, more and more designers are being called upon to create professional-quality icons. Many people think that if you have the artistic ability to create a business card, web page, or magazine ad, then you should also be able to leverage your skills to create icons. In some cases, they are correct.

This chapter will teach you some simple, yet professional techniques for creating icons in Photoshop. It will also demonstrate how you can use the same tools to create icons that you use to create various illustrations and other graphic design work.

Icon overview

When icons first emerged, they were generally restricted to 32 X 32-pixel black-and-white designs. As computers became more advanced, color was added. Icon design has evolved over the past three decades to become what we see on computer screens today.

The following are common characteristics of today's icons:

- **Angle and perspective**: No longer do icons appear as flat, 2D objects. Angle and perspective are key attributes that lend a dynamic energy to today's icons.

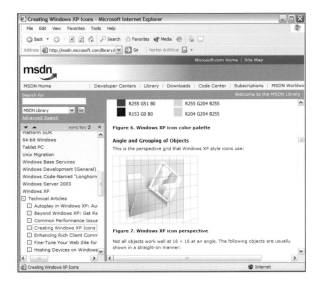

- **Colors**: Icons are no longer restricted to few colors. Colors today are richer and complementary to the operating system. In addition, the added color capabilities allow for softer and more rounded edges.

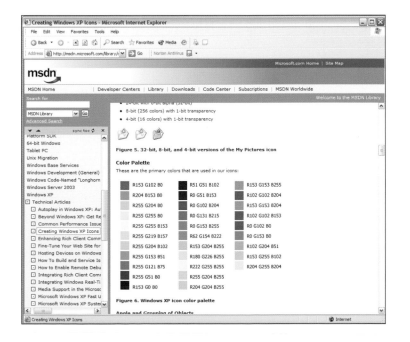

- **Gradients**: Gradients are commonly used to add dimension. They help icons appear to contain depth and help a flat, 2D icon look three-dimensional.

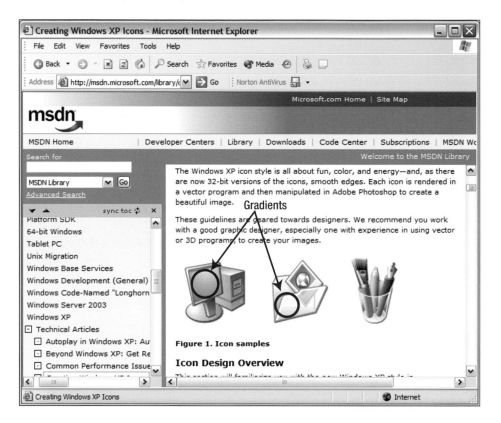

- **Drop shadows**: Again, dimension is vital to today's icons. Drop shadows help achieve this look.

In general, icons have become more modern. They reflect the objects and trends of the world we live in. For example, many computer icons now incorporate a flat-screen monitor image instead of the traditional CRT monitor (see the previous image for an example).

Emoticons

A chapter focusing on icons would be incomplete without a discussion of the icon's little brother: the emoticon. "Emoticon" isn't really a word—I know this because every time I type it, Microsoft Word puts a little red squiggly line underneath it. However, there are many people out there who would disagree. Emoticons have become a common theme in millions of people's everyday computer use.

So what exactly is an **emoticon**? An emoticon is a combination of keyboard characters used to signify a facial expression. They're frequently used in electronic communications to convey meaning that, in offline life, would be conveyed nonverbally. The most popular of emoticons are as follows:

:) The smiley

;-) The wink

:-(The smiley's polar opposite: the sad face

Instant-messaging software makers began to realize people commonly used these key combinations and began adding small icons in their place. It was at this point that the emoticon was born. Today, many programs recognize the common key combinations that people use to create an emoticon and insert the appropriate icon in the emoticon's place. Microsoft's MSN Messenger, one of many similar instant-messaging applications, has a huge library of preset emoticons to choose from.

As you can see from the preceding image, MSN Messenger has gone far beyond the basic smiley and sad faces and created an emoticon for just about any emotion you can think of. In addition, most applications offer a way for you to create your own emoticons and add them to a library for a more personalized experience.

Conceptualization

The conceptualization phase is an important one. It's often good to start out with general concepts on paper first so you can visualize what needs to be done before you ever move your design into Photoshop.

Sketches

When you design icons, sometimes the best way to begin is by sitting down with a pencil and paper. It helps to first sketch out some of the basic characteristics of your icon. Your initial drawing doesn't have to be perfect—it should just get you going in a general direction.

Here are a few samples of some icons I drew that you're going to create in this chapter:

As you can see, these sketches are far from being complete works of art. But they gave me a good sense of the direction I wanted to go in and what I needed to create once I sat down at my computer. In the last one, you can even see that I took my pencil and a blending stick and shaded some of the edges to simulate a gradient I knew I would apply once I started creating the image on my computer.

Guidelines

It's good to follow some general guidelines when creating icons. This helps ensure that any icons you create are of professional quality and follow the general standards for icons in an operating system.

- **Color**: Many operating systems and applications use a specific color palette for icons. Visit the appropriate company's website for more information on this topic and to see if it applies to your icons.

- **Concepts**: Try to use established concepts when creating icons. Users have grown accustomed to certain meanings being associated with icons. For example, a question mark typically indicates a way for users to receive help. A garbage can usually denotes the operating system's trash or deleted items area.

The following links will bring you to the respective operating system's guidelines for icon design:

- **Microsoft**: `http://msdn.microsoft.com/library/default.asp?url=/library/en-us/dnwxp/html/winxpicons.asp`
- **Apple**: `http://developer.apple.com/documentation/UserExperience/Conceptual/OSXHIGuidelines/index.html`

Designing and illustrating icons

The exercises that follow will cover some ways that icons can be created in Photoshop. An important point to remember, though, is that Photoshop isn't the only tool in which icons can be created. Adobe Illustrator is a popular tool for icon illustration. Many times, icons are created using a combination of the two programs. However, Photoshop now offers many of the same tools that draw designers to Illustrator, and it can be a great tool on its own for icon creation.

Exercise: Creating a simple, cartoonlike icon

1. Create a new RGB 800 × 600-pixel Photoshop canvas. Set your foreground color to R:255 G:167 B:99.

2. Select the Rounded Rectangle tool (*U*). In the tool options bar, be sure that the Shape layers button is selected, and enter 50 px as the Radius setting.

3. Create a large rounded rectangle on the canvas that is approximately 350 pixels wide and 320 pixels high. Name this layer HEAD.

4. Press *CTRL/⌘+T* to enable Free Transform for the HEAD layer and display a bounding box around it. Hold down the *CTRL/⌘+ALT/OPTION+SHIFT* keys and drag the bottom right of the bounding box outward slightly. Notice how the left side also expands outward in the same way. Don't apply the transform yet, though.

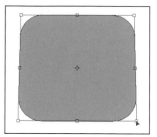

5. Apply the transformation, and your image should look similar to this:

6. Using the technique you learned in Chapter 3, click the Add To Shape Area button in the tool options bar. Note that the Rounded Rectangle tool must still be selected for this option to appear.

7. Create two more shapes on either side of the head to serve as ears. Notice how they become part of the original head shape.

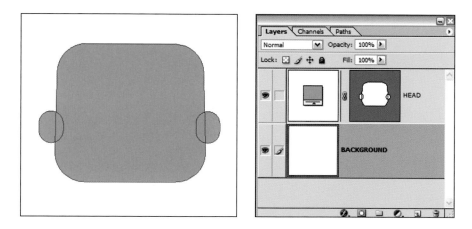

8. Add the following Stroke layer style to the HEAD layer.

Layer Style

Styles	Stroke
Blending Options: Custom	Structure
☐ Drop Shadow	Size: ───── 3 px
☐ Inner Shadow	Position: Outside
☐ Outer Glow	Blend Mode: Normal
☐ Inner Glow	Opacity: ──── 100 %
☐ Bevel and Emboss	
☐ Contour	Fill Type: Color
☐ Texture	Color: ◄── **R: 180**
☐ Satin	**G: 73**
☐ Color Overlay	**B: 21**
☐ Gradient Overlay	
☐ Pattern Overlay	
☑ **Stroke**	

OK Cancel New Style... ☑ Preview

9. Next, set your foreground color to R:238 G:198 B:163. Select the Ellipse tool (*U*) and be sure that Create new shape layer is selected in the tool options bar. Create a circle approximately 150 pixels in width and height on the left side of the face. Name this layer LEFT EYE.

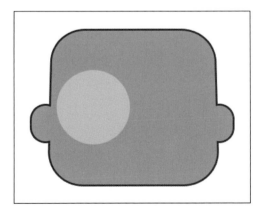

10. Add a black stroke by applying the following Stroke layer style to the LEFT EYE layer.

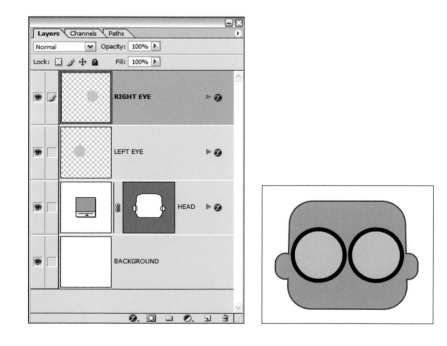

11. Duplicate the LEFT EYE layer and move it over to the right. Name this duplicate layer RIGHT EYE.

12. Set your foreground color to white. Using the Ellipse tool once again, create a small oval in the center of the left eye. Add the following Stroke layer style to this shape.

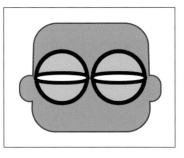

13. Duplicate the thin oval and move it over to the right eye as well.

14. To complete the eyes, set the shape color to black by clicking the color swatch in the tool options bar and then choosing a color from the Color Picker. Also note that your layer style may seem to "stick" to newly created shape layers. If this happens, just set the layer Style to the default (none) in the tool options bar.

15. Create two small black circles with the Ellipse tool in the center of each eye. This is a good time to place the eye-related layers into their own layer set.

16. Now for the nose. Set your shape color to R:255 G:167 B:99. Use the Ellipse tool and create a small oval shape just below the eyes. Name this layer NOSE. Copy the Stroke layer style from the HEAD layer and paste it into this layer.

17. Set the shape color to black. Select the Rounded Rectangle tool once again. This time set Radius in the tool options bar to 80 px. Create a rounded rectangle that encompasses the top two-thirds of the head but also extends outside of the head on the top, left, and right sides. Name this layer HAIR and position it below the HEAD layer in the Layers palette.

Next, you're going to create the body.

18. Set the shape color to R:0 G:114 B:187. Select the Pen tool (*P*) and make sure that Shape layers is selected in the tool options bar. Create a shape similar to this image. This is a fairly simple shape to create, but I've included some instructions in the image here as well to help you along.

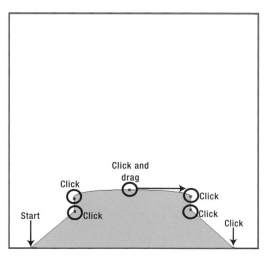

19. Name this layer BODY and ensure it's positioned below the HAIR layer.

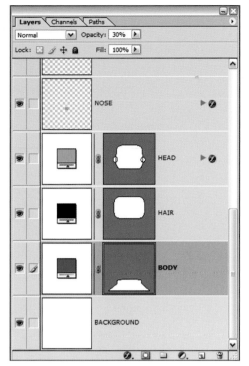

20. Set the shape color to black and use the Ellipse tool to create an oval for the neck area.

You'll now create the neck.

21. Set the shape color back to R:255 G:167 B:99. Use the Eyedropper tool (*I*) on the face for a quick color change. Use the Rectangle tool (*U*) to create a rectangle that extends from inside the bottom of the head toward the bottom of the body. Apply the same Stroke layer style you used on the HEAD layer to this layer.

22. Name this layer NECK and position it above the BODY layer but below the HAIR layer in the Layers palette.

23. You'll notice that the neck extends down too far. To fix this, *CTRL*/⌘-click the black neck-hole layer you created in step 20. Then click the NECK layer once to make it active and click the Add Layer Mask button at the bottom of the Layers palette to create a layer mask out of the selected area. This will hide the unwanted area of the neck.

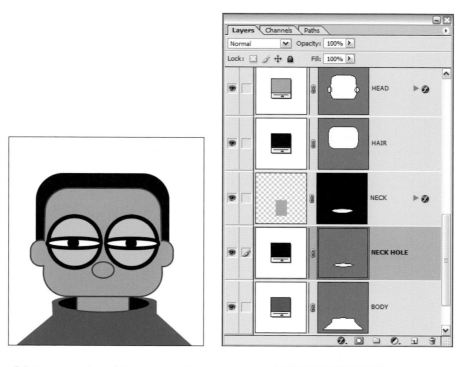

24. You can also add a rectangular stripe down the front of the body if you'd like.

25. For the mouth, select the Brush tool (*B*) and choose a 15-pixel hard-edged brush. Set the foreground color to R:177 G:97 B:54. Create a small mouth on a new layer named MOUTH. Position this layer above the HEAD layer.

26. Lastly, you can use the Brush tool to add some highlights to the hair. Create a new layer above HAIR named HIGHLIGHTS. Paint small streaks with the Brush tool. Don't worry if the streaks go outside the hairlines, because you can just use the HAIR layer selection as a layer mask on the HIGHLIGHTS layer to remove the unwanted area.

6

Exercise: Creating icon people

1. Create a new 500 × 500-pixel Photoshop canvas. Fill the background with a nice blue color. I used R:111 G:146 B:250.

2. Using the Pen tool (be sure the Shape layers button is selected in the tool options bar), draw a shape similar to this image. Rename the new shape layer BODY. The color of the shape doesn't matter at this point.

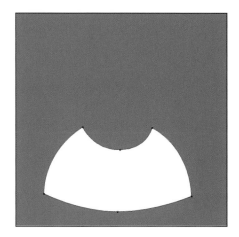

3. Set the foreground color to a light gray (R:171 G:171 B:171) and the background color to a dark gray (R:108 G:108 B:108). Double-click the BODY layer to display the Layer Style dialog box. Choose Gradient Overlay and use the following settings:

A nice trick is that you can move the Layer Style dialog box out of the way and use your cursor to position the gradient. Just click the image with the gradient overlay and drag the center point of the gradient around until it appears in the correct position.

4. Add the following Drop Shadow and Inner Glow layer styles to the BODY layer.

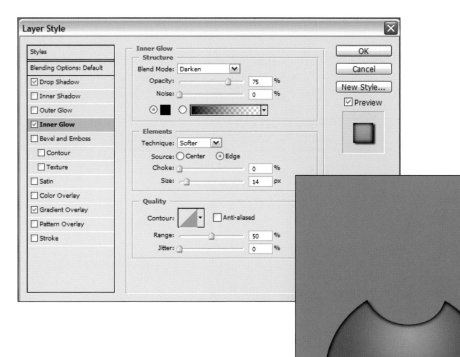

5. Create a new layer named HEAD above the BODY layer. Draw an oval shape filled with white with the Elliptical Marquee tool (*M*) or the Elliptical Shape tool.

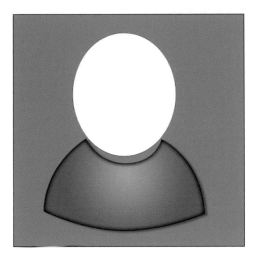

Use the shape tools whenever possible, because you'll always be able to transform or scale them later if needed.

6. This time, set R:252 G:173 B:62 as the foreground color and R:214 G:138 B:42 as the background color. Add a Gradient Overlay layer style to this layer with the following settings:

7. Add the following Drop Shadow and Inner Glow layer styles to the HEAD layer.

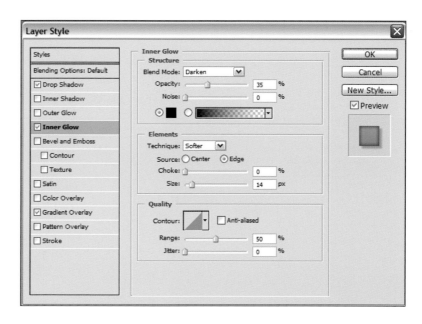

8. You should now have an image similar to this:

Next, you have some selections work to do on the head to create some hair.

9. First, create a new layer named HAIR above HEAD. Then, using the Elliptical Marquee tool, draw a large oval selection that encompasses an area of the head. Don't worry about the area that extends beyond the head shape.

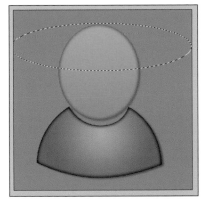

10. *CTRL/⌘+ALT/OPTION+SHIFT*-click the HEAD layer. This intersects your HEAD layer selection with the active selection you created in the previous step.

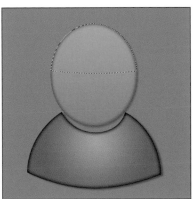

11. Be sure the HAIR layer is active and fill this selection with R:171 G:116 B:15. Then apply the following Drop Shadow and Inner Glow layer styles to the HAIR layer.

12. Use the Polygonal Lasso tool (*L*) to create a selection of small jagged shapes toward the front of the hair.

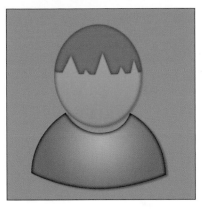

13. With the HAIR layer active, press *Delete* to remove the selection from the hair, and you're done creating the hair.

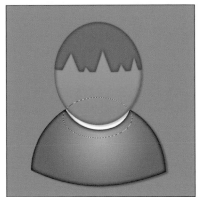

14. Now create a new layer below BODY named TSHIRT. Make an oval selection with the Elliptical Marquee tool and fill it with white. You should see only white in the small area between the head and the body.

6

15. A nice touch to add is to use the Pen tool to create a few highlights throughout the icon. Then reduce the opacity of the highlights slightly.

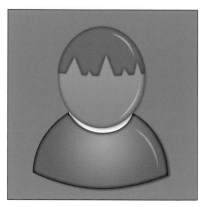

16. With some creative shape selections and use of the Pen tool, you could even put a baseball cap on him if you wanted.

Exercise: Shiny, happy emoticon

Although icons and emoticons are typically small in size when displayed onscreen, it's a good idea to create them large. That way, you can easily repurpose the file if you need to at a later date.

A perfect example is the icon you'll create next. When I first created this icon, I had no idea that I would eventually use it in a book. Had I created it too small initially, I would have had to re-create it for use here.

1. Create a new canvas that is 700 × 700 pixels in size. Press *ALT/OPTION* and double-click the Background layer to make it a real layer, Layer 0.

2. Select the Elliptical Shape tool (*U*) and make sure that the Shape layers button is selected in the tool options bar. Draw a circle on your canvas. Rename the Shape layer that is created as FACE.

3. Double-click the circle to display the Layer Style dialog box. Select Gradient Overlay
and apply the following settings:

4. Select Inner Glow and use these settings:

5. Finally, select the Inner Shadow layer style and apply these settings:

Layer Style		
Styles	**Inner Shadow**	OK
Blending Options: Default	Structure	Cancel
☐ Drop Shadow	Blend Mode: Multiply	New Style...
☑ **Inner Shadow**	Opacity: 56 %	☑ Preview
☐ Outer Glow	Angle: 120 ° ☑ Use Global Light	
☑ Inner Glow	Distance: 70 px	
☐ Bevel and Emboss	Choke: 11 %	
☐ Contour	Size: 78 px	
☐ Texture	**Quality**	
☐ Satin	Contour: ☐ Anti-aliased	
☐ Color Overlay	Noise: 0 %	
☑ Gradient Overlay		
☐ Pattern Overlay		
☐ Stroke		

6. You should now have something that resembles this image:

The basic face shape is done. Now let's add a highlight and some features.

7. Create a new layer above the circle named HIGHLIGHT and make sure it's the active layer. Use the Elliptical Marquee tool (M) to draw an oval similar to this reference image:

8. Press *D* and then *X* to set your foreground color to white. Then select the Gradient tool (*G*) and use the foreground-to-transparent gradient. Drag a linear gradient from the top of the selection to the bottom.

There are a few ways you can create the mouth. I favor using the Pen tool, which is pretty straightforward. It's simple to make the same mouth shape that you're going to create in the next step with the Pen tool. However, here I'll demonstrate how to use the Elliptical Marquee tool to achieve nearly the same result.

9. Create a new layer named MOUTH above the HIGHLIGHT layer. Again, use the Elliptical Marquee tool to create an oval.

6

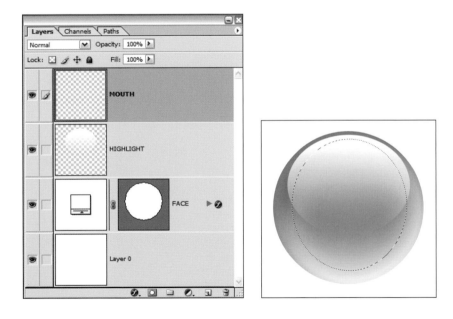

10. Now press the *ALT/OPTION* key to subtract a selection and draw another oval to subtract from the original. When you release your mouse button, you should be left with this shape:

> You can also use the Pen tool to draw this shape if you'd like.

11. Fill this selection with white. Choose Edit ➤ Stroke. Enter 2 px for the width and change the color to R:184 G:133 B:15. Click OK.

12. The mouth is nearly done. Create a new layer named DIMPLES. Set your foreground color to R:184 G:133 B:15. On the same layer, select the Brush tool (*B*). Using a 2-pixel hard-edged brush, paint some small dimples on the edges of the mouth.

13. Now for the eyes. Create a new layer named EYES. Use the same technique you used to create the mouth. Draw a circular selection with the Elliptical Marquee tool, press the *ALT/OPTION* key, and then draw another selection below it to subtract most of the area. In the end, you should be left with a selection similar to this reference image.

14. Fill this selection with R:184 G:133 B:15. Then duplicate the layer and drag it over to the right for the other eye. Merge the two eye layers so you're left with only one EYE layer. He's very happy and squinting a bit, so we'll leave the eyes like this.

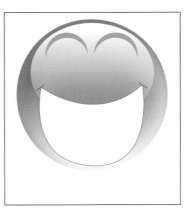

Next, you can add some lines to form the appearance of teeth.

15. Create a new layer named TEETH above the MOUTH layer. Use the Pen tool (be sure Paths is selected in the tool options bar) and draw a curved line through the center of the mouth.

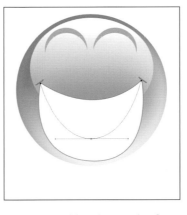

16. Select the Brush tool. Set the brush to a 4-pixel hard-edged brush. Set the foreground color to R:191 G:211 B:247.

17. Move to the Paths palette and select the Stroke path with brush button at the bottom of the palette. This should put a nice rounded stroke through the center of the mouth.

18. Next, on the same TEETH layer, use a 4-pixel hard-edged brush to paint some lines. Use the color R:191 G:211 B:247.

19. Finally, you can add a white-to-blue gradient background to make it look as if the face is sitting on a surface. This is mainly for display purposes, as your emoticons will most likely not contain this background. You can also hide all layers except for those with the smiley face objects on them. Then, select all (*CTRL*/⌘+*A*) and use the Copy Merged command (*SHIFT*+*CTRL*/⌘+*C*). Paste the contents on a new layer. Then choose Edit ➤ Transform ➤ Flip Vertical. Reduce the opacity a bit and you've got a reflection.

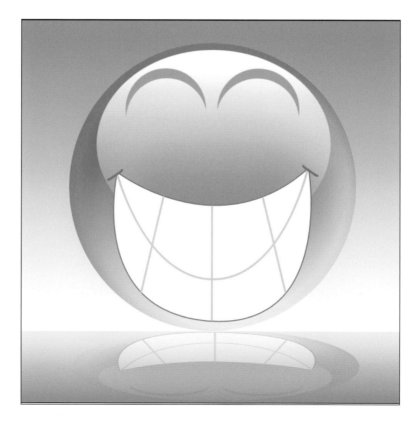

20. With a few small changes to the preceding steps, you can create an angry emoti-con. Note that the layers for this version are included in the final PSD file in the download for this book.

Creating the actual icon file

Microsoft Windows and Apple Macintosh icons are very similar. They both have several image formats embedded in the same icon. But the file formats are totally different and are not compatible. You can't use Macintosh icons under Windows, nor can you use Windows icons on a Macintosh operating system. You must convert them to the appropriate operating system file format first.

It's also important to know that you can't save your icon file directly from Photoshop without a third-party plug-in. In addition, various companies offer stand-alone applications for creating icons. These plug-ins or applications create the appropriate operating system icon out of your image file and save it to your hard disk. At this point, your icon is ready for distribution and installation.

Listed here are a few popular applications that can be useful in this process:

- Axialis Software: www.axialis.com
- IconEdit2: www.iconedit2.com
- IconBuilder: www.iconfactory.com

Summary

I hope this chapter has shown you that icon design in Photoshop can be a great addition to your skill set. In previous years, icon design was so restrictive that it didn't offer designers the ability to truly express themselves. However, with the increasing power of computers and their operating systems, icon design has not only progressed in recent years, but has become an art form of its own. Today, icons can be just as complex and inspiring as traditional graphic design and illustration. I encourage you to create your own library of icons as you progress in your design career, as it is not only great practice to help hone your design skills, but also can lead to many useful future applications.

Traditionally, cartoon and comic book artists created their works solely with pencils, brushes, inks, and paints. With the advent of affordable computer technology, many artists have swapped those tools for PCs and Macs. In the past, many traditional artists resisted the change because computer-based drawing simply didn't allow them to use their individual style of drawing or painting. Photoshop's paint engine has changed many people's minds about this, however. In fact, some artists have started using Photoshop to create output that so closely resembles traditionally painted work that few realize the art was created on a computer.

In this chapter, you'll learn how professionals use Photoshop to create cartoons and comic book art. As you've discovered in previous chapters, Photoshop may not have been built specifically for the tasks that you'll perform here, but artists have learned to push the program to its limits and make it work in ways that many thought were impossible.

Getting your drawings into Photoshop

For the most part, cartoon and comic book artists still tend to create their work on paper first. While this may not hold true for everyone, a pencil and paper is typically the place where many cartoons and comics are born. From there, the artwork is scanned into Photoshop and digitally enhanced, colored, and saved. Other artwork may be added to it, text may be incorporated, and scenic elements may be created at this point.

Scanning

So how do you go about getting that artwork into Photoshop so you can work on it digitally? You scan it. This is typically accomplished via the Import submenu under the File menu (File ➤ Import ➤ *Your scanner name*). Most artists use a flatbed scanner to move their work from paper to digital form.

While the methods used to create the artwork before scanning may be different, the actual process of scanning is typically the same. The following scanning tips can help you to create professional-looking work:

- Scan your work at as high a resolution as possible. A minimum of 300 dpi is usually recommended. You can always reduce it later if needed.
- Try to scan as clean a copy of your work as possible. Remove any eraser dust, stray drawing marks, or anything that may interfere with the image in Photoshop.
- Attempt to straighten or remove any folds that may appear in your artwork.

While it's true that Photoshop can repair, remove, and retouch nearly everything, why not make your life as easy as possible by taking the extra few steps ahead of time to make this process easier? The better the quality of work put into Photoshop, the better the quality of output.

Using the Levels adjustment

When drawing a comic or cartoon, some artists begin with pencil and then retrace their work with ink when they've finalized their sketches. They then scan the artwork into Photoshop, and use the inked lines as the outlines for the piece. Conversely, some artists prefer to simply sketch their artwork with a pencil and trace the sketch in Photoshop (or Illustrator) with the Pen tool. This produces a totally different look, as the outlines typically don't look hand-drawn. However, the artist need not worry about any stray marks on the paper, or the color of the paper itself, since the drawing serves only as a template from which to trace.

Artists that use the first method may sometimes need to scan an image into Photoshop and use the Levels adjustment to prepare it for coloring. Using Levels, a designer can make black areas blacker and remove all other areas of the drawing.

Color palettes

Color palettes are big timesavers for professionals—for that matter, they're timesavers for anyone who wants to streamline their workflow. In cartoon and comic book art designs, color palettes are a must. Photoshop's Swatches palette is well suited to this type of application because you can create different swatch files depending on the type of work you're doing. This capability allows you to consistently reuse colors instead of having to search for them each time you create a new piece of artwork. Remember, time is money. And even if it this weren't the case, most likely you'd rather spend your time creating art instead of searching around for colors you know you've used in the past.

Saving and using swatches

Using and saving swatches is a fairly straightforward process. First, if the Swatches palette isn't visible, you can display it by choosing Window ➤ Swatches.

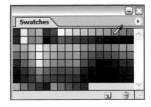

For this chapter's purposes, assume that you'd like to create a palette of colors to use and save with the source file. Choose an appropriate foreground color. Right-click in an empty area in the Swatches palette, and the Color Swatch Name dialog box will appear.

Give your swatch a descriptive name and click OK. Your new swatch will appear in the palette.

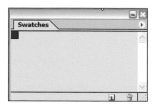

It's just as easy to load an existing Swatches palette from an external file. To help you work through the next exercise in this chapter, I've created a set of swatches for you to use in the exercise. To load it, select Load Swatches from the Swatches palette options menu. Navigate to the source file included for Chapter 7 named Chapter_07_Swatches.aco, and click the Load button. If Photoshop asks you to Replace the current color swatches with the swatches from your new file? click the OK button. Clicking the Append button will simply append the new swatch palette to the end of the existing one, which can get confusing.

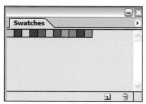

As you'll notice, a new Swatches palette will appear with various colors used in the following exercise. While I'll include the colors to use throughout the exercise, you can refer to this color palette for coloring as well. In addition, I've named all the swatches, so when you hover your mouse pointer over a swatch, a tool tip with a descriptive name will appear.

Various cartoon and comic book styles

Before you begin the exercises, let's take a look at the various styles that exist within this art genre. Keep in mind that these are very distinct styles. There are probably many cartoonists who would be appalled that their work is being compared to comic book art, and most likely the reverse holds true for comic book artists. However, the point here isn't necessarily to compare the different art forms. Instead, I'd like to point them out and show how, when it comes to Photoshop, they have similar characteristics and use many of the same tools within the application.

Comic book art

Comic book art and the Japanese manga/anime-style artwork (described in the next section) are similar to each other. However, people typically associate comic book art with large, muscular heroes and scary villains. The details associated with this style of drawing and coloring demand that a painting tool such as Photoshop be used, as you can see in the following examples.

http://homepage.ntlworld.com/michael.collins17

www.simonfraser.net

Japanese manga/anime-style art

My favorite style of art, the Japanese manga/anime style, has become extremely popular over the past few years worldwide with the rise in interest in cartoons such as Yugioh and Pokemon. This style is characterized by large eyes, funky hair-dos, and small, pointy noses.

Manga is an art form that has been around for many years in Japan. Japanese comic books were actually popular in Japan before most of the comic books such as *Spiderman* and many of the Marvel comic superhero series that many consider to be the pioneers of the genre.

Here are a few samples for you to check out.

www.polykarbon.com

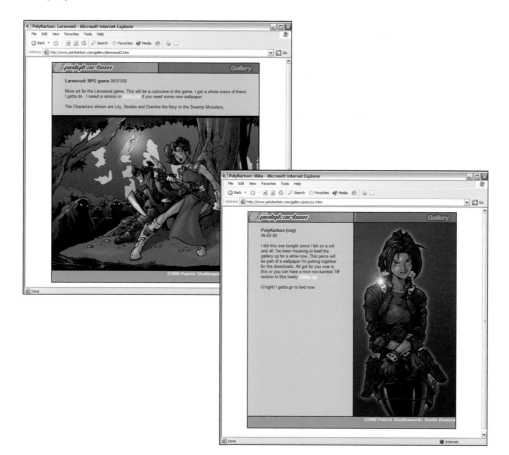

www.stevenpreston.com

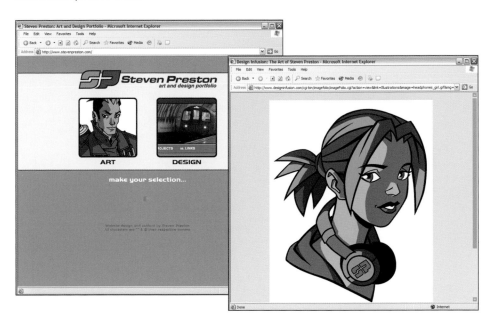

If you visit these websites, you'll see that the artwork within them has similar characteristics. Many of these characteristics allow the same rules to be applied to them in Photoshop. While the results may differ tremendously, the steps taken to achieve qualities such as highlights, shadows, texture, and depth are quite similar.

Also keep in mind that the main area that differentiates Photoshop from Illustrator is the need for control. When you create flat, colored-based cartoon illustrations, Illustrator may be your tool of choice. To achieve the detailed shading and highlighting effects that the professionals use in comic book and Japanese manga-style art, Photoshop is a must-have.

Exercise: Coloring line art

In this exercise, you're going to color a manga/anime-style line-art drawing. Before your jaw drops in amazement at my superior drawing skills, I must first confess that I didn't create this drawing. It's the work of Patrick Shettlesworth (www.polykarbon.com), a talented and award-winning manga/anime artist. His work is fascinating to look at, and it's a great starting point for learning how to color line-art.

Before you begin, be aware that this tutorial and this type of design in general is a great candidate for using a digital drawing tablet. The pressure sensitivity of the pen really helps with accuracy and speed in this area. If you don't have a digital drawing tablet, you can still complete the exercise, but the process will easier if you do.

1. Start by opening `Chapter_07_AnimeLineArt_Start.psd` from this chapter's source files.

2. You'll see this file contains two layers: BACKGROUND and ORIGINAL LINE ART. First let's take care of some housekeeping. Create a copy of the ORIGINAL LINE ART layer and name it LINES. Hide the ORIGINAL LINE ART layer just in case you need it later for some reason.

> *It's always good to create a copy of your original file just in case you damage the original and need to revert back to it without losing your changes.*

3. You'll create your color layers underneath the LINES layer. This will ensure that the lines always stay on top of the color. To do this, you'll use a layer blend mode called Multiply. The Multiply blend mode leaves the black lines intact and essentially makes the white areas transparent so any colored layers below them show through. Change the Blend mode of the LINES layer to Multiply.

4. Now that you have the file ready, it's time to color. Create a new layer below LINES named SKIN. Set your foreground color to R:253 G:211 B:151.

5. Select the Brush tool (*B*) and choose a large, hard-edged brush (90–100 pixels). Be sure the brush Mode is set to Normal, and the Opacity and Flow are set to 100%. Loosely paint the areas inside the face with the large brush.

6. Choose a smaller hard-edged brush for more precision, and paint along the inside of the outlines.

If I could give only one tip during this chapter, this would be it: memorize the keyboard shortcuts for changing brush sizes, the left and right bracket keys ([ ]). Pressing the left bracket key decreases the size of the brush, and pressing the right bracket increases the size of the brush.

When you've finished coloring the skin, you should have an image similar to this:

One thing to keep in mind at this stage is that it may take some time to color each area precisely. However, it's well worth it to spend the time now—it will make your life much easier later when you add detail.

7. Create a new layer above SKIN named HAIR. Set the foreground color to R:95 G:82 B:76 (or just click the swatch labeled SKIN in the Swatches palette mentioned in the "Saving and using swatches" section earlier in this chapter) and color the hair in the same way as the face.

Now is a good time to use the Swatches palette instead of entering in each color's RGB values. You'll notice you can pick up the labeled colors from the palette to make the color selection process quicker.

8. Repeat the process of creating new layers and naming them according to their place within this illustration. You can be as specific as you like. For instance, while I've created a separate layer for the belt and one for the body suit, I didn't create a new layer for the left arm and a new layer for the right arm. This is something that you'll get a better feel for the more you work on this type of art.

I've included several images here for reference purposes to help you break out the layers and colors that you'll use throughout this exercise. Don't forget that the source files for this chapter include a custom swatch palette. Here's a breakdown of the layer names and colors:

- BELT: R:104 G:103 B:99
- END PIECE: R:158 G:142 B:127
- MOUTH
  - LIPS: R:165 G:74 B:17
  - TONGUE: R:253 G:145 B:83
- LINE: R:135 G:172 B:141
- BODY ARMOR: R:253 G:192 B:85
- INNER BODY SUIT: R:138 G:110 B:160
- GEAR STRAPS: R:217 G:199 B:161
- BODY SUIT: R:94 G:84 B:75
- BODY SUIT STRIPE: R:185 G:185 B:185
- HAIR: R:95 G:82 B:76
- SKIN: R:253 G:211 B:151

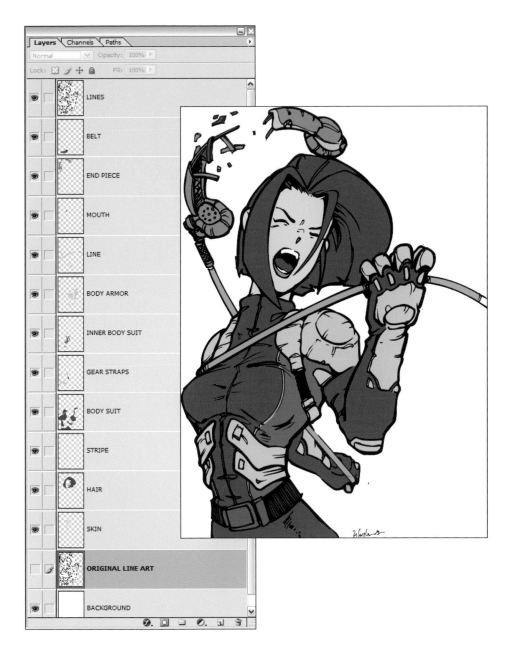

When you've finished coloring, you need to complete a few housekeeping steps once again to keep things tidy and make your file easier to work with. You'll create two layer sets and store the colored layers inside them. One layer set will be for the flat colors that you've just created, and the other will hold the more detailed color layers that you're about to create. The flat colors will be hidden and will serve only as a backup and reference point for you to revert to if needed.

9. Link all of the flat color layers that you just created.

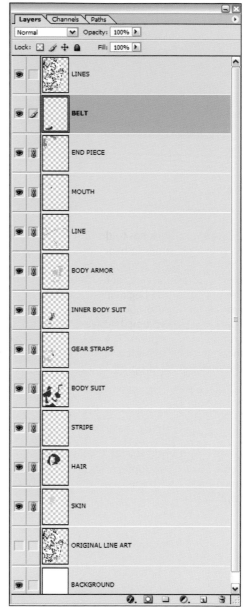

10. Choose New Set From Linked from the Layers palette options menu. Name this layer set FLATS.

11. Duplicate the layer set by choosing Duplicate Layer Set from the Layers palette options menu. Rename this layer set COLOR DETAILS.

12. Hide the FLATS layer set. This layer set will serve as a backup. If you ever color, distort, or destroy one of the colored areas beyond repair, you can always revert to this backup and start from the flat color again.

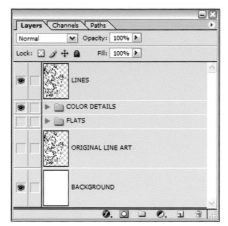

Another nice trick has to do with locking the transparency of a layer. This comes in handy during this exercise because, at this point, you've spent a good amount of time up front to create the outlines and color fills for this drawing. Remember in the beginning when I mentioned how it's well worth the time to color each area carefully? The time you spent will pay off now because Photoshop offers you a **lock transparency** option. The button to turn on this option is located in the top-left area of the Layers palette, just below the blend mode drop-down list.

You'll know this option is turned on when you see a small lock icon to the right of each layer that this setting is applied to.

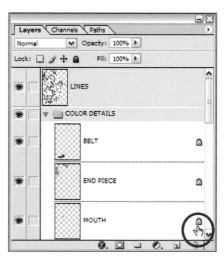

The lock transparency option allows you to lock all transparent areas of a layer. This means that if you apply it to a layer with nontransparent pixels (the flat colored layers are a perfect example of this), all editing of that layer will be confined to opaque areas.

13. Lock the transparency of all layers within the COLOR DETAILS layer set by clicking the Lock button in the Layers palette. Now you can paint on these layers as much as you'd like, and you'll never have to worry about ruining the integrity of the original color areas that you spent so much time painting at the beginning of this exercise.

Now that your flat color areas are in place, it's time to start adding some detail. This will mainly consist of highlights and shadows throughout the drawing to make it look more realistic. Here's a screenshot of the final image compared to the point at which you are currently:

As you can see, there's quite a difference. Even though the flat colored drawing looks great, the final version really stands out. Also, as you'll soon find, once you learn a few simple techniques to achieve the texture, highlights, and shadows shown in the final version, you can apply them to the entire coloring process.

Most of the shading techniques revolve around using the Brush tool. At first, you may think that you need to choose shadow and highlight colors with which to color various areas. But there's a much better way: blend modes. Yep, brushes have them too. If you observe the tool options bar when the Brush tool is selected, you'll see a Mode setting.

From the drop-down list, you can select blend modes that correspond to the same blend modes located in the Layers palette. With these blend modes, you won't have to hunt around for the perfect shadow or highlight color—you can just let the brush, blend modes, and opacity settings do the work for you.

The tool options bar contains two other settings: Opacity and Flow. Opacity specifies the maximum amount of paint coverage applied by the brush. Flow specifies how quickly the paint is applied. The values for these settings can range from 1% to 100%. To achieve a weak or transparent effect, specify a low value. For stronger, more opaque effects, specify a high value.

Before you move on to shading and highlighting the colors, I'd like to display the options that you should turn on if you're using a graphic pen and tablet.

14. Choose Window ➤ Brushes (*F5*) to display the expanded Brushes palette.

15. Select Shape Dynamics. Set Size Jitter to 0% and select Pen Pressure in the Control drop-down list.

16. Select Other Dynamics. Choose Pen Pressure from the Control drop-down list underneath the Opacity Jitter setting.

Now when you use your pen, the amount of pressure you apply will cause the shape and opacity of the brush to change. Pressing harder will achieve the full size of the brush at full opacity. Pressing softer will result in lighter and smaller brush strokes.

Again, if you plan on creating this type of artwork, often a digital drawing tablet is almost necessary. It will not only significantly improve your artwork, but also reduce the amount of time you spend on it.

OK, now you're ready to start shading and highlighting. You're going to start with the body suit. This is one of the largest areas in the drawing, and it's a great place to get familiar with the shading techniques.

17. Expand the COLORS layer set. Click the BODY SUIT layer to make it active.

18. Press *D* to reset your foreground and background colors to their defaults.

19. Select the Brush tool and set the mode to Multiply. For the most part, you'll use the Multiply mode when shading the flat colors. Select a 35–40-pixel soft-edged brush, and reduce the opacity of the brush to around 15%. Now shade the bottom of the chest area. The more you color over the area, the darker it gets.

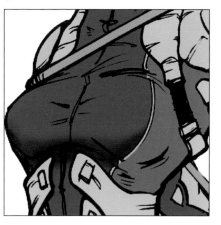

It's a good idea to start with a low-opacity brush. It's much easier to increase the opacity and apply more shading or highlighting later than it is to undo and recolor your artwork.

20. Start shading toward the center of the chest, but reduce the opacity and brush less as you move toward the brighter areas.

7

21. Add a few more shaded areas near the neck, belt, and pants areas.

Highlighting is very similar to shading. You'll use the Screen mode to accomplish this task. Like Multiply, the Screen blend mode will save you from having to hunt around for the perfect highlight color. Varying the opacity of the brush stroke will produce different degrees of highlights on your flat colors.

22. Set the foreground color to white. Set the brush Mode to Screen and set Opacity to 25%.

23. Add some highlights in the center of the chest area. The highlights will be brightest at the center point and become weaker as the area transitions toward the darker shaded points. You can achieve this effect by lowering the opacity of the brush (using the Opacity setting in the tool options bar) or by pressing softer with the pen.

24. Add a few highlights at the top of the suit near the neck.

25. Another nice effect is to highlight the marks, stretches, and imperfections in the body suit. Do this by selecting a small, soft-edged brush. With white as the foreground color and the mode set to Screen, paint the bottom and inside the small marks you see on the body suit. These highlights will be brighter than some of the others, so you may need to increase the opacity of the brush slightly.

Another trick that comes in handy is the process of **blurring**. Often, it can take a long time to shade and highlight areas to perfection. You'll find yourself shading an area, and then highlighting it and realizing that you may have caused a harsh transition between the two. You can spend a lot of time switching back and forth trying to get it just right. A great alternative to this is blurring the area to produce the transition automatically. You have two options when you do this: one for small controlled areas that require a fine touch and one for large areas that you can select with the Marquee tools. The chest area is the perfect place to try out this technique. Follow along to see how.

26. The highlight areas along some of the stretch marks on the suit are a bit harsh. To fix this, select the Blur tool (*R*). It's located just below the Eraser tool and to the left of the Dodge and Burn tools in the toolbar.

27. With a soft-edged brush, brush with the Blur tool along the highlighted areas in question. Notice how they become slightly blurred. The effect isn't harsh, and it's best used for small areas where you want to retain control of the blurring process.

The second method involves the Gaussian Blur filter.

28. Using the Lasso tool (*L*), create a selection around the chest areas where the transitions may appear to be too strong.

29. Choose Filter ➤ Blur ➤ Gaussian Blur. Experiment with the Radius settings, but be aware that lower values seem to work better. You can always reapply the filter (*CTRL*/⌘+*F*) to heighten the effect.

30. Now that you have a good foundation, repeat the highlight and shading process on the brown area inside the body suit.

31. Now click the GEAR STRAPS layer to make it active. This will be the next area you'll shade and highlight.

32. Using the same highlight and shading techniques as before, shade these straps in way that creates a beveled look. This entails shading two adjacent sides and highlighting the other two sides (this is similar to the Bevel & Emboss effect). This process will raise the straps from the body suit and add some depth to their overall appearance.

33. The next area to concentrate on is the BODY ARMOR layer. Shade and highlight this layer in the same way as you did the others. When I worked on this layer, I changed the shading blend mode from Multiply to Color Burn in some places, namely the shoulder plate. As you can see in the following image, this enhances the color while still maintaining a darker shaded effect.

34. Now move to the HAIR layer. No special tricks here—just pick your shadow and highlight areas according to the light source, as in the rest of the drawing.

35. Color the remaining layers in the same way. The SKIN layer is the only area where I varied the usual settings used so far. Instead of shading with just the Multiply blend mode, I shaded with Color Burn and Multiply.

36. For the mouth, all that's needed is a small highlight on one of the lips.

Summary

Whether you have traditional cartoon drawing experience or digital cartoon experience, or you simply enjoy coloring other people's line art, Photoshop offers something for all. It's painterly effects, such as brushes, when it comes to re-creating traditional media make it the tool of choice when coloring and shading line art.

7

PART THREE ADVANCED ILLUSTRATION

Silhouette illustration is a trend in today's design community that has become very popular. This form of illustration is focused on using and extracting the most basic forms of an object and turning them into art. It can be seen everywhere from Web graphics, Flash movies, and magazine ads, to full-blown TV ads. Although simple, silhouette illustration can reduce an object to its most simplistic form and still convey an emotion, style, and energy with little actual color and definition. In this chapter, I'll dissect the use of silhouettes for illustrative purposes and show how Photoshop can be used to create this type of artwork. You'll see potential and real examples involving this type of design and how they may have been created. Finally, you'll delve into two exercises that will help build your portfolio, inspire you to add a new style to your design portfolio, and push you to use Photoshop in ways that you may not have thought of before.

What is a silhouette?

There are many definitions for the term *silhouette*. However, most have two core concepts in common. First, a silhouette generally entails the drawing of an outline of an object. Second, the background is typically removed from this drawing leaving only the object in focus. In short, a silhouette drawing includes only the images of the most visually important curves on the surface of an object, person, or structure.

Why use a silhouette illustration?

The techniques you'll see here are popular among today's design trends. You'll often see silhouette illustrations and graphics used on the Web and in Flash movies. Not only do they look great and are easy to create, but they involve few colors, providing quick download times.

Mood

Mood is a vital consideration when planning a silhouette illustration. You must select objects that are simple enough to work for this form of design, yet communicative enough to achieve your goal. Oddly enough, images without any detail can be excellent in communicating mood, leaving enough room for text and not detracting from the overall goal of the piece. Here are a few examples of silhouette illustrations used to convey various moods.

Nighttime, scary, threatening.

Love and intimacy.

Playful, energetic, hip.

All of these samples have several things in common. They are simple in nature, none of them contain many details, and they use a combination of a communicative pose and color to convey various moods. The basic techniques to create these images in Photoshop are fairly easy, it's what you do with the theory, knowledge, and overall goal of the illustration that sets you apart and makes your work worthy of professional recognition.

Picking an image to silhouette

Picking an image from which to create a silhouette is not a difficult process. After all, this is art and you are the artist. If you have a vision, who's to say it's right or wrong? However, there are a few guidelines that can help save you some time and keep you from choosing an image that may not produce the intended results.

Complexity

Most often, you want to choose simple shapes to silhouette. The goal with this type of illustration is to draw the viewer's attention to the overall elegance of the artwork. You want the shape of the object to communicate for you. If you choose a woman with long hair that is blowing in the wind, it may not only be difficult to draw every piece of the windblown hair, but it may also be challenging for the viewer to concentrate on what's important in the image. The hair may draw all of the attention as opposed to the overall illustration.

8

Viewing angle

View angle is very important. By this, I mean the way the silhouette object is viewed. For example, take a silhouette image of a woman with a hand on her head and a handshake.

Now take a look at the source images. As you can see, the silhouettes of the woman and handshake are barely distinguishable and aren't representative of the source image from which they were created.

Image by www.PhotoSpin.com.
© All rights reserved.

Image by www.PhotoSpin.com.
© All rights reserved.

When attempting to draw a silhouette from these two images, the detail that conveys the key characteristics is lost. Overlapping shapes within the object, no definable curves, and images in which the details do most of the communicating may not be the best choices for silhouettes. In fact, in this example you really can't even tell that this is a woman.

However, if you were to draw a silhouette from a different image like a sports or dancing pose, the movement and energy of the original image is usually much more recognizable. Be careful to select a pose that doesn't rely on details to convey what's happening in the image.

Composition

Be mindful of the overall composition in the image you choose to silhouette. While a silhouetted image of a snowboarder flying through the air may be communicative, it may not be very practical on its own. Often, your images may require other objects to put them in context. If the image requires too many other objects, then it may begin to detract from the whole appeal of a silhouette illustration: simplicity.

Creativity

Be creative when picking a suitable silhouette image. I know it's a lot easier said than done, but I urge you to do what you can to make your work your own. For example, take a look at the before view of the image used for the exercise later in this chapter.

From this image, I created this silhouette.

Although the silhouette retains many of the characteristics of the outline in the original image, it's not a perfect traced replication of it. I added and subtracted a few details. When I viewed this image, I saw the folds in the shirt. To me, they conveyed motion and stretching. You can almost feel the effort involved in the twisting of the body to achieve the golf swing. So, instead of just tracing the outline of the pose, I chose to leave much of the back out. In addition, you'll see that I added some details that weren't there in the first place, such as some of the folds and shapes in the hat. The point here is to make this your own work. Add your own signature style to it. This is a large part of achieving and keeping a professional status in the design community. Anyone can go out and trace something and call it art. Examine your work and contemplate how to take it a step further.

Extracting your image

Photoshop offers many ways in which to subtract your image from a background and trace the outlines of the object in focus. However, I bet you can probably guess what I'm going to say is the best method—the Pen tool (*P*) naturally. The Pen tool offers the greatest amount of flexibility when trying to create the core outlines and curves of your image or remove your focus image from the background. Not only will it allow you to draw around every curve and contour, but the path created remains editable so you can always go back and modify it at a later date. The process is fairly straightforward and you've already seen most of the methods involved, but take another look as a quick refresher course.

First, start with the image to trace, like this woman.

Image by www.PhotoSpin.com. © All rights reserved.

Using the Pen tool, trace around the edges of the woman. Now there's a path in the Paths palette.

From here, create a new layer in the Layers palette to hold the silhouette painting. Then, the path can be filled using the Fill path with foreground color button at the bottom of the palette.

Alternatively, a selection can be created from this path using the Load path as selection button at the bottom of the Paths palette. From there, you can paint the selection. (In this example, I chose black in the Layers palette.)

8

A gradient often looks nice as well.

OK, you've heard me preach about the Pen tool and its many uses throughout this book. I do need to mention a good alternative to using the Pen tool—quick masks. A *quick mask* is basically a selection. However, instead of using the traditional selection tools to create it, you can use the Brush tool (*B*) to create a much more precise selection.

Using the same example, load an original file into Photoshop as normal. Then, click on the Edit in Quick Mask Mode button in the Toolbox (*Q*).

Photoshop switches to Quick Mask mode. In this mode, you have a choice of painting with black or white. Anything painted with black will show up as pink while in this mode. Anything painted with white will not show up at all. When you return to Standard mode, the pink areas will be left intact and the remaining areas will be selected. At that point, you can delete the unwanted background, leaving only the area that was painted (or selected) in pink while in Quick Mask mode.

This method offers you the ability to zoom in and be very precise in your selections because you can increase or decrease your brush size as much as you'd like. Plus, it allows a much more natural way of selecting because you're essentially painting on the image.

8

Which method is better? I'll leave that one up to you to decide. Often, it depends on the task at hand and your skill level. Many people prefer the Pen tool because it's precise and quick. However, some designers feel more at home with the Brush tool. A brush coupled with a graphic pen tablet can be a powerful selection tool as well. In the end, it really depends on the tool with which you feel most comfortable.

Exercise: Creating a golf apparel ad

1. Open `Chapter_08_GolfPose_Start.psd`. This file contains an image of yours truly posing with a golf club.

If you can't find a picture, just snap one with a digital camera. It can be a great time-saver, provide endless amounts of potential, and spark your creative process.

The first task is to visualize what areas you'd like to draw in this illustration. As I mentioned earlier, I decided that I wasn't just going to trace the entire outline of the pose. Instead, I felt the highlights and shadows produced by the folds in the shirt conveyed a certain sense of motion and I wanted to re-create them. A common question when I discuss this technique is how to discern those details. Practice is definitely one of the ways, but another way is to use the adjustment tools right within Photoshop to help spark your creativity. By manipulating the reference image and reducing the amount of colors, you'll begin to see patterns that can help when trying to create your own artwork. Follow along to see one example.

2. Click once on the ORIGINAL POSE layer to make it active. Then, click on the New Adjustment Layer button at the bottom of the Layers palette. Choose Posterize from the list that appears.

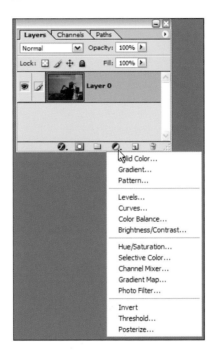

Note that adjustment layers are a great alternative to using the Image ➤ Adjustments menu. When applying an adjustment through the menu commands, the changes to the image are permanent. Using an adjustment layer allows you to go back and change these settings (or hide the adjustment layer completely) at any time.

3. This action will present you with the Posterize dialog box.

4. Change the Levels setting to 3. This will reduce the number of tonal levels within the image.

> *What is **posterizing**? The* Posterize *command lets you specify the number of tonal levels (or brightness values) for each channel in an image, and then maps pixels to the closest matching level. For example, choosing two tonal levels in an RGB image gives six colors: two for red, two for green, and two for blue.*

As you can see, the image has been reduced to only a few colors. Now you can begin to see some patterns and definable shapes taking place within the image. Notice how the back, much of the face, and the hat become almost totally black. It's the highlights on the hat and face and the folds and stretch marks on the shirt that attract your eye.

8

By drawing those highlight shapes and filling them with a light color on top of a dark background, this shows that the golfer pose would still be distinguishable as a silhouette.

5. We'll create the illustration using shape layers. Select the Pen tool and be sure Shape Layers button is selected in the tool options bar. Also, press the *D* and *X* keys to set your foreground color to white.

6. Now draw or trace the highlight areas along the shirt up to the shoulder. It doesn't have to be perfect. In fact, I suggest that it's not. Just follow the basic shapes, but also allow your instincts to take over and feel free to stray if you see an opportunity.

> *If the white foreground color of the shape layer is preventing you from seeing the reference photo beneath, just reduce the opacity of the layer to around 20%. You should still see some of the white, but you'll also see the reference below.*

7. When you're done, name this layer SHIRT.

8. Repeat this process for the face, keeping in mind that you'll only draw the front highlighted area. Also note that part of the nose doesn't have any light shining on it, so you'll want to draw around it. Name this layer FACE.

9. Next, draw the hat. After experimenting, I found that when I drew that hat based off of the original highlights, it didn't look much like a hat. So, I've taken more artistic liberty here and added some areas that didn't appear as highlights to retain more of its shape.

10. Next, draw the ear.

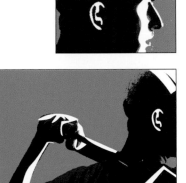

11. Now draw the hands and the arms. No need to get too detailed here. Just some basic free-formed shapes will work fine.

12. Last, draw the golf club. After reviewing my golf stance, I thought my club was pointing down a little too much so I also straightened it a bit.

13. OK, the shapes that make up the golfer are now in place. Hide the Posterize adjustment layer and create a new layer above ORIGINAL POSE named BACKGROUND. Fill this layer with (*ALT/OPTION BACKSPACE*) R:64 G:181 B:73. Now you should be able to see your silhouette image.

13. To keep things tidy in the Photoshop file, link together all of the shape layers and create a new layer set from the linked layers named GOLFER.

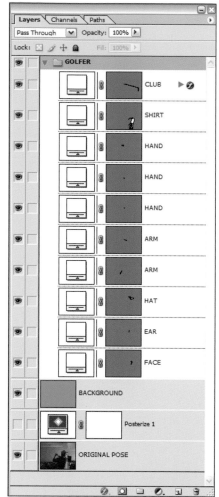

Next, incorporate this image into a magazine-sized ad.

14. Open Chapter_08_ExtremeGolfAd_Start.psd from the source files. This is a large Photoshop document based on the ISO-standard paper size system. Since the final output for this design will be a magazine ad, I chose A4 as the size when I created the new file in Photoshop.

15. Switch back to the golfer window. Now drag the GOLFER layer set into the large magazine ad file just opened. Position it above the BORDER layer, but below all of the text layers.

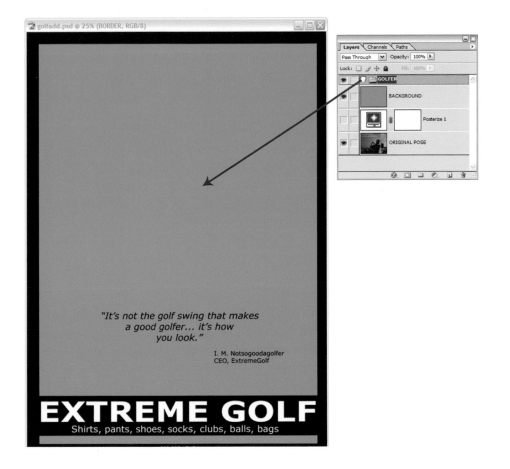

OK, it looks nice, but it's rather small for this ad. This is no problem though because the silhouette was created using shape layers. Now you can scale them up as large as you'd like.

16. Click on the GOLFER layer set and choose Edit ➤ Transform ➤ Scale. Hold down the *SHIFT* key and extend the bounding box until the golfer silhouette encompasses most of the area in the center of the ad.

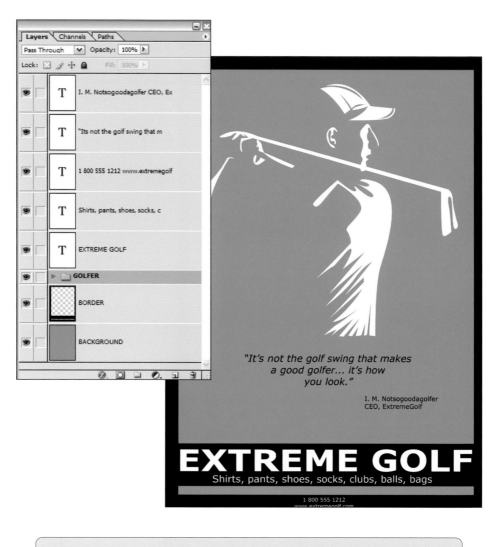

Move your cursor inside the bounding box to reposition the layers while still remaining in Scale mode.

17. Adding a layer mask with a slight gradient to fade the bottom of the golfer makes a nice finishing touch.

Summary

Silhouette-styled illustration has been around for many years. Traditional artists have successfully drawn artistic focus to the outline of an object with nowhere near the tools and assets available to today's digital designer. In this chapter, you learned how easy it is to create this style of art. As you've seen, a simple photograph can be turned into a silhouette-styled illustration with little time and effort. As a professional designer, the ease of creating this type of art will allow you to concentrate on the overall illustration and the impact you'd like to make to your clients. In the end, you'll produce eye-catching work for your clients quickly and inexpensively.

Artists, illustrators, and designers have been incorporating 3D into their artwork for many years. However, wireframe illustration is a fairly new trend in the design industry. With roots based in 3D modeling and rendering, wireframe illustration involves similar characteristics as silhouette illustration (discussed in Chapter 8). However, instead of using filled shapes with few details as focal points, wireframe illustration focuses on the outlines around and within an object to represent the edges of the form being designed. In this chapter, I'll focus on the origins of this type of illustration, and then you'll see how this type of illustration is useful and how to incorporate it into your designs. Finally, several exercises will be presented to give you a firm understanding of real-life examples that incorporate this type of work and how you can start using it in your personal and professional projects today.

What is a wireframe?

To begin, let's examine the foundation of wireframe illustration—the wireframe. Essentially, a *wireframe* is a geometric representation of a 3D object as outlined by its outer edges. In other words, a wireframe is a view within a 3D modeling program that shows only the edges, intersecting points, and lines of an object's contours.

Historically, wireframe rendering is a fast rendering method in which objects are drawn as if they've been made of wires, with only their edges showing. This allows 3D artists to quickly view their object without having to wait for the surface to be shaded and textured.

The following two images represent a wireframe view of a 3D object and the actual object produced by the wireframe.

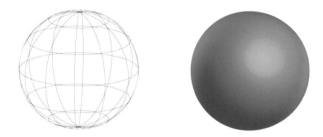

As you can see, this is the simplest type of representation for a 3D object.

Wireframe history

Wireframe illustration became popular during the technology boom of the late 1990s. Often wireframe objects were added to websites, company financial reports, ads, and other marketing collateral to enhance designs. They became a key staple of the graphic designer to communicate a high-tech message to potential viewers.

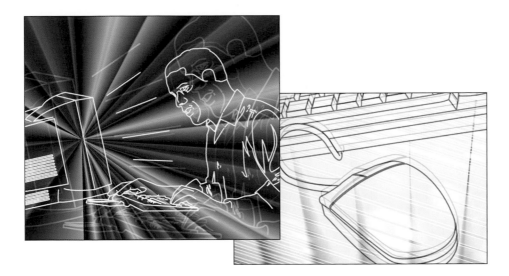

Today, wireframes in graphic design have become even more pronounced, sometimes occupying the entire focal point of an illustration. However, this style has also evolved in its purpose as well. While still maintaining its technology focus, wireframe illustrations have branched out to designs for other industries. Trendy, young, spontaneous, hip, and edgy designs have all been the focus of a wireframe illustration in the past few years.

Finally, wireframe illustrations don't need to specifically retain all of the properties of a traditional wireframe. The key messages throughout this book have been to not only show you how to push Photoshop to its extreme limits and demonstrate various types of graphic design skills to use in your personal and professional development, but also to show you how to evolve as a designer. This is one area that can set you apart from other designers and help you get or keep that key designer job. One way to extend the wireframe-based illustrations is to keep the old saying, "Sometimes less is more", in mind. Often, you can utilize the same concepts covered earlier in the book to create logos, fine art, and illustrations that retain many characteristics of wireframe illustration, but are not as obvious.

Picking an image to wireframe

Picking a reference image from which to create a wireframe illustration is somewhat more forgiving than with silhouette illustration. Since wireframes allow you to incorporate some of the details that help make an object distinguishable, you have more flexibility when looking for inspiration. However, there are still several concepts to keep in mind. Picking an image or object with a casual yet communicative pose or angle is still a process that must be given the appropriate amount of thought and attention. Here are a few guidelines that can help save you some time and keep you from choosing an image that may not produce the intended results.

Complexity

Complexity was a characteristic that I warned you of with silhouette illustration. However, with wireframe illustration, you have more flexibility when it comes to this characteristic. You'll utilize more detail with this type of illustration, so you can use more lines and shapes to help distinguish a complex object. The only caveat is that the more complex an object you decide to draw, the more time it will take. However, it's time well spent as you can create some truly fantastic objects utilizing this type of design.

Viewing angle

The same principles apply to the viewing angle. Since you can add details to an outline, even objects that weren't suited for silhouette illustration may work just fine when converting to wireframe drawings.

For example, examine the following image that will be used for one of the exercises in this chapter.

If you were to attempt a silhouette illustration from this image, you wouldn't be able to tell that it was a hand holding a mobile phone. However, if you were to reduce this photograph to only outlines by using the Pen tool (*P*), you can immediately recognize the image. This is a perfect example of how the two styles differ.

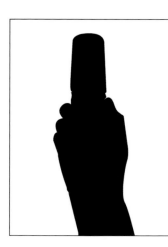
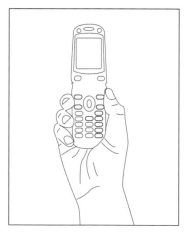

Creativity

Be creative when picking a suitable wireframe image. I know it's a lot easier said than done, but I urge you to do what you can to make your work your own. For example, take a look at the before view of the image used for the exercise later in this chapter.

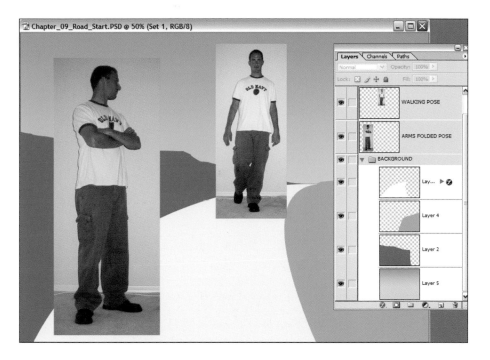

By using your creativity to envision the results of combing multiple photographs and images, you design with very few limitations. If you can't find the perfect reference photograph, make your own. As you can see from the final output of the image, I've done just that.

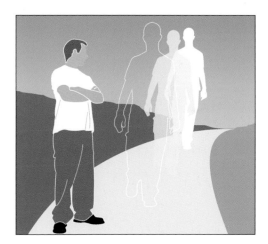

Creating outlines

For most purposes, you'll use the Pen tool to produce wireframe illustrations. As you may know from previous discussions throughout this book, you have several options available in the tool options bar when using this tool. In this situation, the Paths option typically works best.

However, there's one key point to keep in mind when using this option. If you select the Paths option and begin drawing on a layer with the Pen tool, you would create a work path in the Paths palette.

A *work path* is a temporary path that appears in the Paths palette and defines the outline of a shape. However, once you begin drawing another path, your work path is lost and another is created because they are only temporary. To make your paths permanent so this doesn't happen, click the Create New Path button in the Paths palette before you begin drawing. This will automatically save the work path as a named path.

Exercise: Basic wireframe drawing

This first exercise introduces you to the basics of creating a wireframe illustration in Photoshop. Using a simple photograph taken of a hand holding a mobile phone can be a great way to start.

1. Open Chapter_09_PhoneHand_Start.psd from this chapter's source files. This file contains one layer containing a photograph of a hand holding a mobile phone.

2. Select the Pen tool. Be sure the Paths button is selected in the tool options bar. This means that every path you create will be stored in the Paths palette.

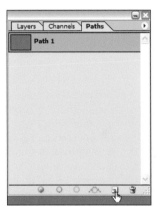

3. Display the Paths palette. Click on the Create New Path button at the bottom of the palette. Now you're ready to begin drawing paths.

The next step entails drawing paths based on the visible outlines in the photograph as a reference. The best way to tackle this exercise is to break the hand up into two parts—one part for the portion of the hand on the left of the phone and one part for the area on the right.

4. Using the Pen tool, draw a path on the new Path layer for the left side of the hand. Note this path is not closed.

9

5. When you're finished with the left side, press the *Esc* key. This ends the path even though it's not closed but keeps focus on the current path layer so you can begin drawing another path on the same layer.

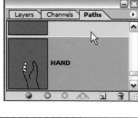

6. Next, draw the right side of the hand. When you're done, rename this path layer HAND.

7. While still on the HAND path layer, pick some lines and wrinkles to draw from the reference photo. Again, most of these paths will not be closed so you'll have to press the *Esc* key after each segment to end the path and begin drawing another on the same path layer.

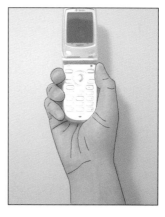

8. Now draw the fingernails and any other key areas of the hand that will help distinguish it. However, don't get too bogged down in the details. While this form of illustration tends to be more detailed than a silhouette illustration, it doesn't require you to trace every small detail. One way to help plan what details you'd like to keep is to zoom out and examine the hand every so often to determine which lines and shapes really give the hand its shape.

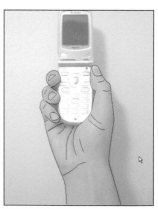

9. Next, create a new path layer named PHONE and draw the outline of the phone. Don't worry about the areas that appear behind the hand at this time. Just loosely estimate the outline behind the hand and continue precisely drawing the path where it emerges into view again.

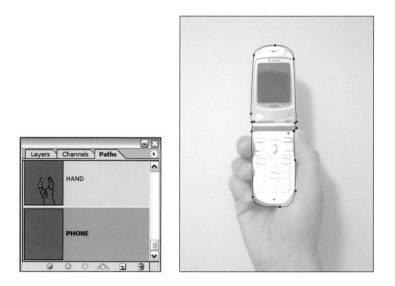

10. When you're done drawing the outline of the phone, you should have a closed path. Click the Rounded Rectangle tool (*U*) and set the Radius to 30 px in the tool options bar. Also be sure that the Add To Path Area button is selected next to the Radius setting. This will ensure that each shape you draw with one of the shape tools will be added to the current path.

11. Draw a small rounded-rectangle shape over one of the buttons on the phone.

9

12. Select the Direct Selection tool (*A*). Drag around this small rectangle to select it.

13. Copy (*CTRL/⌘+C*) this shape and paste it (*CTRL/⌘+V*). You won't see the duplicate, but if you press the down arrow key, you'll notice that the original will still be in place and your duplicate will be nudged down. Continue to nudge the duplicate down until it's in place.

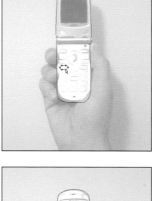

14. Another point of interest is that the duplicate will still be selected. This means that once in place, you can copy and paste another button shape without having to use the Direct Selection tool again. It will be placed over the existing one, ready for you to nudge with the arrow keys again.

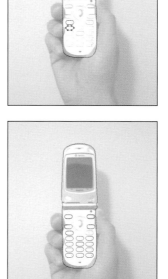

Hold down the SHIFT key to increase the nudge amount from 1 pixel to 10 pixels for each key press.

Now we need to add some of the final details that will help enhance the mobile phone. One key technique with which to become familiar involves using the shape tools whenever possible. In this illustration, it's OK to use them even if they don't perfectly match the original shape on the phone. You won't notice the difference in small details once reduced to outlines.

15. Using the Ellipse (*U*) and Rounded Rectangle tools, I created several more shapes near the display screen on the phone.

16. Finally, one last path is drawn around the screen.

At this point, the hardest part is complete. Next, we'll stroke the outlines just created and turn this into a wireframe.

17. Switch back to the Layers palette. Create a new layer above the ORIGINAL PHOTO layer named BACKGROUND. Fill this layer with R:197 G:53 B:195.

9

18. Create a new layer above BACKGROUND named PHONE.

19. Now select the Brush tool (*B*) and choose a 3-pixel, hard-edged brush with which to paint.

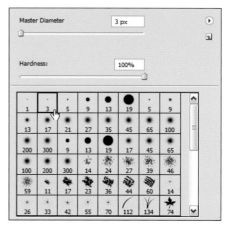

20. Set your foreground color to white and click once on the PHONE layer to make it active.

21. Switch back to the Paths palette and click the PHONE path to select it. Stroke this path by clicking the Stroke path with brush button at the bottom of the palette.

If your results aren't as expected, try making sure that the Brush tool was selected before you clicked the stroke path button. Keep in mind that the path will always be stroked with the current tool and its associated settings.

22. OK, now for the hand. Create a new layer above PHONE named HAND.

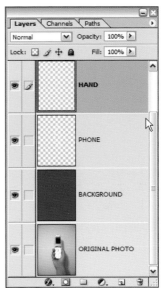

23. Using the same settings as before, stroke the hand path on this new layer.

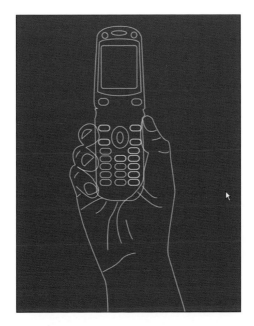

9

We're almost done. All that is left is to clean up the outlines. Remember in step 9 when you created the outline of the phone regardless of whether it was actually behind the hand? This was a big time-saving step, as it allowed you to quickly create the outlines without have to retrace around various areas. However, as with many quick fixes, they must eventually be dealt with.

24. Select the Eraser tool (*E*) and erase any areas on the phone layer that shouldn't be seen (mainly, the areas between the fingers). Remember to use the shortcuts for increasing and decreasing brush size quickly (the *[* and *]* keys) as they hold true for the Eraser tool as well.

Exercise: Using outlines with fill colors and animation techniques

This next exercise shows a slightly different approach to wireframe illustration. As you've seen in the first exercise, creating the actual outlines and wireframe components isn't too difficult once you become familiar with drawing paths. However, there's much more that can be done with this form of illustration. One area that comes to mind is the addition of color. A simple outline drawing similar to the first exercise may work well for many projects, but often color is needed as well. Fortunately, this style lends itself well to both methods of drawing.

To encourage you to be creative when composing this type of illustration I've taken two photographs of myself against an ordinary wall. Keep this in mind when you can't find a perfect picture to use as a reference. Many times a digital camera and some creative thinking will allow you to compose whatever scene you need.

1. Open `Chapter_09_ColorWireframe_Start.psd`. This file contains a layer set named BACKGROUND and two additional layers with pictures of myself.

2. Select the Pen tool and choose the Shape layers button in the tool options bar this time. Since we're going to be using color, the use of a shape layer will save you some time later in the process. Each shape you draw will automatically contain a color as well as allow you the use of the Stroke layer style to add outlines.

3. Set your foreground color to R:253 G:185 B:128. Start with the photo on the left with the arms crossed. Begin drawing around the head. Don't worry about the area where the skin meets the hair because you'll create a separate layer for the hair. Name this layer FACE.

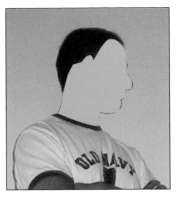

4. Next, set your foreground color to R:134 G:103 B:77 and draw the hair. Name this new layer HAIR. Be sure this shape layer is above the FACE layer and don't forget that you'll have to be more precise with this path where the hair meets the skin.

5. Continue drawing shapes for each area on the body. Use separate layers for each arm, the shirt, pants, and shoes.

When all of the shapes are drawn, you'll need to add some outlines to give an outlined wireframe appearance. Note that this illustration will not contain as many lines and details as the previous exercise did. In fact, as you progress through these exercises, you'll notice that they will begin to take on a form that's a combination of a silhouette illustration and a wireframe design.

6. Now double-click the HAIR layer to display the Layer Style dialog box. Add a Stroke layer style with the following settings and click OK.

7. Link all layers containing the body shapes together and choose New Set From Linked in the Layers palette options menu. This will help keep things manageable as more layers are added to the file.

8. Next, right-click the HAIR layer and choose Copy Layer Style. Then, right-click another one of the shape layers and choose Paste Layer Style to Linked. This will paste the layer style to all layers at once. Very handy, isn't it?

9. Finally, switch over to the Paths palette and create a new path. Select the Pen tool and choose the Paths button in the tool options bar this time to create paths only.

10. Draw several lines in any key areas where you feel details were lost by just using solid shapes. The pants and shirt were the only area that needed more detail in this illustration. Note that you may need to reduce the opacity of the layer set to see through and use the original reference image as a guide.

9

11. Create a new layer within the same layer set created in step 7. Be sure this layer is above the PANTS and SHIRT layers. Select the Brush tool and pick a 3-pixel, hard-edged brush similar to the one used in the previous exercise. Then, stroke the path created in step 10 with this brush.

12. You should now have an image similar to this one. This completes the process for the left photograph.

Now let's move on to the right photo. Since the left photograph will be the focal point of this illustration, we're not going to repeat the entire process for the right image. Instead, you'll create an outline of the walking pose and add a couple of silhouette shapes.

13. Set your foreground color to white. Select the Pen tool and create a new shape layer in the form of an outline around the photo on the right. When you're done, you can delete the two original photograph layers.

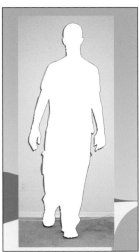

14. Duplicate this layer and change its color to R:215 G:242 B:253. Press *CTRL*/⌘+*T* to display the Free Transform bounding box and scale this shape up slightly. Be sure to hold down the *SHIFT* key to maintain the aspect ratio.

15. Now move it to the left and down slightly.

16. Duplicate this layer once again. Double-click the layer to display the Layer Style dialog box. Reduce the Fill Opacity to 0%. Then, add the following Stroke layer style used earlier for the other pose in this exercise. Scale this layer so it's even larger than the previous one. Move it into position as well.

The illustration is complete. However, in the beginning of this chapter, it was mentioned that this type of illustration works well for animations. It's a very powerful effect to watch the outlines of an object being drawn and then see the object filled with color or texture toward the end of an animation sequence. Well, in case you don't know, Photoshop ships with another program that's perfect for creating animations—ImageReady. If you've used ImageReady in the past, you've most likely noticed that it can create GIF animations. However, a new feature has been added to ImageReady CS. This feature allows you to export your animations as SWF files instead of animated GIFs. This comes in handy for larger animations. While animated GIFs work well for many short animations, SWF animations tend to compress longer animations better to allow for quicker download times.

In the next part of this exercise, you'll add motion to the static illustration. You'll utilize the general shapes that we've already created, but also make some creative use of masks along the way.

17. Open `Chapter_09_ColorWireframeAnimate_Start.psd` in Photoshop. This file picks up where we left off earlier in the exercise. The layers and shapes correspond to the steps above so if you'd like to use your own illustration, feel free. However, I have made one change to this file that you'll need to make in your own. The original file was 1,600 X 1,200 pixels in size. This is very large for a Web animation, so I reduced the dimensions to 800 X 600 pixels by choosing Image ➤ Image Size.

Next, you'll create the frames needed for the animation. You'll use Photoshop for this process because ImageReady is more of a Web design tool and is more difficult to use for tasks such as drawing and painting. When you're ready to animate, you'll move the image to ImageReady.

18. First, duplicate the FOLDED ARMS layer set. Hide the original and rename the new one to TEMP OUTLINE.

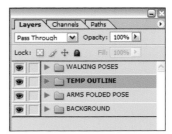

19. Choose Merge Layer Set (*CTRL*/⌘*+E*) from the Layer palette options menu. This will merge all layers within the layer set into one. You still need the original shapes that were in this layer set so the original remains hidden.

20. The previous step left you with one layer with the folded arms pose. *CTRL*/⌘-click this layer to put a selection around the entire shape. Create a new layer and click it to make it active. Then, stroke this selection by choosing Edit ➤ Stroke. Use the following settings.

21. Name this new layer OUTLINE and hide the TEMP OUTLINE layer.

22. Add a layer mask to the OUTLINE layer by clicking the Add Layer Mask button at the bottom of the Layers palette.

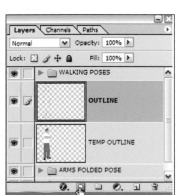

9

23. Select the Brush tool and pick a 19-pixel, hard-edged round brush.

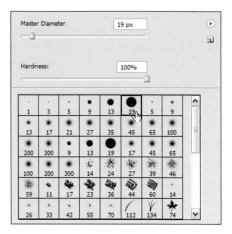

24. Click the layer mask. Press *D* to set black as your foreground color and paint around the outline so you can no longer see it. This will be the first frame for the animation once you move it to ImageReady.

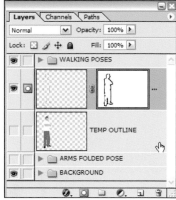

> *Remember the old saying when painting on a mask: "black conceals, white reveals".*

Next, create the remaining frames that will draw the outline. It's a slightly repetitive process, but follow along as the results are well worth it.

25. Press *CTRL*/⌘+*J* to duplicate the OUTLINE layer. Click the layer mask of the duplicate to make it active.

26. Set your foreground color to white and select the same brush used in step 24. Paint a small white area toward the bottom of the outline to unmask this area so you can see the black outline on the actual layer. Remember, you're painting on the layer mask, not the actual layer.

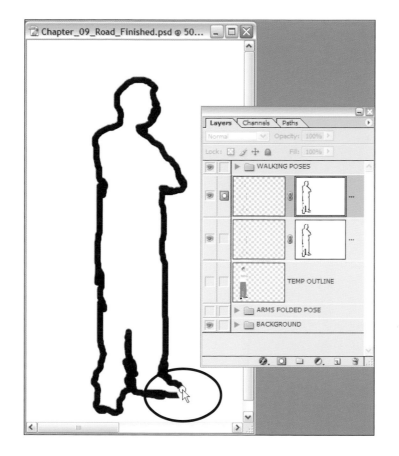

ALT/OPTION-click the layer mask to display only the mask in the window. This is helpful as the small thumbnail image in the Layers palette is often not large enough. To revert back to the normal image view, simply ALT/OPTION-click the layer mask again.

27. Duplicate this layer and click the new duplicate's layer mask once again. Paint a small area with white to reveal even more of the black outline.

28. Repeat this process around the outline until the whole outline is displayed and the mask on the last duplicate is entirely white. I used about 25 duplicate layers to complete this process. The more layers you use, the smoother the animation, but the longer it will take you.

29. After you've finished, flatten all layers into one except for the TEMP OUTLINE layer and all of the masked outline layers created in the previous three steps. Then, position the flattened layer beneath all of the layers. Your Layers palette should now look like this image.

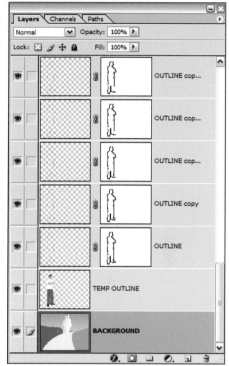

> *Completing the previous step will make life 100% easier when moving over to ImageReady in the next step. Too many layers makes animating very difficult, so it's good to flatten in advance if possible.*

30. The next steps involve using ImageReady. To open this file in ImageReady, just click the Edit In ImageReady button at the bottom of the toolbar in Photoshop and wait for your file to open in ImageReady.

31. If it's not already displayed, choose Window ➤ Animation to display the Animation palette.

32. Choose Make Frames From Layers from the Animation palette's options menu.

The previous step will convert all layers into animation frames within the Animation palette. While this is a useful shortcut, it's not without its flaws. One of those flaws is that it creates frames for all of your layers, so you'll need to make some changes.

33. First, delete all frames that don't contain part of the outline that you just created. If you're following along with the steps, this should consist of frames from 1 and 2.

34. Add a new frame at the end of the other frames.

35. Click the new frame and unhide the TEMP OUTLINE layer in the Layers palette and hide the complete black outline layer.

36. Choose Select All Frames from the Animation palette options menu. Unhide the BACKGROUND layer to make sure it's visible in all frames.

37. Select the last two frames by clicking on one and *Shift*-clicking the other. Choose Tween from the Animation palette options menu. Enter the following settings and click OK. This will use the entire black outline and final colored pose as reference points to add frames between them and make it look as if the black line is fading out and the color is slowly building.

> **Tweening** *is the process of automatically creating a series of frames* **between** *two existing frames (also known as key frames). In the animation industry, higher paid (or skilled) artists create the key frames and poses of an animation. To save money, animation studios would then hire lower paid or less experienced artists to create the in-between frames that would fall between each key frame. You'll see many animation programs contain a command for creating a tween as it's still an important concept today.*

38. You're now ready to test your animation. You can test it within ImageReady itself by clicking the Play button at the bottom of the Animation palette or in a Web browser by choosing File ➤ Preview In ➤ (*Your Web browser*).

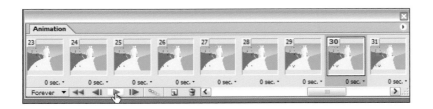

39. When you're satisfied with the final animation use ImageReady's new SWF export feature by choosing File ➤ Export ➤ Macromedia Flash SWF. You will be presented with a dialog box.

40. Enter the settings in this screen and click OK. These settings will not only create the SWF file for you, but it will create the HTML page with the SWF file already embedded inside of it. You will be asked where to store your new SWF file. Choose a location and click OK. Then, navigate to where your file was saved and open the HTML page in a Web browser to view your animation.

Exercise: Blending wireframe images with real ones

The next exercise is a popular effect when working with wireframe images. Often, instead of using Photoshop to fake a wireframe look, you may actually create or be given a real wireframe model generated with a 3D program. One effect is to merge the wireframe version of an image and its true shaded or colored version. This is an easy task using layer masks and perfectly suited for Photoshop.

1. Open `Chapter_09_WireframeMerge_Start.psd`. This file contains three layers: BACKGROUND, SHADED, and WIREFRAME. The SHADED and WIREFRAME layers are objects that were generated in Adobe Illustrator using 3D effects.

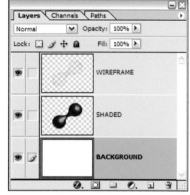

2. Add a layer mask to the SHADED layer by clicking the Add Layer Mask button at the bottom of the Layers palette.

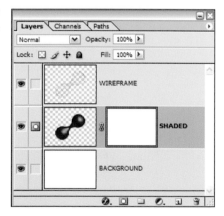

3. Select the Gradient tool (*G*) and click once on the layer mask. Drag a black to white gradient across the mask as shown in this image.

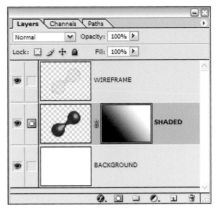

4. You should now have an image where the SHADED layer fades into the wireframe.

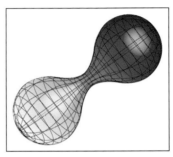

5. *ALT/OPTION*-click the layer mask to display only the mask, not the contents of the layer. Select all (*CTRL/⌘+A*) and copy (*CTRL/⌘+C*).

6. Add a layer mask to the WIREFRAME layer.

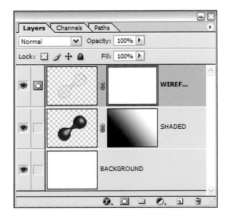

9

7. *ALT/OPTION* -click the layer mask to display only the mask. Paste the black to white gradient that was copied in the previous step into this layer mask.

8. Press *CTRL/⌘+I* to invert the black and white colors so the mask is opposite of the previous one.

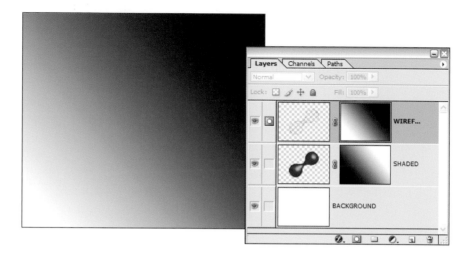

Finally, your image should look as if the shaded and wireframe object blend into each other.

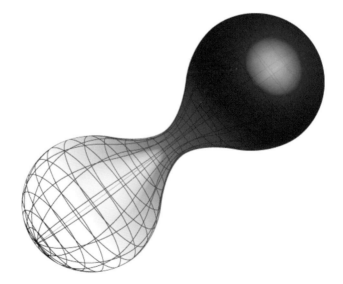

Exercise: Adding text to create a t-shirt

In this final exercise, we'll look at a practical application of using the outline and wireframe techniques discussed in this chapter. Often, images must be accompanied by text. While the style of illustrations created in this chapter looks great, there are few cases where it would stand alone. In Photoshop CS, Adobe has added even more features for using text by incorporating type on a path. Illustrator users have had this feature for quite some time, but it's a welcome addition to Photoshop and worth exploring further. In this exercise, you'll create a t-shirt and add some text to it to show off the new illustration style as well as one of Photoshop's new features.

1. Open `Chapter_09_TShirt_Start.psd`. This file contains several layers: BACKGROUND, T-SHIRT, CIRCLE, and OUTLINE.

9

2. Create a new layer below OUTLINE named COLOR. We'll use another method for coloring the wireframe illustration on the OUTLINE layer.

3. Set your foreground color to R:232 G:210 B:155. Select the Brush tool and pick a 19-pixel, hard-edged brush. Now brush between the lines of the pants and the hat. This is a free-form style and part of the appeal is that you don't need to color exactly between the lines.

4. Next, set your foreground color to R:253 G:178 B:115 and paint on the arms, face, and neck. You may need to decrease your brush size slightly to be more accurate.

5. Now paint with white over the t-shirt and hair areas.

9

Next, let's add some text. Photoshop has added the ability to place text on a path. If you recall from earlier discussions, shape layers are actually paths. If you were to click on the Shape layer in the Layers palette, you would actually see a path in the Paths palette for this shape. That said, we can use this layer as a guide in which to place text.

6. Click once on the CIRCLE shape layer to make it active. Select the Horizontal Type tool (*T*).

7. Position your cursor over the outline of the circle. You should notice the cursor changes and has a small diagonal line through it when it intersects with the path. This indicates you can click to place text on the path.

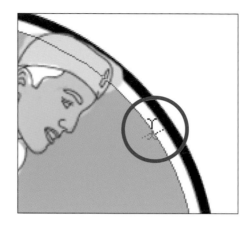

8. Click and type the word **Extreme**. I used a thick, black font set at 14 pt for this example.

9. When you've placed your type, you can use the transformation commands located in the Edit menu to rotate, scale, or skew the text.

10. Click the CIRCLE layer once again and add the word Photoshop on the other end of the circle.

Summary

Much like silhouette-styled illustration in Chapter 8, producing wireframe illustrations offers designers a powerful yet simple way to communicate energy and style. As you've seen, composing various photographs and background elements enables you to creatively build an illustration with few resources. Armed with a digital camera or Web browser and a bit of creative thinking, you can create illustrations that appeal to many types of audiences.

9

At the moment, nothing cries hip more than photographs converted to stylistic paintings or vector illustrations. Armed with little more than a photograph, designers are able to create powerful, stylistic, trendy, and visually stunning illustrations. While once the territory of highly skilled vector-based software users, these illustrations are now easier than ever for Photoshop users to create. However, the recent advances in Photoshop can leave many wondering just what tools to use to create such work. The rates at which the program has changed and styles have evolved make it more crucial than ever that designers stay ahead of the game.

This chapter will introduce you to some simple techniques for creating stylized illustrations from photographs. You'll quickly delve into harnessing Photoshop's power to make use of its vector and painting tools to create these illustrations.

Stylizing techniques

You can create stylized photographs in many ways. Some involve the use of the Pen tool (*P*) and paths, others involve using filters, some utilize Photoshop's powerful paintbrush engine, and some consist of working with all of the above. As you complete the exercises in this chapter, you will not only gain a good working knowledge of how to use all of these techniques, but also finish with artwork ready for your portfolio.

Picking a photograph

Picking a photograph for this style of illustration is even more forgiving than the styles covered in Chapters 8 and 9. Stylizing photographs allows you the utmost of flexibility when creating your artwork because you can choose what details to incorporate or omit. However, keep the following few guidelines in mind when choosing your reference photograph.

Complexity

Just as in the previous two chapters, the complexity of the reference picture is very important. Trying to envision your final illustration and the methods you're going to use to get there will help with this process. Look at the reference you plan to use and decide if and how it can be re-created to your satisfaction, and what will be required.

Hair

Stylizing portraits are one of the most popular techniques within this genre of illustration. Be cognizant of the hair within a photo before you select the picture to stylize. Often the hair can be the most difficult part to create, and it can also be the most damaging to an illustration if not done well.

Copyright issues

You should always take copyright issues into account. When creating silhouette or wire-frame illustrations, the final image usually doesn't closely represent the original. However, stylized illustrations like the ones you'll create in this chapter often resemble the original reference very closely. Be aware of the copyright issues surrounding the reference photograph and be sure to abide by them.

Getting started

One of the best things about many of the design styles and techniques covered in this book is that they're accessible to everyone. The process of stylizing photographs is no exception. In fact, after you've selected a reference image, you can start immediately if you feel up to it. However, if you need some inspiration on how to attack a new project, then you're not alone. While many designers can look at a reference photograph and instantly determine the highlights, shadows, tones, and colors that will help bring the reference photo to digital life in Photoshop, many great artists are not blessed with that talent. However, the good news is that many talents and skills aren't instantly acquired at birth. Instead, they're learned through practice. Graphic design is no exception. By following a few simple methods in Photoshop, you can also develop an eye for spotting these details when working. Here are a few tips to help you on your way.

Bringing out highlights and shadows

Adjustments (located under the Image menu) are a great way to get some ideas on what parts of a photograph you'd like to concentrate on. One in particular is the Threshold adjustment (Image ➤ Adjustments ➤ Threshold). This adjustment can quickly display the brightest and darkest areas of an image by reducing it to only two colors: black and white.

Using the slider, you can move the adjustment until you have a good feel for what areas are important to keep when bringing your reference image to life.

10

Image by www.PhotoSpin.com © All rights reserved.

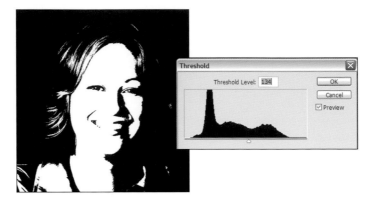

Another technique used by many designers, both professional and amateur, is the Posterize adjustment. As you can see from the following image, posterizing an image provides defined areas of highlights and shadows to give a better idea of the tones.

This adjustment produces a special effect in an image by reducing the number of shades of gray or colors to a specified—usually low—number. This adjustment is useful with photographs because it reduces the tonal levels of complex areas and produces large, flat areas instead. It tends to work very well when used on a grayscale image, but it also produces some interesting results when used on color images.

These techniques are only meant to help aid you in your projects. It's important to not use them as a crutch, but as a learning tool. Examine the results produced by these adjustments and try to anticipate their effects before you even apply them. This will not only make you a better overall artist, but it may also help you when a digital reference photograph isn't available. Yep, believe it or not, people used to create artwork before computers. All kidding aside, there may be times when you can't use the previous tips to help you. If you've practiced enough and have a good understanding of light, shadows, depth, and color, you may be able to create your artwork without them.

1. Find a suitable photograph or use Chapter_10_Snowboarder_Start.psd from this chapter's source files. Extreme sports photographs always work well for this type of illustration.

Image by www.PhotoSpin.com.

One of the first areas of Photoshop that received a large upgrade in the past release is filters. Photoshop CS now includes a filter gallery. This gallery allows you to work with filters like never before. You can now apply multiple filters at once and preview the results right within the dialog box.

2. Choose Filter ➤ Filter Gallery. This dialog box contains most of the filters that ship with Photoshop CS.

10

3. The filters are broken up into folders, which coincide with the filter categories visible in the Filter menu. Just click the arrow to the left of the folder to see the available filters.

4. Try picking the Glowing Edges filter under the Stylize folder.

5. Note the small area with the eyeball icon to the left, near the settings for this filter. In essence, this is a layer in the Filter Gallery.

6. Click the New Effect Layer button to add another layer. Then pick the Stained Glass filter located within the Texture folder.

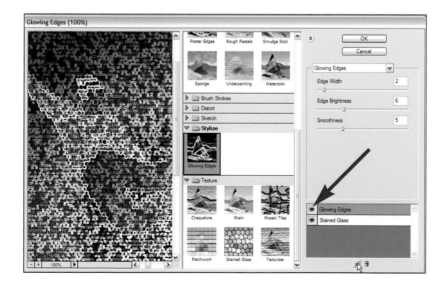

OK, now you're familiar with the Filter Gallery, but the image it produced may not be very useful. Let's actually apply a filter that can help the stylized image project.

7. Choose Filter ➤ Artistic ➤ Cutout and enter the following settings.

Note the image preview produced by this filter begins to consolidate the color ranges. It's beginning to look as if you used the Pen tool to create small paths through the image to produce this effect. In fact, if you clicked OK now, you would have a nicely stylized image from the photograph. However, let's take it a step further.

8. Click Cancel so the cutout filter isn't actually applied.

9. Next, using your preferred selection method, remove your focal point (the snowboarder) from the background in your photograph so it resides on its own layer.

10

10. Apply the cutout filter to this layer. This keeps the background intact and applies the filter to the snowboarder only.

At this point, you could leave the background layer as is, or create your own.

11. In this image, I created a new layer below the snowboarder named BACKGROUND and applied a blue gradient across it.

12. Then I applied a Lens Flare filter (Filter ➤ Render ➤ Lens Flare) to the BACKGROUND layer with the following settings.

13. Finally, I created a custom brush from one of the default brushes within Photoshop.

14. Paint in some snow on a separate layer and you're done. If needed, apply a Gaussian Blur filter to the snow to soften it a bit.

Exercise: Portrait illustration

Often, it's best to start out with a good foundation when working with this type of illustration. The skin is one area that's most likely below all other features, so it's best to start there.

1. Begin by picking a skin color. I used R:255 G:215 B:163 for this illustration. Then, using the Pen tool with the Shape layers option selected, draw around the shape of the face.

Image by
www.PhotoSpin.com

Don't worry about the hair at the moment. You'll create a new layer for that later, and it will cover up the outlines of the face. Just be sure to extend your path into the hairline enough so you won't have to manipulate it later.

> *You'll develop a palette of colors you use most often as you create these types of illustrations. Be sure to save them to a swatch palette so you can reuse them at a later date.*

2. Name this layer FACE when you're done.

3. Do the same for the neck area. Name this layer NECK and be sure it's below the FACE layer.

10

This is a great opportunity to expand on the reference photograph and add your own elements into it. Next, you'll draw the mouth and teeth. However, in this example, the woman wasn't smiling and looked a little too stern for this illustration. To fix this, I simply found another photograph of another person smiling and used that person's mouth as a reference.

> *You may be scared to try techniques like this because it looks rather silly at the first. Be open-minded. Once the final illustration is complete, you won't notice the difference.*

4. Draw the mouth and fill it with R:222 G:118 B:93. In this case, it's best to draw the entire mouth first.

5. Draw the teeth on a new layer on top of the mouth. Notice how placing the entire mouth shape below the teeth also takes care of the gums between the teeth for you.

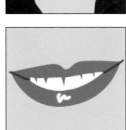

6. Using the Brush tool (*B*), set your foreground color to R:134 G:61 B:129 and paint two small lines on either side of the mouth on a new layer. Also, add a small highlight on the bottom lip.

7. Duplicate the MOUTH layer and fill it with R:181 G:115 B:81. Place it under the original mouth layer and nudge it down a few pixels. This serves as a small shadow under the mouth.

Next, let's tackle the nose. This task can be surprisingly simple, but largely depends on the reference photo you're using. Many times, a few simple lines and small shapes are all that is needed to define the nose and cheek areas. Sometimes these shapes will be very obvious. In the case of this reference photo, they aren't too apparent. When this happens, use some of the techniques discussed earlier in this chapter to help bring out any highlights or shadows to make them easier to see.

8. Hide all layers except the reference photo layer. Click the reference photograph layer and add a Threshold adjustment layer on top of it.

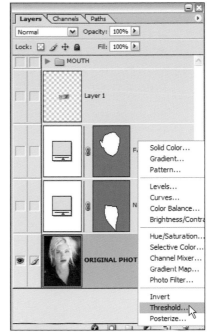

9. Move the slider left and right until you start seeing some details appear over the photograph. They should give you a good place to start. When you're done, hide the adjustment layer. Remember that it's there in case you need it again later.

10. If needed, hide the FACE layer. Set the foreground color to a light brown color and create small crescent shapes with the Pen tool based on the details you saw using the Threshold adjustment. Remember, a reference is just that—a reference. Feel free to add your own details or reshape existing ones slightly. I did just that on the right side of the nose, as the Threshold adjustment didn't reveal any lines there. However, from looking at the reference photo with no adjustment, I realized that I could get away with a small shape there to maintain some symmetry.

10

11. If the person in your reference photograph is looking straight at you, then you should be able to duplicate these layers, choose Edit ➤ Transform ➤ Flip Horizontal, and place them on the other side. If not, as in this photograph, you'll need to redraw them for the other side of the face.

12. Next, draw the eyebrows with the Pen tool using a foreground color of R:190 G:45 B:90. Try to reuse the same shape for the other side of the face if possible. Also, you may need to hide the FACE layer again in order to use the reference photo as a guideline.

OK, now it's time to work on the eyes. This is one of the most important parts of the illustration. Very few elements within a portrait can affect the entire portrait like the eyes can. If you zoomed in, the task of drawing eyes may look a bit daunting. However, the key idea is to not try to re-create every detail. Just as you didn't draw every small area when creating the lips, nose, and mouth, you don't need to draw every detail of the eyes.

13. Zoom in on an eye. Set the foreground color to R:200 G:161 B:106. Using the Pen tool, draw one shape around the eye.

14. Next, on a new layer, draw the white area of the eye. Remember to name your layers accordingly to help keep things in order.

15. Now use the Ellipse tool (*U*) to add a brown-colored iris in the center of the eye.

The iris will most likely extend beyond the original eye shape. To fix this, just add a layer mask.

16. *CTRL/⌘*-click the white eye layer to put a selection around it. Then, click the iris layer to make it active and click the Add Layer Mask button at the bottom of the Layers palette. Since a selection is active, the action restricted the mask to the area within the selection, hiding the area of the iris that extended beyond the selection.

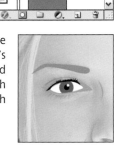

17. Next, draw the black eyelashes with the Pen tool. This can be one of the most tedious areas to draw within the eye, but it's worth the time. Alternatively, you can use the Brush tool and a graphic pen tablet, if you have one, to draw this area. Each method has its benefits and drawbacks, so it's best to try both if possible.

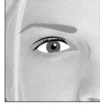

18. Finally, many eyes produce a strong shadow due to the shape of the forehead meeting the eye socket. You can re-create this effect by drawing a small, black crescent shape with the Pen tool.

OK, the first eye is done. If you're lucky and the person in your reference photograph is looking at you (or close to it), then you should be able to duplicate the layers and flip them horizontally. If not, you'll need to use the previous steps and create the other eye. Since this reference photograph is nearly straight on, you can just duplicate the eye layers.

19. Select the bottommost eye layer and link all other eye-related layers together with it. Don't forget the eyebrow. Then, create a layer set from the linked layers by clicking the Create new Layer set from linked option in the Layers palette. Name this set LEFT EYE.

20. Duplicate the layer set by choosing Duplicate Layer set from the Layers palette option menu. Name this layer set RIGHT EYE. Click the duplicate once, choose Edit ➤ Transform ➤ Flip Horizontal, and then move the copy into place.

10

21. If your reference isn't looking straight forward, press *CTRL/⌘+T* and rotate the layer set counterclockwise slightly. Press Enter to confirm. The eyes are done.

One of the final parts to complete in this illustration is the hair. Depending on your reference photograph, this could be an easy or difficult task. As mentioned earlier in this chapter, hair is one of those details that you should take into consideration when picking a reference photo. However, regardless of the complexity, the steps to follow are generally the same. It's the amount of time it takes to complete them that will vary.

22. Using the Pen tool, draw a path around the hair. I used R:242 G:211 B:120 as the fill color for this illustration. It seems to work well for blondes. Be sure to position this layer above the FACE layer. You'll have to do some creative decision-making at this point and decide what areas of the hair you'd like to keep and what areas you won't re-create. Try to restrain yourself from drawing every small area of hair, and just concentrate on the overall shape of the hair in comparison with the head.

When you're done with the hair, you need to add highlights. This is a great chance to use the Posterize adjustment and examine the color differences in your photograph. This will give you a good feel for how you can reduce the hair to only a few colors.

You can use the Pen tool for this process as usual. However, using the Polygonal Lasso tool (L) also works well in some circumstances. It's good to explore both methods. The Pen tool tends to work better when you need to contour the highlight along the shape of the head, as in this image.

The Polygonal Lasso tool works well when you need to select a large jagged area in which to color. See the accompanying image for an example.

Finally, all that's left is the body.

23. First, reduce the opacity of the NECK layer, so you can see the chest.

24. By now you should have a good idea of the various methods that allow you to see the highlights and shadows. In this example, I used the Posterize adjustment to help. Then I added several shadows on the chest area to reduce the flat color appearance.

10

25. Add a small shadow under the chin area to separate the head from the neck.

You can use the same methods to create any clothes. The Posterize adjustment will give you a good idea of how to visualize a shirt and how you can re-create it in Photoshop.

You can also use another method to quickly stylize the shirt that fits well with this illustration.

26. Using your selection method of choice, select the entire shirt. Don't worry about the area over the neck and chest. It's OK to select that as well because you won't see it when this effect is applied.

27. Once you have the shirt selected, be sure the original reference photo layer is active and press *CTRL*/⌘+*J* to create a new layer from this selection. This will duplicate the shirt onto a new layer.

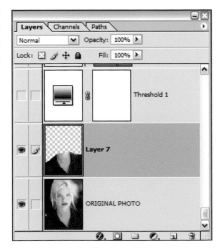

28. Choose Filter ➤ Artistic ➤ Cutout and enter the following settings. Click OK.

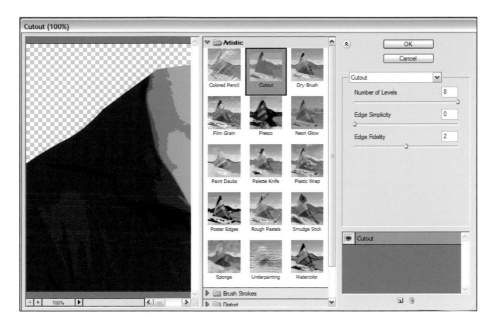

Not bad results for a fraction of the time it would take to draw the shirt manually!

29. While quick, this method is not perfect. Be sure to repair any problem areas such as the stray piece of hair near the bottom right side of her face that interferes with the shirt. To fix this, simply sample the shirt color with the Eyedropper tool (*I*). Then, zoom in and use the Brush tool to paint in the problem areas.

30. Create a new layer above the reference photograph, below all others. Fill it with an appropriate background color.

Summary

Hopefully, you now realize just how powerful the technique described in this chapter is. While it may seem simple, vectorizing photographs can be a difficult task to master. It requires a strong sense of composition. You need to be able to look at a photograph and determine which details are necessary to keep and which can be discarded in the transition from photo to vector. Even though you may trace much of your work, vectorizing really is an art form.

Also, keep in mind that this effect is not limited to photographs of people. Photographs of scenery, buildings, cars, and just about any other objects you can think of are good candidates. So, in the spirit of what I've said many times throughout this book, *get creative.* Look at the world around you. Take pictures with your camera and import them into Photoshop. Create certain objects from one photograph and merge them with objects from other photographs. The sky's the limit, so enjoy and have fun!

10

PART FOUR RETRO AND VINTAGE ART

Let's face it, vintage and retro styles are a part of our current culture. What was popular 30, 40, or even 50 years ago is popular again today. As with many trends, roots can be traced to the fashion industry. Take a look around you—bell-bottom pants are everywhere! Within the last three years, many styles have been revived from the 1960s and 1970s and made to fit today's culture. This holds true for graphic design as well. The worn vintage look is as popular and thriving today as it ever has been. Coupled with the increase in computer technology, this style is an appealing subject for graphic designers.

This chapter will walk you through the application of retro and vintage art styles to your illustrations. You'll create artwork that not only conveys the visual appeal of these styles, but also maintains the quality and technical advancements of today's computer graphic design power.

A sampling of retro styles

Pop art, art deco, and Bauhaus/constructivist are samples of classic styles that I cover in this chapter. However, keep in mind that these styles are just a taste of what exists. Many books could be filled with artwork from the twentieth century. I chose a few popular examples to get you started, but I urge you to research this topic further if this chapter's topic interests you.

Pop art

When you think of pop art, what comes to mind? The repetitive prints of soup cans and Marilyn Monroe created by Andy Warhol, or maybe the bold comiclike paintings created by Roy Lichtenstein. If you're not familiar with these specific styles of art, just search www.google.com for these artist's names, and you'll quickly see that they have a huge following in the design community.

Art deco

Art deco is a 1920s and 1930s style characterized by geometric motifs and shapes, luxurious materials, and strong colors. Zigzags and sharp angles were popular with this style, rather than the curves of the previous era. New York's Chrysler Building is a perfect architectural example of this style. Skyscrapers were rising fast, setting new height records, and cities such as New York demanded that additional floors could only be built if they were set back from the main wall. This created the stepped pattern, as seen in the Chrysler Building, to the top of an element, either the building itself or even a column on the side.

This style also marked a time where technical advancements in machinery were achieving huge strides, both figuratively and literally. Boats, trains, airplanes, tanks, and many other machines were reaching sizes never seen before. As a result, much of the artwork resulting from this period has some manmade industrial marvel incorporated in it.

Bauhaus/constructivist

Established in 1919, the Bauhaus was a design school in Germany. This school is known as one of the most influential of the twentieth century. While radical at the time, the goal of the Bauhaus was to marry structural and decorative arts. This created a philosophy of using art and design principles to design machine technology for mass production. The Bauhaus was rooted in a minimalist and functional style of design that carried through to what later became modernist and constructivist styles.

Research and inspiration

Researching artists from the past and their styles is a great way to learn about the roots of art as well as improve your work going forward. In fact, as with many areas in life, when you learn about the past masters in a particular field, you can draw on their knowledge and add it to your own. It is at that point that you can move toward becoming a master in your own field. Researching the art styles mentioned in this chapter can not only help you understand the roots of graphic design and illustration, but also provide you with inspiration for future projects of your own. Here are a few websites that can help get you started:

- Artcyclopedia.com: A definitive and effective guide to museum-quality art on the Internet. It provides a search engine based on many aspects of art, such as physical and online museums, posters, image archives, and other websites.

- AllPosters.com: This site represents its name very well. It's a website full of posters on nearly everything imaginable. If you're ever looking for inspiration, AllPosters.com is a perfect place to visit. You can browse by artist, subject, style, time period, and many other options.

Finally, if you ever get the chance to visit a museum or art gallery, take it. The knowledge and inspiration you gain from walking through a museum is immeasurable. Admission to many is either free or reasonably priced, and it's well worth your time if you get the chance to visit. Also, art galleries are another great place to gain knowledge and inspiration. You might see some great artwork while visiting, and you never know who you might meet inside. Often, relationships with other designers can be a huge asset to your design career as well as your skill set.

11

Exercise: Using the art deco style

In this exercise, you'll create an art deco–style poster. As mentioned earlier, large industrial buildings and machines were prevalent in this style, so you'll add a few of those elements to help match the reality of the time period.

> **1.** Find a suitable reference photograph to use as the focal point of the illustration. If you're having a hard time coming up with ideas, try searching www.google.com for inspiration. Since tall buildings like those in New York City were often the centerpieces in art deco–style posters, I found this image of the Chrysler Building.

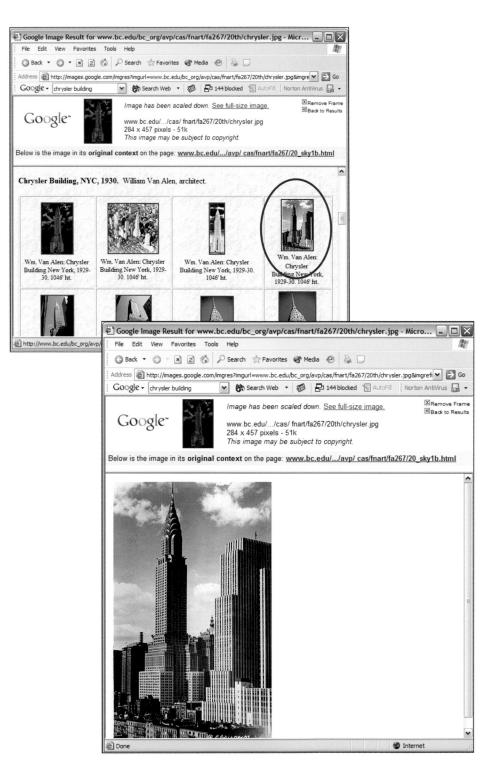

2. The first task is to remove the building from its background. Use the Pen tool (*P*) for this task and create a new path in the Paths palette to hold the outline of the building.

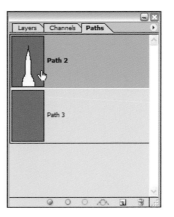

3. Click the Load path as selection button at the bottom of the Paths palette to turn the path into a selection.

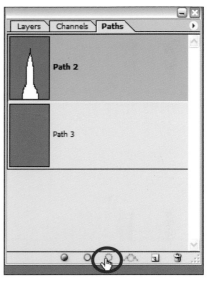

4. Switch back to the Layers palette, and with the reference photo layer active, press *CTRL*/⌘+*J* to create a new layer from the active selection. Go ahead and delete or hide the reference photo layer at this time.

11

5. Now is a good time to enlarge the dimensions of your image in case your reference photo is too small. As you can see, my reference photo was extremely small in comparison to what's needed for a poster-sized image, so I increased it significantly. Don't worry about the loss of image quality at this point, as you won't need much detail from the existing image.

6. Using the path in the Paths palette, activate the selection around the building once again. Create a new layer above the original building named BUILDING COLOR and fill it with R:132 G:152 B:183.

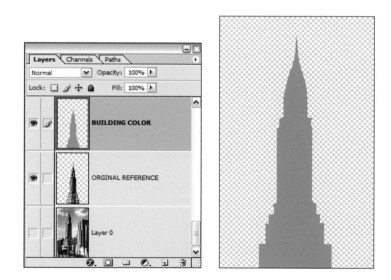

7. Decrease the opacity of the BUILDING COLOR layer to 50% so you can see most of the original reference photo below it. Use the Polygonal Lasso tool (L) to select the dark shadowed areas along the center and right side of the building. However, don't worry about the actual edges on the right side. Simply extend your selection well beyond that area as shown.

8. Next, *CTRL/⌘+ALT/OPTION+SHIFT*-click the BUILDING COLOR layer. This will intersect your existing selection with the actual outline of the building (see below left).

9. Fill this new selection with a darker blue, such as R:44 G:80 B:134 (see below right).

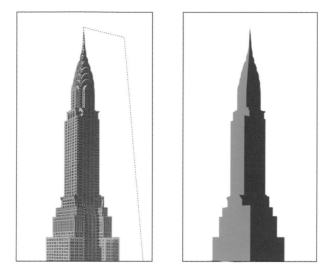

10. Create a BACKGROUND layer below all other layers and fill it with R:43 G:28 B:69.
Then, decrease the opacity of the BUILDING COLOR layer to 90% so you can see
some of the detail from the original reference photograph through it.

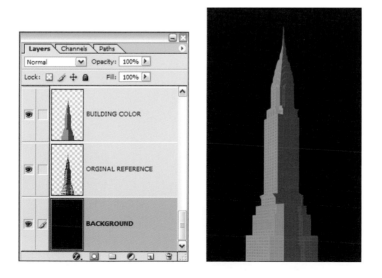

The art deco poster is coming along nicely. The primary elements are in place. Now it's
time to add some secondary artwork to showcase some of the themes of the art deco
style. One theme found across many art deco examples is spotlights.

11

11. Create a new layer above BACKGROUND named BLUE SPOTLIGHTS. Use the Polygonal Lasso tool to create large triangular shapes and fill them with R:147 G:174 B:203.

12. Now create a new layer above BUILDING COLOR named YELLOW SPOTLIGHTS and repeat the previous step, but fill the shapes with R:255 G:244 B:173. Also, change the blending mode of this layer to Hard Light.

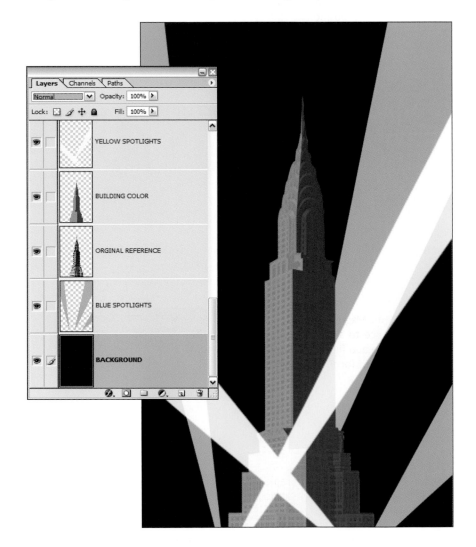

Great! Now you'll add one more key element to the center of this poster: an airplane. While researching art deco artwork for this chapter, I noticed that many classic posters contain large airplanes, trains, or boats.

13. Find a suitable picture of an airplane. Clip art and old photographs are great sources of inspiration and material for this task. Alternatively, you can open Chapter_11_Airplane.psd from the download files for this chapter, and drag this image of the airplane into the art deco illustration, positioning the layer directly below the YELLOW SPOTLIGHTS layer.

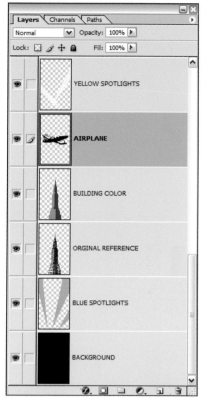

14. Use the Magic Wand tool (*W*) with a low tolerance to select the white areas of the airplane and fill them with the same yellow color used for the spotlights.

OK, the illustration is nearly complete. All that remains is to add some text. This can be a deciding moment in your illustration's impact and overall appeal. As in many cases, the success and impact of the type you add to an illustration depends not only on the words, placement, and size of your type, but also on the style of font. Since this is an art deco poster, it's imperative that you use a font representative of this era.

How do you go about finding fonts? Once again, the answer is www.google.com. A search on "free art deco fonts" should turn up many possible sources from which you can download fonts. In fact, the first result from my search turned up a hit. The following link contains a set of free art deco fonts that you can install on your computer: www.softpile.com/Desktop/Fonts/Review_05999_index.html.

Once you've found your font, follow along with the next few steps to finish the poster.

In Windows, you can install a font by copying the font file to C:/Windows/Fonts. *In Mac OS X, copy the font file to* ~Username/Library/Fonts. *The font should appear immediately in Photoshop without your having to restart the application.*

15. First, create a rectangle at the bottom of the poster and fill it with the same blue used for the background. Using the Rectangular Marquee tool (*M*), create a small orange separator line at the top of the dark blue rectangle. This will help offset the type so it doesn't interfere with the actual elements within the illustration.

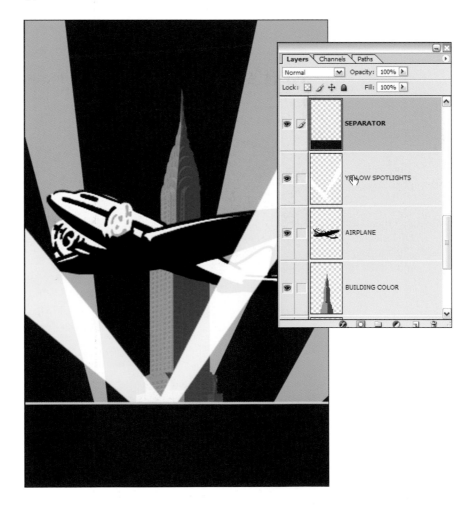

16. Now add some appropriate type using various fonts. For the white **New York** text at the top, I used the Big City font from the sample font package previously mentioned. I also added a black 2 pt Stroke layer style to help offset the font from the background. I used Viva Standard for the **Overnight Express** text and Dalith for the **Special Reduced Fares** text.

Exercise: Creating pop art, Roy Lichtenstein style

In this exercise, you'll create a small poster inspired by the comiclike illustrations of Roy Lichtenstein.

1. Open `Chapter_11_Lichtenstein_Start.psd` from this chapter's download files. This file contains black-and-white line art of a woman's face. You'll use this as the basis of the exercise.

2. First, set the blending mode of the LINEART layer to Multiply.

By itself, this action doesn't do anything. However, if you recall from Chapter 7, when you colored the line art drawing, setting the blending mode to Multiply allows you to see through the white areas when placing color layers beneath the original line art.

3. Create a new layer below LINE ART named FACE.

4. Set the foreground color to R:246 G:222 B:205 and use the Brush tool (*B*) to paint the area within the face. Don't worry yet about the eyes and lips. It's OK to paint over them as well.

5. Create a new layer above FACE named HAIR. Set the foreground color to R:245 G:09 B:13 and paint the hair color. Try to paint within the black outlines along the outer edges of the hair. However, when you get near the face, you'll have to make a decision about where to stop, as there are no black outlines to guide you.

6. Create two new layers for the lips and eyes. Color the lips red (R:164 G:47 B:37) and the iris of the eye blue (R:0 G:96 B:255).

At this point, the line art should be completely colored. Now it's time to add the pop art elements. A key element of Lichtenstein's pop art style is the use of a halftone pattern to produce the appearance of stylized dots (also known as *Ben Day dots*) within certain areas of his artwork. Fortunately, this effect is simple to re-create in Photoshop.

> *Benday is a trade name for a method of laying a screen (dots, lines, and other textures) on artwork or plates to obtain various tone and shading effects. Today, many people refer to the halftone pattern/styled dots mentioned in the previous paragraph as Ben Day dots.*

7. Click the FACE layer once to make it active. Set your foreground color to R:246 G:222 B:205 (the original foreground color used to paint the face). Set the background color to R:238 G:194 B:162.

11

8. Choose Filter ➤ Stylize ➤ Halftone Pattern and enter the following settings. Instant Lichtenstein style!

The Halftone Pattern *filter uses the foreground and background colors as a base from which to apply its pattern.*

9. You could use the same filter for the lips, but I found it easier to simply change the opacity of the LIPS layer to around 50%. If you colored the area under the lips when you colored the face, you should be able to see the halftone pattern through the lips.

Another key characteristic of Roy Lichtenstein's work is the extreme close-up views he presents. Often, the only area that's visible is the face and hair of the person in his artwork.

10. Select the Crop tool (*C*). Drag a rectangle around the image so that only the face and hair remain visible. Press Enter when you're done.

Finally, Lichtenstein often incorporated talk bubbles in his work and some type of colorful border. To re-create this effect, you'll need to expand the canvas to allow for the extra artwork.

11. Choose Image ➤ Canvas Size. Enter the following settings to expand the canvas, while leaving the actual artwork at its original size.

12. Create a new layer under all other layers and fill it with R:239 G:0 B:19. Also, link the layers that make up the face together and drag them all down.

13. Next, select the Pen tool and be sure Shape layers is selected in the tool options bar. Set the foreground color to white and draw a talk bubble similar to the one in this image.

14. Add a black, 5-pixel Stroke layer style to the talk bubble and some Lichtenstein-styled text within it. I used a font called Comix that you can download for free from many places on the Internet, if you don't have it already.

15. Last, add a layer above the red background layer and create a black rectangle with the Rectangular Marquee tool. This serves two purposes: it helps to emphasize and set apart the bright colors used to color the woman from the strong red in the background, and it helps the black stroke around the talk bubble blend better with the background.

Exercise: Creating pop art, Andy Warhol style (part 1)

Andy Warhol's artistic style has been re-created many times throughout the years. As you may imagine, Photoshop's popularity has caused it to become a key catalyst in this process, and many tutorials have been written explaining how to make a photograph appear to have the Warhol-esque, pop art style to it. The problem is that Warhol's style has many different elements to it, and one Photoshop tutorial often will produce very different results for various photographs. I'll present you with several methods, varying in complexity and results. This will get you familiar with Warhol's style and how to re-create it in Photoshop.

This first method is simple. It's almost an instant Warhol style tutorial.

1. Open your photograph in Photoshop. The first step is to remove the color by choosing Image ➤ Adjustments ➤ Desaturate (*CTRL/⌘+SHIFT+U*).

2. Next, choose Image ➤ Adjustments ➤ Gradient Map. Select the present gradient named Spectrum and click OK.

3. Create a new layer below your photograph and fill it with R:255 G:0 B:0. Merge the two layers together when you're done.

That's way too easy, isn't it? Well there's one more step you can take to make this image more Warhol-like. Often, Warhol tiled various shades and colors of the same image across the canvas. If he only had Photoshop, he might have saved himself an incredible amount of time, as this is simple to accomplish.

4. First, choose Image ➤ Canvas Size. Note the width and height settings for your image. Multiply each of them by 3, and enter the new proportions. Also, be sure to click the top-left arrow in the Anchor settings area.

Canvas Size

Current Size: 272.0K
　　　　Width: 278 pixels
　　　　Height: 334 pixels

New Size: 2.39M
　　Width: 834　pixels
　　Height: 1002　pixels
　　☐ Relative
　　Anchor:

Canvas extension color: Background

OK
Cancel

5. Next, duplicate the image across and down so the entire canvas is filled with a total of nine images.

6. Finally, select each individual layer and use the Hue/Saturation adjustment (*CTRL*/⌘+*U*) to vary the colors. Bright colors tend to work best and resemble the actual Andy Warhol style, but feel free to use whatever colors you see fit.

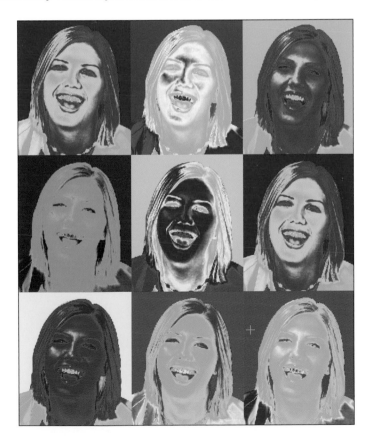

11

Exercise: Creating pop art, Andy Warhol style (part 2)

The next exercise is slightly more involved and creates a different effect than the first.

1. Open a suitable photograph. Photographs with or without a background will work fine for this exercise, but keep in mind that some of the background elements will show up if you don't remove them. If you don't wish to have this happen, now would be the time to extract your subject and place it on a white background.

2. Create a new Threshold adjustment layer.

3. Move the slider to produce an image in which enough black detail exists to distinguish the subject, but not so much that the entire image is too dark.

> *Using an adjustment layer leaves the original image intact so you can modify the adjustment later.*

4. At this point, you should have a black-and-white image. Next, click the photograph layer and select all (*CTRL*/⌘+*A*). Then, move over to the Channels palette and create a new channel. Finally, paste the selection into the new alpha channel. Your image should still look exactly the same.

5. Press *CTRL*/⌘+*I* to invert the alpha channel. The whites will become black and the blacks will become white.

6. *CTRL*/⌘-click the alpha channel. This selects the white areas in the channel.

7. Switch back to the Layers palette and create a new layer above the others named FILL. Set the foreground color to R:34 G:79 B:129, and press *ALT*/*OPTION*+*BACKSPACE* to fill the selection with a dark blue.

8. Create a new layer named BACKGROUND below the FILL layer. Fill this layer with R:210 G:41 B:41, and you have another Andy Warhol effect.

11

9. Use the same technique as the previous exercise to tile the image across a larger canvas. Placing the BACKGROUND and FILL layers into a layer set and duplicating it across the new larger canvas helps you change the foreground and background colors more accurately, as you can control each color individually. Alternatively, you can merge the two layers and use the Hue/Saturation adjustment to vary the colors.

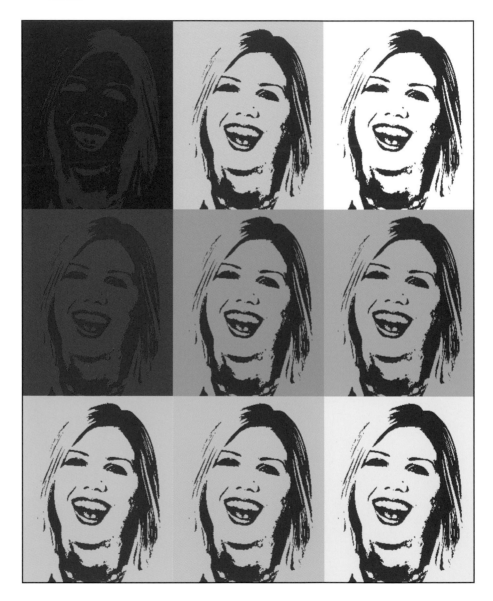

Exercise: Creating vintage art

1. Open `Chapter_11_VintagePizza_Start.psd` from this chapter's source files. This file contains many layers used to create a retro-style pizza poster.

2. Create a new layer above all others named GRUNGE.

3. Press the *D* key to set the foreground color to black and the background to white. Then, choose Filter ➤ Render ➤ Clouds.

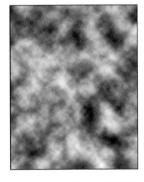

4. Next, add some noise by choosing Filter ➤ Noise ➤ Add Noise. Use the following settings.

5. Choose Filter ➤ Stylize ➤ Emboss and use these settings.

6. Now choose Filter ➤ Distort ➤ Diffuse Glow and use these settings.

7. Duplicate the GRUNGE layer. On the top copy of the layer, apply the Palette Knife filter (Filter ➤ Artistic ➤ Palette Knife) with the following settings.

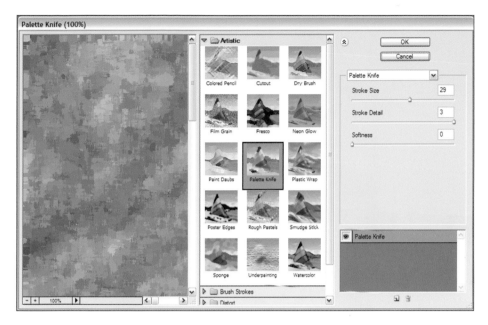

8. Drop the opacity of the top copy to 75%. Then, click the top copy and merge it (CTRL/⌘+E) with the GRUNGE layer underneath it.

The texture you'll use to create the worn vintage look is now done. Next, select a random area from this texture to complete the technique.

9. With the GRUNGE layer active, choose Select ➤ Color Range. Pick the Highlights option and click OK.

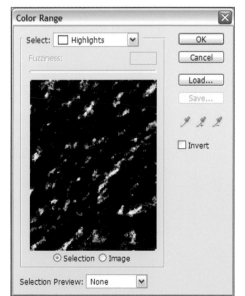

This selects the white areas from the texture and produces a nice random selection.

10. With your selection still active, create a new layer above GRUNGE named VINTAGE TEXTURE and hide the GRUNGE layer. Fill this selection on the new layer with R:255 G:254 B:203 (this also happens to be the yellow background color of the entire poster).

This should produce a nice, vintage-styled poster. It looks almost as if the painted areas are faded and have worn into the background. However, there's one more thing you can do to further randomize this effect. Follow along the next few steps to add the finishing touches.

11. Add a layer mask to the VINTAGE TEXTURE layer.

12. Set the foreground color to R:182 G:182 B:182 and the background color to white.

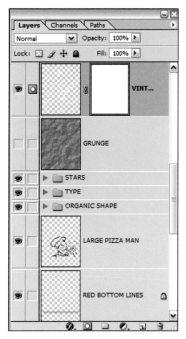

13. Click the layer mask once to make it active, and apply the Clouds filter (Filter ➤ Render ➤ Clouds) to it. This helps randomize the vintage texture by decreasing the opacity of the original texture in certain areas.

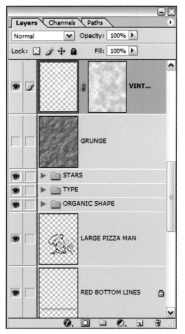

11

Here's the final image. The changes are very subtle, but it's often small enhancements that make a big difference.

As you may have already noticed by the fact that I haven't mentioned them yet in this book, I'm not a huge fan of special-effect third-party plug-ins and filters. However, after writing this chapter, I came across an excellent product that I wanted to draw your attention to. If you find yourself creating the effects discussed in this exercise often, then the Machine Wash Image Filters group of filters produced by www.misterretro.com is for you. This product contains 60 image filters to texturize, age, and weather layered artwork in

Photoshop. I must say that these effects are top-notch (and no, they're not paying me to say this)! Here are a few examples of their filters applied with just one click of a button to the image you used in the previous exercise.

Exercise: Creating Bauhaus/constructivist artwork

Due to the fairly minimalist roots of this style, Photoshop is a great place to create a Bauhaus/constructivist style illustration. In fact, some simple tools, such as guides, grids, and the Rectangular Marquee tool, provide a quick and easy way to become familiar with this style.

1. Create a new canvas using the file size settings shown in this image.

2. First, take care of a few housekeeping tasks. Since this style is grid-based, turn the grid on in Photoshop by choosing View ➤ Show ➤ Grid (*CTRL*/⌘+').

3. Then, display the Ruler by choosing View ➤ Rulers (*CTRL*/⌘+R).

4. Turn snapping on by choosing View ➤ Snap (*SHIFT*+*CTRL*/⌘+;).

5. Make sure you start with a white layer named BACKGROUND.

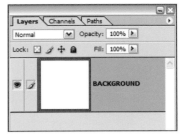

6. Next, select the Rectangular Marquee tool and begin drawing rectangular shapes within the grids. Notice how turning Snap on forces the marquee selection to snap to the edges of the grids.

7. Using the SHIFT key, add to each selection until you've selected an area on all four sides of the canvas. Create a new layer named BORDER and fill this selection with black.

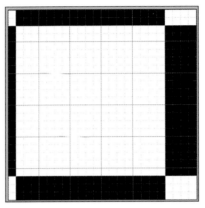

8. Now comes the fun part! Create a new layer named INSIDE BORDERS and use the Rectangular Marquee tool to create various black rectangles, both thin and thick. Remember that Snap is turned on, so you can quick create selections that match up with each other.

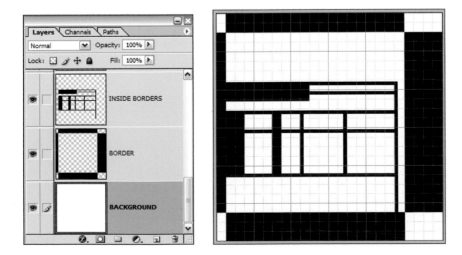

11

9. Next, select the Magic Wand tool and click certain rectangles within your inner black lines and fill them with various colors. This styles tends to use simple primary colors such as blue (R:2 G:105 B:180), yellow (R:224 G:50 B:39), and red (R:255 G:252 B:0).

To complete the exercise, you need to add some text. The same holds true for the type in this illustration as did in the previous art deco exercise. The type used must match the style of art that you're trying to create. Fortunately, the same method of finding the fonts holds true as well. A quick search on www.google.com for "free bauhaus font" turned up the following link: www.fontseek.com/fonts/bauhaus.htm.

Toward the bottom of this web page is a font called Bauhaus 93. I downloaded this font and added some red text to the illustration.

10. Finally, keep in mind that you're not restricted to squares and rectangles. Here, in the lower right, I used the Elliptical Marquee tool (M) to create a circle inside the grid. Having Snap turned on makes circles snap to the grid as well. Then, I stroked (Edit ➤ Stroke) the circle with black and created a couple lines and a small blue fill area inside to keep with the constructivist style.

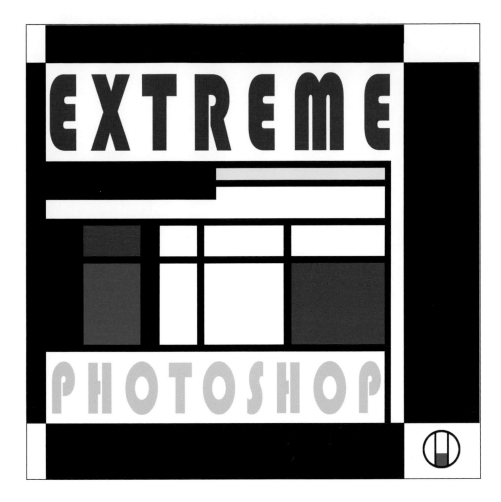

Summary

In this chapter, you've sampled various retro and vintage effects that exist today and learned how to create them in Photoshop CS. I encourage you to now go beyond this chapter in search of retro ideas in illustration and design. Inspiration exists everywhere. Old magazine ads, new magazine ads, TV, books, and the Web all contain many examples of retro-styled artwork. I urge you to attempt to study and re-create these effects in Photoshop on your own, as it's an emerging trend that seems to be here to stay for a while. Once you begin to see the thought process that other designers go through when creating this type of artwork, you'll begin coming up with your own ideas. At that point, you'll be well equipped to create illustrations that not only contain vintage and retro effects, but also carry your own unique and individual style with them.

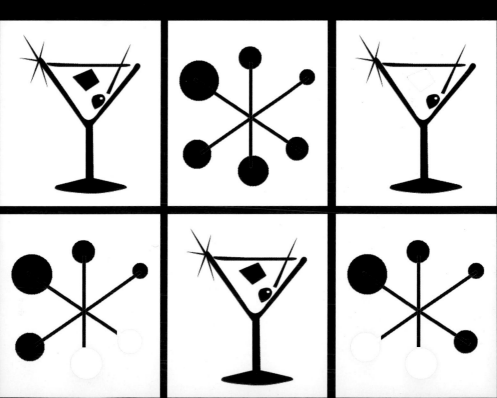

This final chapter is where I leave you with the tools and techniques to go forth and design. They're essential techniques if you wish to take your design career to the next level—or, if you're already in a design career, they're techniques that you can look at to improve. I'll cover these techniques under the common theme of retro design and illustration, so you'll pick up a few tips on a very popular theme in the design community today. One thing to keep in mind: you can apply the tools, tips, and techniques described in this chapter to any style or area of workflow in Photoshop. I cover them here to help you tie everything together within this retro theme, but they're certainly not limited to this style of artwork.

Shapes

Wavy lines, atoms, kidneys, boomerangs, and twinkling stars are common shapes used in retro-styled illustrations. Retro shapes almost seem to have been inspired from organisms you'd find under a microscope. Regardless of the shapes' origins, there is a common theme to shapes that inspire a retro theme. Once you realize this common theme, creating these shapes is a fairly simple process with the Pen tool. However, as a designer, you probably don't want to create the same shapes every time a new project arises. You could always save the files and re-open them when needed, but that can get messy. Photoshop has provided **shape tools** for this very purpose. Ranging from simple to complex, the shape tools can be a considerable asset if used correctly.

When you draw with the Pen tool in Photoshop, you create vector shapes. **Vector shapes** are objects made of mathematically defined curves and lines. As a result, the shapes are resolution independent and maintain crisp edges when resized or printed. The basic shape tools, however, are somewhat limited, as you can create only rectangles, ellipses, polygons, and lines with them. Enter **custom shapes**. A subset of the shape tools, custom shapes are even more versatile, as you can use the Pen tool to create whatever shape you can imagine. You can even use other shapes and the intersection choices in the tool options bar to create custom shapes.

If you've never created custom shapes before, here are a few tips for how to go about doing so.

Exercise: Creating a custom shape from scratch

1. Create a new Photoshop canvas.
2. Select the Pen tool (*P*) and make sure the Shape layers button is selected in the tool options bar.
3. Draw an organic kidney shape with the Pen tool.

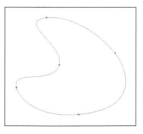

4. After you've drawn the shape, select Edit ➤ Define Custom Shape. Give your shape a meaningful name, and then click OK.

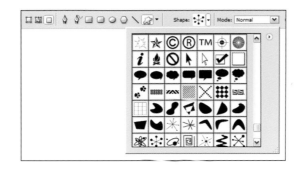

5. The shape will now be stored within the Custom Shapes palette.

Exercise: Creating a custom shape using other shapes

1. Create a new Photoshop canvas.

2. Select the Ellipse tool (*U*) and make sure Shape layers is selected in the tool options bar.

3. Hold down the *SHIFT* key and draw a circle on the canvas.

4. Now select the Add To Shape Area button in the tool options bar.

5. Draw five more circles on the canvas. Notice how they all remain on the same Shape layer.

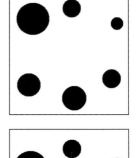

6. Select the Line tool (*U*) and increase the line weight to the desired amount. I used 10 pixels here. Connect each circle and define this shape as a custom shape. You now have another retro shape with no drawing required.

Reasons for creating shapes

Now that you know how to create shapes, let's tackle *why* you should create them. It's actually a fairly simple explanation. The first reason is reuse. Shapes can be saved and reused many times over with little effort. A perfect candidate for this is a logo. Take, for example, this logo, which was created for a website of mine:

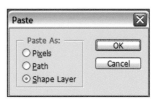

By defining a logo as a custom shape, you have an instant method of re-creating the logo whenever it's needed. This can come in handy when you design a website, make a desktop, or create stationery and business cards for a company. You can use the same custom shape throughout, since it's resolution independent.

Another great benefit of custom shapes is that they don't need to be created in Photoshop. You can take nearly any path created in Adobe Illustrator and paste it directly into Photoshop. You'll be presented with a dialog box similar to the following:

At this point, you only need to choose Shape Layer and define the shape as a custom shape, just as you usually would (Edit ➤ Define Custom Shape).

Starting a library of retro custom shapes

Starting a library of custom shapes is easy. Just begin creating shapes and save them in your own custom shape set. Previously created shape sets can also help you get moving. The following link to the Creative Mac website features a nice retro custom shape set: www.creativemac.com/2002/10_oct/features/retrodaddyo.htm.

The custom shape set at the Creative Mac website is a great place to begin, as it provides many popular retro shapes. You can just add to them as you create more.

Opening third-party custom shape sets

Third-party custom shape sets can be libraries of custom shapes that you've purchased or downloaded, or simply a custom shape set that a friend or coworker has given you. Regardless of where the shapes came from, their file names should end with .csh. Normally, when you receive one of these files, it's best to store it in the Photoshop application folder under the Presets subfolder. Within this folder, you should see another folder named Custom Shapes. Here is an example if you've installed Photoshop in its default location:

- **Windows**: /Program Files/Adobe/Adobe Photoshop CS/Presets/Custom Shapes
- **Mac OS X**: /Applications/Photoshop CS/Presets/Custom Shapes

If you place your file in the appropriate location, when you restart Photoshop the custom shape set will appear in the Custom Shapes palette's pop-out menu. If you choose to place the file elsewhere, you'll need to point Photoshop to the location where it's stored. You can replace the shapes in the current palette by choosing Replace Shapes from the Custom Shapes palette's menu, or you can append shapes to the existing palette of shapes by choosing Load Shapes. Either way, just navigate to the appropriate folder and click OK to load the new shape set.

Fonts

As you saw in the previous chapter, a font can make or break an illustration. Luckily, the retro theme of this chapter is a great way to showcase the usefulness and flexibility of fonts. Diners, bowling alleys, and old television shows are a great place to see this concept in action. They are perhaps some of the best places to see retro-styled fonts. The problem lies in finding these fonts. As with many font styles, the Internet is one of the best places to begin your search. Searching for "free retro fonts" through www.google.com will often yield some useful results. To get you started, here are a few links to help.

12

www.fontdiner.com

www.devicefonts.co.uk

Another great site that hosts mostly fonts for purchase is www.T26.com (see the following image). You can find some great inspiration on this site, and if you can't find what you need for free, then purchasing fonts is the next step. You can also browse fonts by category on this site; one of the categories happens to be Retro.

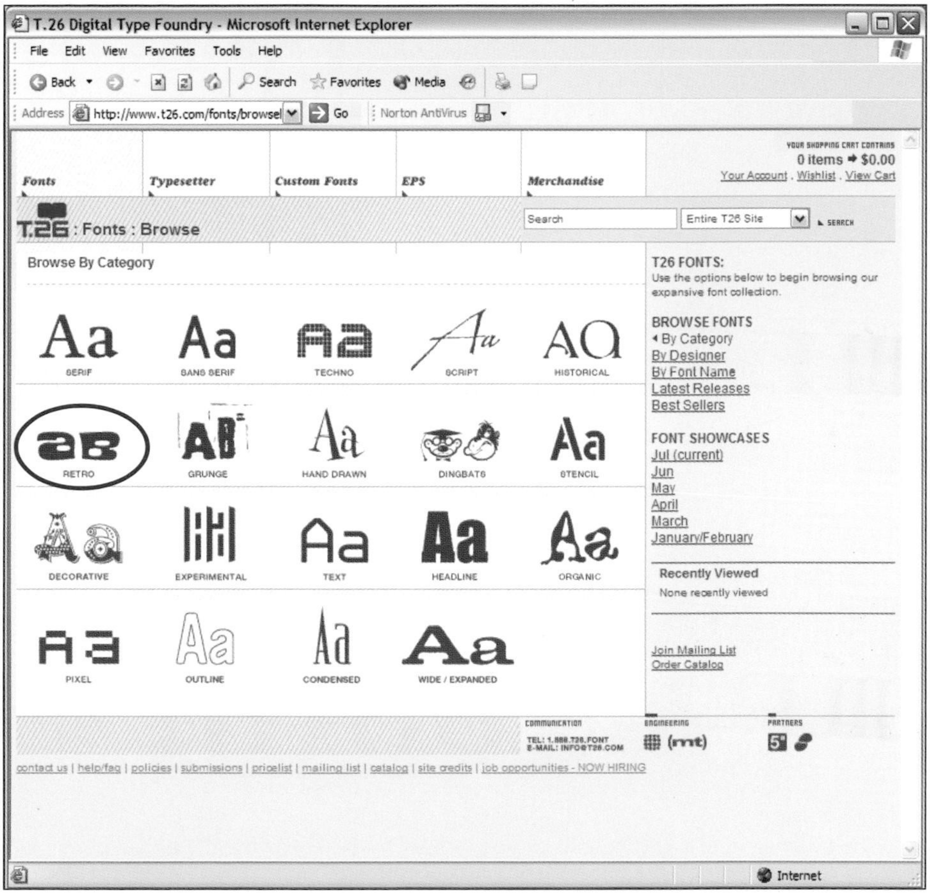

Once you've downloaded the fonts, you now need to choose the right font for your project. Since you'll undoubtedly have many fonts installed on your system, it can be difficult to test each font in your illustration to see what works. Adobe (www.adobe.com) and Extensis (www.extensis.com) provide font-management programs that may be worth checking out, but I'd like to show you a few ways to help you manage and work with fonts right within Photoshop.

12

Font preview

First, there's an easy trick to cycling through the fonts in Photoshop. Enter the text you'd like to see displayed in various fonts.

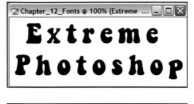

Double-click the small text icon in the Layers palette or select your text with the Type tool. It should appear highlighted to indicate that it's selected.

Then click the font drop-down list in the tool options bar once. This will highlight the current font. Now you can use the arrow keys to cycle through the installed fonts and watch your text change as you switch fonts.

If the text highlighting is getting in your way, press *Ctrl*/⌘+*H* to hide the highlighting. Your text will still be selected, though, so don't forget to unhide your selections later.

Creating font sample files

The second method is slightly different in nature from the first. While the previous method works great, it can be difficult and time consuming to cycle through all the fonts installed on your computer. This second method is more customized, but it will allow you to see how your type works with multiple fonts at once. I call it a "font sample file."

Before we begin, though, did you know Photoshop CS now has spell-check and find/replace capabilities? It's about time, right? Well, here's a great way to speed up your font selection and inspiration process, and use Photoshop's new features. When working with a style such as the retro theme, fonts can play an important part in your design. Often it's the case that you spend more time searching for a new font or one that you've used before than you actually spend applying the text. In this situation, I find the font sample file very useful. There are font-management portfolios available that often are very useful, too, but they cost money and they're mainly useful for managing a large number of fonts. This method is better for picking a font to use or experimenting quickly with how a certain font looks. Try this:

1. Create a new Photoshop canvas. Type the text that you'd like to appear in your project and select a retro font.

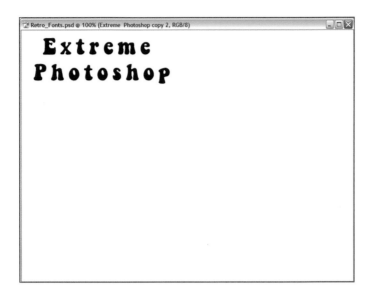

2. Duplicate this layer and reposition the layers throughout your canvas. Then change each text layer to a different retro font.

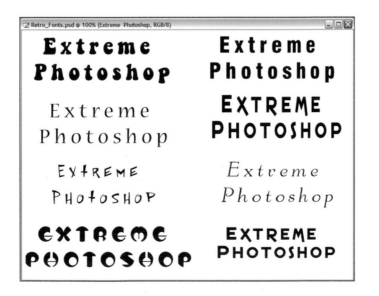

12

Great—now you have a quick visual sample of various retro fonts.

3. Save this file as `retrofonts.psd` and store it in your Inspiration/fonts folder (covered at the end of this chapter).

The next time you're looking for the perfect font to use, you can just open this file to view a sampling of the retro fonts you have available.

4. Better yet, once you open the file, choose Edit ➤ Find and Replace Text. Enter the text to find and the text to replace it with, and click the Change All button. This will replace the current text with whatever words you happen to be working with to give you a better idea of what your work will look like.

Symbol fonts and repurposing

Now that you know all about fonts and how to pick that perfect retro font, I'd like to turn your attention to one more tip about fonts. In a nutshell, this tip is just to think outside the box when it comes to working with fonts. Fonts are a lot like custom shapes. They're resolution independent and can be scaled to very large sizes and still retain crisp edges. As you may know already, not all fonts consist of letters. There are many font sets made entirely of symbols. These sets are typically referred to as **dingbats**. The following is a picture of a font called 60s Chic.

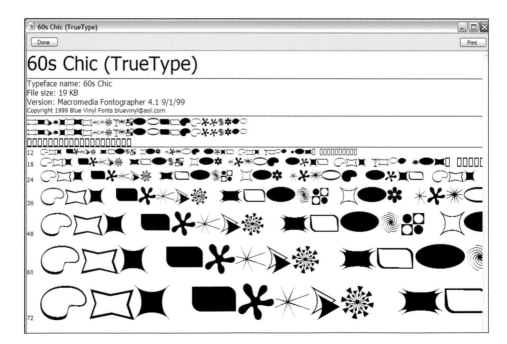

You can download this font free of charge from www.bvfonts.com/free/fonts10.shtml. Just be sure to abide by the owner's license agreement.

If you find a useful symbol within a font, then nothing is stopping you from using just that one letter in your design. Even better, why not turn it into a custom shape so it's easy to reuse at a later time?

12

1. Enter your text as normal. Here, I've typed the letter L using the 60s Chic font, and then I chose Layer ➤ Type ➤ Convert to Shape.

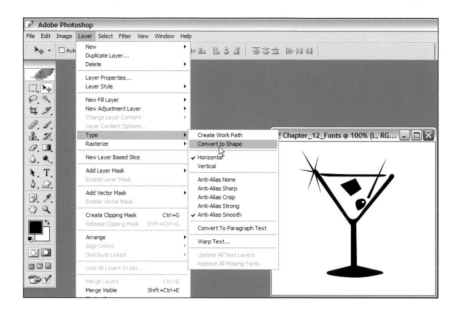

This creates a shape layer in the Layers palette.

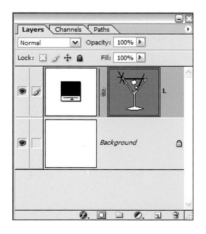

2. Then choose Edit ➤ Define Custom Shape and the shape will be saved in your custom shapes palette, ready to use with the Custom Shape tool.

This process does two things. First, you can save the custom shape set with your new symbol and have access to it whenever you access your custom shapes. Now, if you're on another computer that doesn't have the font installed, but you've been good about backing up your custom shapes (see the section "Backing up your work" at the end of this chapter), you can just load the shapes into Photoshop and your symbol will be ready to use.

Second, the process of converting a font to a shape produces another inadvertent advantage. On their own, fonts don't have all of the transformation capabilities that other objects have. For example, you can't use distort and perspective transformations on a font. Go ahead try it for yourself. Select an actual type layer and choose Edit ➤ Transform. The Distort and Perspective options are grayed out.

But if you choose Layer ➤ Type ➤ Convert to Shape and look at the transformation options available, you'll see that Distort and Perspective are not grayed out anymore.

Patterns

Just as kidney shapes and wavy lines are often used in retro designs, polka dots, flowers, and nonsymmetric squares, circles, and rectangles are often seen in retro patterns. In fact, a pattern is probably one of the most obvious ways to add a retro theme to an illustration.

Patterns can be used in several places within Photoshop.

- Edit ➤ Fill

- Layer Style: Pattern Overlay

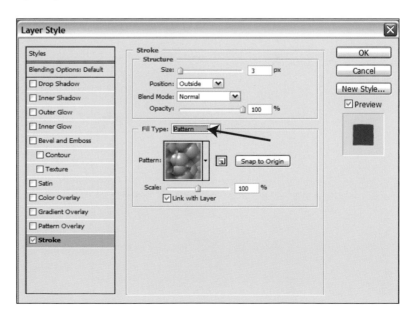

- Layer Style: Stroke

- Adjustment Layer: Pattern

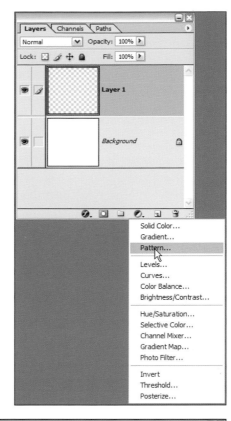

- Brushes: Texture brush

The good thing about patterns is that once you define them, they're available throughout the program. You don't need to redefine them anywhere else for use with another tool. Also, keep in mind that pattern sets can be saved from any of the Pattern palette options menus or the Preset Manager (more on this toward the end of the chapter).

Color palettes

Many elements influence the nostalgic appearance of a retro-style design. Of these, color selection can be one of the most important. Good color selection can make an illustration stand out and truly feel as if it has a retro theme. At the same time, poor color selection can have an adverse effect on a design.

Regardless of the color palette you're working with, though, having a good set of color swatches to work from is essential when you're trying to quickly produce predictable designs for your clients. Fortunately, Photoshop makes it easy to create, save, and reuse color swatches with just a few clicks.

To view the Swatches palette, choose Window ➤ View. If you click the small arrow to view the palette's options menu, you'll see that Photoshop has many other preset swatches that you can load. In addition, you can load other swatches that better suit a retro-styled illustration when you begin work. This will help you easily select colors and stick to a standard palette, making your work easier and more predictable.

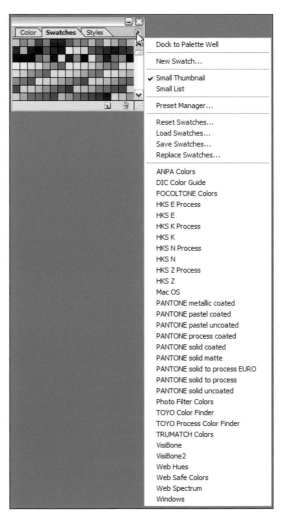

To help get you started, I've included several retro color swatch files in this chapter's source files. If you download them, you'll see that they all have an `.aco` file extension. Place these files into the following folders and restart Photoshop.

- **Windows**: /Program Files/Adobe/Adobe Photoshop CS/Presets/Color Swatches
- **Mac OS X**: /Applications/Photoshop CS/Presets/Color Swatches

If you view the options in the Swatches palette now, you'll see the new retro swatches in the list.

The Adobe Illustrator connection

I realize this is a Photoshop book. For that reason, I've taken great care to ensure that no exercises rely on other programs that may limit your ability to complete the exercise. However, I don't want to leave out a key asset in producing and using retro-styled material: Illustrator. Illustrator is a great complement to Photoshop for a few reasons. First, if you bought the Adobe Creative Suite package, you already have Illustrator. Second, the integration between the two programs is outstanding. Not only can you copy and paste between the two applications freely, but Illustrator operates much like Photoshop in that it's layer based, and many of the tools are shared between the two applications. Finally, if you don't have Illustrator, that shouldn't stop you. Photoshop can open Illustrator (`.ai`) files as well. You'll be presented with a slightly different dialog box when you attempt to open an Illustrator file, but this is just to confirm that you'd like to rasterize the vector image within the Illustrator file.

In addition, many download sites such as Adobe Exchange may list an .eps file as an Illustrator file type, but Photoshop can open that file type as well.

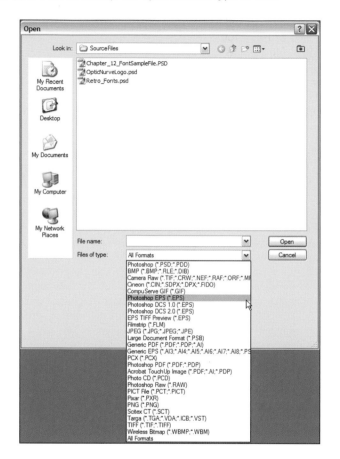

Inspiration and material

Inspiration for retro and vintage artwork is all around you. Knowing where to look for it can be tricky, but here are a few good places to start:

- **Google** (www.google.com): I've mentioned this search engine many times throughout this book, and I'm going to mention it again here. It's one of the best places to start when you're searching for anything, including inspiration.

■ **Adobe Studio Exchange** (http://share.studio.adobe.com): Adobe Studio Exchange is also a great place to find tutorials, styles, patterns, custom shapes, and many other free gems. Studio Exchange provides downloads for nearly every aspect of Photoshop, categorized by software title. From custom shapes to patterns, color swatches, and brushes, you can find nearly everything here. However, I urge you to not let other file formats intimidate you. Check out the Illustrator area as well. Illustrator files can be opened in Photoshop almost as easily as its native .psd file. And if for some reason you need to open a file in Illustrator to select certain layers or objects within an illustration, have no fear. Illustrator's layers are very similar to Photoshop's, and the fact that you can copy and paste between the two applications makes using Illustrator in conjunction with Photoshop nearly painless.

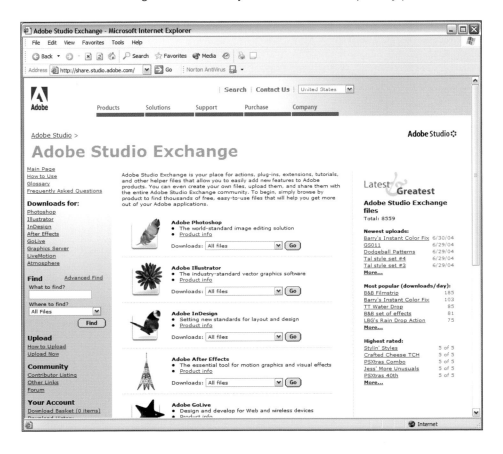

When searching on the term "retro," several results were returned, including retro patterns, clip art, and color palettes.

12

- **Havana Street** (www.havanastreet.com): This site offers a multitude of retro clip art.

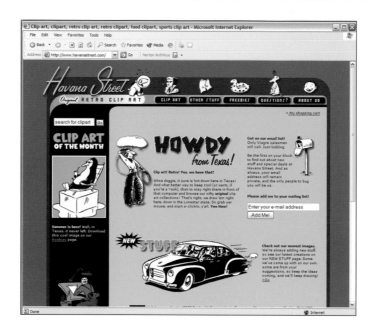

- **PixelDecor** (www.pixeldecor.com): This is a great site for everything retro. Jen Funk Segrest is the webmaster, and she has done an incredible job with her website. Pay her a visit and be prepared to step back in time.

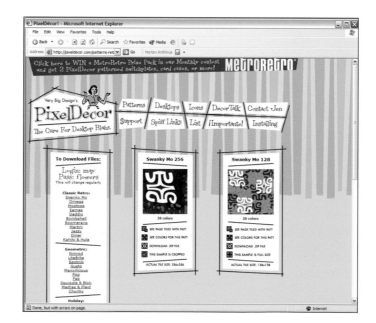

- **Font Diner** (www.fontdiner.com): Another great website I can't say enough about. The free retro-styled fonts alone make it worth the visit. And if you need something more specialized in the way of retro, the site also offers a great library of fonts for purchase.

- **Retro Ad Art** (www.retroadart.com): This site provides retro fonts, clip art, logo designs, tutorials, samples, and more.

Building a library of inspiration

Building a library of reusable artwork is essential to becoming and being a professional designer. At the same time, maintaining a library of inspirational artwork can be just as important. You never know when the creative well will run dry, or when a client will ask for a certain style that you know you've seen before but just can't pinpoint where. Not to mention the fact that an inspirational library can help tremendously during the course of a normal project to provide fresh ideas from which to work.

If you've ever worked for or visited an advertising agency, you've seen that many desks and bookshelves are lined with design annuals that showcase the best in advertising for a current year. These books are often dog-eared or flagged with sticky notes in many places. It's not that the designers are stealing ideas from past advertisements—rather, they're using what has worked to spark ideas of their own.

You can harness this concept in graphic design as well. Saving website URLs, logos, advertisements, and artwork as you surf the Internet can help you quickly build up an inspirational library that you can turn to in times of need.

12

Starting out

Starting your electronic library of inspirational material can be the hardest part. However, once you begin, it's very easy to maintain. You'll first want to create a folder structure on your hard drive.

While this folder structure may differ based on your needs, it's a great place to begin. As you can see, the sample I've provided contains an area for most categories within the design industry. For example, if you were browsing the Web in Windows and found a website with a great retro logo, you could right-click the logo and choose Save Picture As. Then navigate to the appropriate folder and click OK. For Mac users in Internet Explorer, *CTRL*-click and choose Download Image to Disk. Then in Safari, *CTRL*-click and choose Save Image As. . . . If you find yourself saving many logos, and you feel you need to further categorize them, you could always add a Retro subfolder under the main Logos folder. You'll undoubtedly customize this method of saving inspirational images and designs, but this sample should definitely get you moving in the right direction.

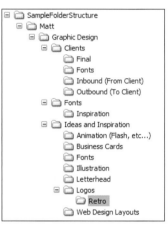

Finding and sorting through your inspirational files with File Browser

The File Browser was added to Photoshop in version 7. While this feature is targeted at digital photographers who need to manage, sort, and tag a large number of photographs, it can be a useful tool for managing images in your inspirational portfolio as well as your file system in general.

Opening the File Browser is simple. Just choose Window ➤ File Browser or click the Toggle File Browser button next to the palette well.

Once the File Browser is open, you can view thumbnails of your images—not just Photoshop .psd files, but Illustrator (.ai), .jpg, and .gif files as well. This is a key advantage to using only the native file explorer that ships with your operating system. You can also search, tag, change the thumbnail size in, rotate, and sort (by 13 different attributes) your files, leaving you with endless methods for finding and managing your artwork.

Backing up your work

Backing up your work is an important part of being a designer at any level. By now, you probably know how to back up your actual source files so you don't lose your artwork. But did you know that you can back up your Photoshop presets so you don't lose them as well? Not only that, but you can take your presets with you to another computer.

Let's first take look at why you'd want to do this. For example, suppose you've created a nice retro shape with the Pen tool. As demonstrated earlier, you save this shape as a custom shape so it will be available to use whenever needed. However, it's important to note that when the shape is saved as a custom shape, you've inserted it into Photoshop's current custom shape library and can use it freely whenever needed. Now, let's say you inadvertently loaded a new custom shape set on top of the existing shape set. What will happen to your custom shape? Unfortunately, it's gone forever. Now, you may be thinking that you'd never do that. However, an even worse circumstance is when Photoshop crashes—something that I'm sure you've experienced at one time or another. If you're lucky, Photoshop will recover and all will be well. But there are occasions when Photoshop crashes and it resets all of your presets (custom shapes, brushes, patterns, layer styles, etc.). Hopefully my point here is clear. The example of one custom shape preset may not seem too terrible, but imagine that you've created hundreds of them. It would certainly not be fun to lose them all. The good news in this discussion is that there's an easy way to avoid all of this. You guessed it—save your presets! Since Adobe clearly wants you to do this, the company has even given you two ways to accomplish this task.

First, you can have access to all of your presets through the Preset Manager by choosing Edit ➤ Preset Manager. This is a great tool that Photoshop provides to manage your presets. In the example of the retro custom shape preset, you can click Custom Shapes from the Preset Type drop-down list and see that your custom shape is indeed stored in this library. However, as I mentioned before, it isn't saved yet. To save it permanently, just click one of the shapes in the set to activate it, and click the Save Set button. You can then overwrite an existing custom shape set to add your new shape to it permanently or create a new set by typing in a new name. Either way, when you click Save, your new shape will now be part of the shape set you named in the dialog box.

12

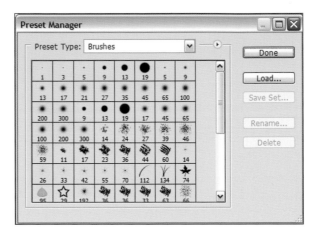

The second way is just as easy. Nearly every preset in Photoshop offers a way to save the current preset library within its palette by clicking the small options arrow at the top left of the palette. If you'd like to find out just what presets this applies to, look in the Preset Type drop-down list mentioned in the previous method. Once you click the options arrow, you'll be presented with a list, of which Save Shapes (or whatever preset you're dealing with) will be listed as an option.

OK, now that you know how to save the presets, you need to take one more step to ensure their survival. If your computer were to crash altogether and your hard drive were unrecoverable, you'd hopefully have your artwork backed up safely. However, your presets will most likely be gone if you've never backed them up. Fortunately, this is an easy process as well. Simply navigate to your Photoshop installation folder, and you'll notice a folder named Presets.

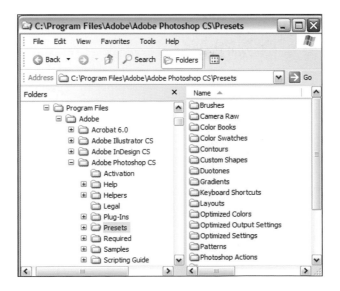

Within this folder are separate folders for each type of preset. You could copy each individually, but I've found it's easier to just copy the entire folder to a safe place. Now you can sleep peacefully at night knowing your Photoshop presets are safe and sound.

Summary

Well, you made it! The last chapter of this book is now complete. At this point, you've gained not only an understanding of how you can use Photoshop to create many different design styles, but also some powerful insight as to how to manage your work as a professional. In closing, I want to thank you for spending your valuable time with this book. Photoshop is an incredible piece of software, and its popularity seems to be growing with each new release.

As I mentioned in Chapter 1, the title of this book is *Extreme Photoshop* for a reason. After having read it, you should be left with the knowledge and real-life artwork to help you take Photoshop to its extremes and go beyond your current use of the program. However, like nearly all books, this book is just a stepping-stone. If I could give you any advice about what to do next, it would be to **practice**. I realize this is a rather empty piece of advice, and you've probably heard it more times than you've cared to. So, let me give you some advice on how to practice. Deconstruct every illustration and design that you can get your hands on. Learn from others' work. But don't just look at what has been done and how it's been accomplished—ask yourself why a certain illustration or design looks good or bad. In fact, ask yourself "Why?" as often as possible. Once you begin to understand why something looks good or bad, you'll be better equipped to apply good practices and techniques to your own work.

Also, don't forget to use the vast resources available to you. My website (www.extremephotoshop.com) is a great place to start. The friends of ED site (www.friendsofed.com) is another valuable resource that includes a popular support forum as well as the source files for this book. Finally, get your hands on industry magazines and join any trade associations that you can. I've found that *Computer Arts* and *Photoshop User* are two wonderful magazine resources for inspiration and learning more about Photoshop. The National Association of Photoshop Professionals (NAPP, www.photoshopuser.com) is a great organization to join for more learning resources and networking opportunities.

Finally, have fun. Often, you can get caught up in the vast amount of information available. Photoshop is meant to make your life easier when working as an illustrator or graphic designer. Remember that, and enjoy it. Good luck!

12

INDEX

Symbols

3D glass fishbowl example 72
  adding depth to fishbowl 79
  adding reflection 89
  Background layer 73
    creating linear gradient 73
    Liquify filter 100
  creating water line 82
  fishbowl shape layers 74
  making shadow more realistic 82
  Marbles layer 98
    Inner Shadow layer style 99
    Spherize filter 98
  Master layer
    Multiply blending mode 80
    Overlay blending mode 82
  Pixel Stretch layer 86
    adding black-to-white gradient across reflection 89
  reflection map 91
    adding black-to-white linear gradient 93
  Shadow layer 97
    Gaussian Blur filter 97
  Top layer 93
    Inner Shadow layer style 94
    Overlay blending mode 94
  Water layer 84
    filling with white 84
    Overlay blending mode 84
  Water Line layer 95
3D modeling
  wireframe illustration 272
3D techniques and concepts 68
  clipping groups 68
  reflections and highlights 70
  refraction 70
  texture mapping 71
60s Chic font 372
  converting symbol into custom shape 374

A

Add Anchor Point tool
  adding anchor point to intersection of shapes 78
Adjustment Layer
  Pattern option 377
Adobe Studio Exchange
  as resource 381
Andy Warhol style exercise (part 1) 346
  reference photo
    adding new layer 346
    adding Spectrum gradient to 346
    desaturating 346
    Hue/Saturation adjustment of tiled images 347
    tiling image 346
Andy Warhol style exercise (part 2) 348
  Background layer
    filling with red 349
  Fill layer
    filling with dark blue 349
  Photograph layer 349
    creating new channel 349
    inverting new channel 349
  Threshold adjustment layer 348
  tiling image 350
  varying colors in tiled images 350
angles and icons 197
angry emoticon exercise 225
Animals custom shape set 13
Animation palette
  Make Frames From Layers option 296
  Play button 297
  Select All Frames option 296
  Tween option 297
Anti-aliased option
  Elliptical Marquee tool 133, 157
  Magic Wand tool 134
  Type tool 168
anti-aliasing
  playing pranks on fellow designers 133
  text 166
Arrange menu
  New Window For (your current document title)
    option 134
art deco 330
  finding fonts 337
art deco style exercise 331
  adding text 338
  Airplane layer 336
    coloring with Magic Wand tool 337
  Background layer 335
  Blue Spotlights layer 336
  Building Color layer 334
    filling selection with darker blue 335
  Chrysler building 331
    enlarging image 334
    removing building from background 333
  Yellow Spotlights layer 336
atmospheric perspective 25, 40
  stuck in the rough example 48

B

Background layer
  activating 50
Bauhaus 93 font 360

Bauhaus/constructivist styles 331
Bauhaus/constructivist styles exercise 358
  adding text 360
  Background layer 359
  Border layer 359
  coloring various black rectangles 360
  creating new canvas 358
  display Ruler 358
  Inside Border layer 359
  turning on grid 358
    drawing rectangular shapes 359
Ben Day dots
  Roy Lichenstein style exercise 341
bitmap fonts 167
blending wireframes images with real ones exercise
  Background layer 298
  Shaded layer 298
    adding gradient to layer mask 299
    adding layer mask 298
  Wireframe layer 298
    adding layer mask 299
    inverting black and white colors 300
Blur tool
  blurring highlights 247
Brush palette
  accessing the expanded view 38
  Control drop-down list
    Pen Pressure 244
  creating custom brush 315
  creating Tool Preset for brush 43
    Brush Tip Shape options 42, 44–45
    Color Dynamics option 43
    Scattering option 43
    Shape Dynamics option 43
  Controls setting
    Pen Pressure option 43
  defining brush for stroking paths 14
  digital drawing tablet 243
    Other Dynamics option
    Pen Pressure 244
  Shape Dynamics option 244
  Texture brush 377
Brush tool
  adding highlights to hair 209
  creating fire example 50
  creating mouth 209
  Flow setting 237
  Mode setting 237
    Color Burn option 249–250
    Multiply option 245, 250
    Screen option 246
  Opacity setting 237
  painting face for Roy Lichenstein style exercise 340
  stroking paths 14

stuck in the rough example 40
brushes
  history 38
  shortcuts for changing sizes 237
bump map 71

C
cartooning 132
  color palettes 231
  comic book art 232
  getting drawings into Photoshop 230
    scanning 230
  Japanese manga/anime-style art 234
  Swatches palette 231
    saving and using 231
cartoonlike icon exercise 201
  adding eye detail 205
  Body layer 207
  Hair layer 206
  Head layer 201
    Stroke layer style 203
  Highlights layer 209
  Left Eye layer 203
    Stroke layer style 204
  Mouth layer 209
  Neck layer 208
  Nose layer 206
  Right Eye layer 204
Channels palette
  creating new channel 349
circle example
  Circle Fill layer 158
    adding radial gradient 160
  Circle Outline layer 158
  Cylinder Fill layer 162
    linear foreground to background gradient 163
  Cylinder Highlight layer 164
    inverting colors 164
  Cylinder Outline layer 160
    duplicating and merging 161
  final view of cylinder 166
  grid-creation process 157
  pixel art 157
  Shadow layer 165
  simple paths with Pen tool 15
clipping groups 68
  correcting inner shadow effect on fishbowl 80
  text with photo fill example 69
Close, Chuck 4
CMYK color mode 10
color
  color palettes for icons 200
  icons and 197

Color Dodge blending mode
   merging fire base layers 54
color modes 8
   CMYK color mode 10
   RGB color mode 9
color palettes
   cartooning 231
   retro library 378
Color Range dialog box
   Highlights option 353
Color Swatch Name dialog box
   saving and using swatches 232
coloring line art exercise 235
   Body Armor layer
      highlight and shading 249
   Body Suit layer
      blurring 247
      Gaussian Blur fillter 248
      highlighting 246
      shading 245
   Color Details layer set 240
      Body Suit layer 245
      locking transparency of all layers 242
      shading 242
   Flats layer set 240
   Gear Straps layer
      highlight and shading 249
   Hair layer 237
      shading and highlights 250
   highlighting mouth 251
   layer names and colors 238
   Lines layer 236
      Multiply blend mode 236
   linking flat color layers 240
   Skin layer 237
      painting face 237
      shading 250
comic book art examples 232
Comix font
   using for Roy Lichenstein style exercise 344
concepts
   established icon meanings 201
Contiguous option
   Magic Wand tool 133, 149, 154
Copy Merged command 224
creating fire example
   adding text layer 50
   Background layer 50
   blending glow layer 57
   blurring fire base layer 53
   changing hue for fire base layer 54
   changing opacity of glow layer 58
   coloring fire base layer 53

   creating flames with Liquify filter 54
   fire base layer 51
      applying Wind filter 52
   heart shape illustration 63
   original text layer 51
      adding to fire 58
   reflection layer 61
   rippling flames with Turbulence tool 56
Crop tool
   cropping image of Roy Lichenstein style exercise 343
CTRL/Cmd shortcuts
   navigating 137
cube exercise 152
   creating cube shape 153
   Cube Fill layer 154
      darkest color 155
   Cube Outline layer 152
      duplicating 152
   Highlight Outline layer 156
      erasing lines 157
      inverting color 156
   merging layers 153
custom brush
   creating 42
   creating in Brushes palette 315
custom shapes
   converting symbol into 374
   creating with Ellipse tool and Line tool 365
   creating with Pen tool 364
Custom Shapes palette
   Load Shapes option 367
   Replace Shapes option 367
   saving symbol as custom shape 374
   Shapes options 121, 122
   storing custom shape 365

D

Dennis, F. Robert 5
   interview 31
   Reflections illustration 8
depth 29
    of field 40
digital drawing tablet
   Brushes palette options 243
   using 235
dingbats, symbol fonts 372
Direct Selection tool
   adding buttons to Phone layer 280
   flattening bottom of fishbowl 79
   flattening top of fishbowl 78
dolphin example
   advanced paths with Pen tool 17

drawing paths with Pen tool 12
Drop Shadow Layer Style dialog box
    Distance setting 26
drop shadows
    icons and 198

E

Edit menu
    Copy Merged option 190
Ellipse tool
    Add To Shape Area button 365
    adding shapes to mobile phone 281
    adding shapes to mobile phone outline 281
    Create new shape layer 203
    creating small oval 205
    drawing eyes for portrait illustration 320
    Fixed Size option 74
    Geometry Options arrow 74
    Intersect Shape Areas button 75
    shape layers button 74, 109, 365
    Unconstrained option 76
Elliptical Marquee tool
    Anti-aliased option 133, 157
    Circle Outline layer 158
    creating circle inside grid 360
    creating eyes 222
    creating Hair layer 215
    creating reflection map 91
    creating Shadow layer 97
    creating top of fishbowl 94
    drawing an oval 161, 165, 213, 217, 220–221
    pixel art 133
    Spherize filter 87, 90, 92
    ZigZag filter 92
Elliptical Shape tool
    drawing an oval 213
    Shape layers button 218
emoticons
    angry emoticon 225
    introduction 198
    shiny, happy emoticon exercise 218
Eraser tool
    erasing areas on Phone layer 284
    erasing outlines on cylinder 164
    Mode setting 154
        Pencil option 156
    removing lines from type outline 171
    removing lines outside basketball 188
Estes, Richard 4
Expanded Brushes palette
    accessing the expanded view 38
experience data 22

Eyedropper tool
    sampling colors and tones 107
    sampling screen color from original 108

F

FFF Forward pixel font 168
File Browser
    sorting through retro library files 384
File menu
    Import submenu
        getting drawings into Photoshop 230
Fill opacity setting
    compared to Opacity setting 95
filling paths with Paths palette 15
Filter Gallery dialog box
    Artistic folder
        Cutout filter 313, 325
        Palette Knife filter 353
    Distort folder
        Diffuse Glow filter 352
    Noise folder
        Add Noise filter 351
    Render folder
        applying LensFlare filter 314
        Clouds filter 351, 355
    Stylize folder
        Emboss filter 352
        Glowing Edges filter 312
        Halftone Pattern filter 342
    Texture folder
        Stained Glass filter 312
Font Diner
    resource for retro fonts 383
fonts
    finding Bauhaus fonts 360
    font sample files 370
    installing 338
    previewing 370
    resources for retro fonts 383
    retro library 367
    symbol fonts and repurposing 372
Forward Warp tool.
    creating flames 54
Free Transform bounding box 288
    creating type 169
    displaying 148
    Head layer 202
    Vertical Skew option 169
Free Transform tool
    scaling down lines 87
Fresnel Effect 85

G

gamut, definition 10
Gaussian Blur filter
blurring distant grass layer 48
blurring fire base layer 53
blurring front grass layer 46
blurring mid grass layer 47
changing opacity of glow layer 58
golf apparel ad exercise
Background layer 265
Ear layer
tracing highlight areas 265
Face layer
tracing highlight areas 264
golf club
tracing highlight areas 265
Golfer layer set 266
hands and arms
tracing highlight areas 265
Hat layer
tracing highlight areas 264
incorporating image into magazine-sized ad 266
adding gradient 268
positioning 267
scaling up image 267
Original Pose layer 262
reducing number of tonal levels 263
Shirt layer
tracing highlight areas 264
golfball. *See* stuck in the rough example 40
Google as resource 380
gradient, adding to golf apparel ad exercise 266
Gradient Editor dialog box
creating gradient 41
Gradient Map adjustment
adding Spectrum gradient to Andy Warhol exercise (part 1) 346
Gradient tool
foreground-to-transparent gradient 221
Pencil tool as alternative 160
Radial Gradient button 159
white-to-transparent radial gradient 90
white to black linear gradient 62
gradients
icons and 198
positioning with cursor 211
Grass brush 42

H

Halftone Pattern filter
adding to Roy Lichenstein style exercise 342
hand holding a mobile phone example 277
Hand layer 283
adding lines and wrinkles 278
path layer for left side of hand 277
path layer for right side of hand 278
Phone layer 282
adding buttons 279
drawing outline 279
using shape tools
Ellipse tool 281
Rounded Rectangle tool 281
Hand tool, navigating 137
Havana Street, resource for retro clip art 382
Help file, color modes 9
highlights 70
adding body suit 246
adding to body armor 249
adding to gear straps 249
adding to hair 250
adding to icon with Pen tool 218
adding to mouth 251
blurring on body suit 247
horizon line 24
horizontal lines
isometric perspective 141
Horizontal Type tool
adding text to iPod screen 116
adding text to T-Shirt 304
Hue/Saturation setting
adjusting saturation of distant grass layer 48
changing hue for fire base layer 54
coloring fire base layer 53
varying colors in tiled images in Andy Warhol style exercise (part 2) 350

I

icon people exercise 210
adding baseball cap 218
adding highlights with Pen tool 218
background color 210
Body layer 210
Gradient Overlay layer style 210
Hair layer 215
creating jagged fringe 217
Drop Shadow layer style 216
Inner Glow layer style 216
Head layer 213
Drop Shadow layer style 214
Gradient Overlay layer style 213
Inner Glow layer style 214
T-Shirt layer 217
icons 196
conceptualization 200
guidelines 200
sketches 200

creating icon file 226
designing and illustrating 201
    cartoonlike icon exercise 201
    icon people exercise 210
overview 196
    common characteristics 197
Illustrator as complement to Photoshop 379
Image menu
    Adjustments menu
        as alternative to Layers palette/New Adjustment Layer
            button 262
        Desaturate adjustment 346
        Gradient Map adjustment 346
        Hue/Saturation adjustment 347
        Posterize adjustment 310
        Threshold adjustment 309
    Canvas Size setting 343
        tiling image 347
    Duplicate option 135
        Rotate Canvas option 52
Image Size dialog box
    enlarging image 334
ImageReady
    exporting animations as SWF files 289, 297
        Move tool 138
    pixel art 137
iPod mini re-creation example 107
    adding depth to screen and controls 114
    adding text to iPod screen 116
    Arrow layer set 120
    Bar layer 120
    Base layer 108
        Drop Shadow layer style 125
    Battery layer 119
        creating Battery layer set 120
        Drop Shadow layer style 120
    creating gradients by sampling colors 111
    creating green version with layer comps 127
        Green Base layer 127
        Green Reflection layer 128
        Green Rounded Sides layer 128
    custom shapes for controls 121
    Forward layer set 122
    Inner Circle layer 110
        Gradient Overlay layer style 116
        Stroke layer style 116
    Outer Circle layer 110
        Inner Shadow layer style 115
        Stroke layer style 115
    Play layer set 122
    Playlists type layer 117
        copying layer style and pasting to other type
            layers 118
        Drop Shadow layer style 118

Reflection layer 123
    adding layer mask 124
    creating fading reflection 124
Reverse layer set 122
Rounded Sides layer 111
    duplicating layer 113
    Gaussian Blur filter 112
    merging layers 113
scaling up shape layers 110
Screen layer 109
Screen Text layer set 119
isometric grid
    creating pixel grid pattern 141
    setting up 141
isometric perspective
    angles used 139
    breaking rules 140
    compared to true perspective 139
    pixel art 138
    setting up isometric grid 141

J

Japanese manga/anime-style art
    coloring line art exercise 235
    examples 234

L

Lasso tool
    compared to Pen tool 11
    Gaussian Blur fillter 248
layer comps
    description and uses 126
    saving Layers palette in particular state 126
Layer Comps palette
    Create New Layer Comp button 127
    New Layer Comp option 127
layer sets, description 117
Layer Style dialog box 59
    Bevel and Emboss layer style 96
    Drop Shadow layer style 118, 212, 214, 216
    Gradient Overlay layer style 60, 116, 210, 213, 219
    Inner Glow layer style 114, 212, 214, 216, 219
    Inner Shadow layer style 79, 115, 220
    Pattern Overlay option 376
    Stroke layer style 115–116, 203–206, 286, 289, 376
Layers palette
    activating layer 14
    Add Layer Mask button 62, 88, 124, 208, 291, 298,
        321, 355
    converting symbol into custom shape 374
    Create a new layer button 41
    Create Clipping Mask option 82

creating new layer from active selection 333
Duplicate Layer Set option 240, 321
Fill path with foreground color button 259
intersecting active selection 83
lock transparency option 241–242
Merge Layer Set option 291
Multiply blending mode 340
New Adjustment Layer button 262
   as alternative to Image/Adjustments menu 262
   Posterize option 262
New Set From Linked option 117, 191, 240, 287
previewing fonts 370
Levels adjustment
  preparing drawings for coloring 231
lighting
  pixel art 150
  position of source 151
Line tool
  connecting custom shapes 366
linear perspective 24
Liquify filter
  brushes 39
  creating flames 54
locking transparency of layer 241–242

M

Mac, installing fonts 338
Machine Wash Image Filters
  examples of filters applied to retro-style pizza poster
    exercise 357
Magic Wand tool
  adding leaf shapes to palm trees 186
  Anti-aliased option 134
  coloring airplane in art deco exercise 337
  coloring various black rectangles 360
  Contiguous option 133, 149, 154
  filling top of cylinder 163
  pixel art 133
  selecting active layer 155
Marquee tools 10
Measure tool
  verifying 26.565-degree angle 140
Monroy, Bert 5
Move tool 122, 138, 143
  duplicating Cube Outline layer 152
  duplicating pixel art 148

N

navigating
  CTRL/Cmd shortcuts 137
  Hand tool 137
  Navigator palette 136
  pixel art 135
  spacebar shortcut 137
Navigator palette
  alternative to using scrollbars 73
  thumbnails 136
Nelson, Felix 5
New dialog box
  color modes 9
New Layer Comp dialog box
  creating green version of iPod 129
  Visibility option 127

O

Opacity setting
  compared to Fill opacity setting 95
out of gamut
  definition 10
outline of woman example
  gradients 260
  Quick Mask mode 260
  tracing outline with Pen tool 259
outlines with fill colors and animation exercise 284
  adding detail lines 287
  animating static illustration 289
    converting layers into animation frames 296
    creating frames for animation 292
    flattening layers 295
    Outline layer 291
    Temp Outline layer set 290, 296
  Background layer set 285
  Face layer 285
  Hair layer 286
    adding Stroke layer style 286
    copying layer style to all layers 287
  right photo 288
    creating outline 288

P

Paste dialog box
  Shape Layer option 366
Path Selection tool 12
  Show Bounding Box option 77
paths
  drawing with Pen tool 12
  filling with Paths palette 15
  stroking with Brush tool 14
Paths palette
  adding text to T-Shirt 297
    Create New Path button 276–277
  creating new path 259
  creating new work path 89
  Fill path with foreground color button 15

Load path as selection button 83, 259, 333
Stroke path with brush button 14, 188, 223, 282
work path as temporary paths 276
Work Path layer 83
Pattern palette
   pattern sets 378
patterned step approach
   isometric perspective 140
patterns, retro library 375
Pen tool 10
   adding highlights to hair for portrait illustration 323
   adding highlights to icon 218
   advanced paths 17
   compared to Lasso tool 11
   creating custom shapes 364
   drawing eye shadow for portrait illustration 321
   drawing eyelashes for portrait illustration 321
   drawing hair for portrait illustration 322
   drawing paths 12
   filling paths 15
   Paths option 15, 89, 188, 223, 277, 287
      creating outlines 276
   quick masks as alternative 260
   reasons for use 11
   Shape layers button 107, 206, 210, 264, 285, 316, 344
   silhouette illustration 258
   simple path exercise 15
   stroking paths 14
   vector shapes 364
   wireframe illustration
      creating outlines 276
Pencil tool
   adding foliage to pixel art building 185
   adding highlights to palm trees 186
   adding palm trees to pixel art building 186
   alternative to using Gradient tool 160
   connecting top and bottom outlines 153
   drawing iPod battery shape 119
   painting pixels 147
   pixel art 132
   stepped approach 179
   two across, one up technique 171
perspective and icons 197
photographs. *See* stylizing photographs
photorealism 2
   artists 4–6
   definition 2
   introduction 4
   re-creating an iPod mini 107
   reasons for using 104
      accessory additions 104
      photo does not exist 106
      photo quality 104
      product shoot modifications 104

      reference images 106
   techniques 104
Photoshop
   3D techniques and concepts 68
   Adjustment Layer
      patterns 377
   Background layer 50
   Brushes palette
      patterns 377
   cartooning 132
   File Browser
      sorting through retro library files 385
   Fill dialog
      patterns 375
   Filter Gallery 311
   Illustrator as complement to 379
   Layer Style dialog
      patterns 376
   Liquify filter 39
   Pattern palette
      patterns 378
   patterns 375
   photorealism 2
   Presets folder 386
   realism 2
   Snap feature 147
   Swatches palette 231
   tools 8
pixel art 132
   building library of reusable pixel art 189
      reusing foliage art 189
   circle exercise 157
   creating from pictures 187
   cube exercise 152
   duplicating 148
   ImageReady 137
   isometric perspective 138
      breaking rules 140
      isometric grid 141
   lighting 150
   mathematics 138
      isometric perspective 138
   navigating 135
   pixel art building exercise 173
      extending 185
   pixel grid pattern
      outline, fill and coloring techniques 146
   shading 151
   text 166
      anti-aliasing 166
      pixel fonts 167
      text exercise 168
   tools required
      Magic Wand tool 133

Marquee tools 133
Pencil tool 132
zooming 134
pixel art building exercise 173
adding foliage 185
adding palm trees 186
adding sidewalk and street 184
Balcony layer 179
Building Fill layer 175
Building Highlight layer 178
Building Outline layer 174
duplicating and connecting 175
Cutout Fill layer 177
Cutout Outline layer 176
Grid layer 174
Window layer 180
adding highlights 181
adding people 181
pixel art, creating from pictures 187
Basketball layer 188
Lines layer 188
pixel fonts 167
resources 168
pixel grid pattern
applying to other illustrations 145–146
creating 141–145
outline, fill and coloring techniques 146–150
reducing opacity of grid 146
pixel stretch reflection 86
PixelDecor, resource for retro art 382
Polygonal Lasso tool
adding highlights to hair for portrait illustration 323
creating large triangular shapes 336
creating small jagged shapes 217
selecting dark shadowed areas of image 334
pop art 330
Andy Warhol style exercise part 1 346
Andy Warhol style exercise part 2 348
portrait illustration exercise
adding highlights and lines to mouth 318
adding shadow under mouth 318
Body layer 323
creating nose 318
drawing eye shadow 321
drawing eyebrows 320
drawing eyes 320
Face layer 316
Hair layer 322
adding highlights 323
Left Eye layer set 321
Mouth layer 318
Neck layer 317
reducing opacity of 323
Right Eye layer set 321

Shirt layer 324
Teeth layer 318
tidying up image 326
Posterize adjustment
adding highlights to hair for portrait illustration 322
drawing body for portrait illustration 323
drawing shirt for portrait illustration 324
stylizing photographs 310
Posterize dialog box
Levels setting 263
posterizing, definition 263
Preset Manager
managing presets 385
pattern sets 378

Q

Quick Mask mode
choice of painting in black or white 260
quick masks as alternative to Pen tool 260

R

realism 2
concepts 22
atmospheric perspective 25
depth 29
linear perspective 24
reflection 27
refraction 28
shadows 26
definition 2
faking realism 3
using brushes 38
realism and 3D 68
3D glass fishbowl example 72
3D techniques and concepts
clipping groups 68
reflections and highlights 70
refraction 70
texture mapping 71
Rectangle tool
creating small rectangle 122
Rectangular Marquee tool
adding black rectangle shape to Roy Lichenstein style exercise 345
creating fire example 60
creating pixel stretch reflection 86
creating rectangle for bar 121
creating separator line 338
creating various black rectangles 359
drawing long rectangle along sides of iPod 112
pixel art 133

square selection around palm tree 190
    Copy Merged option 190
reference images 106
reflection map 71
    3D glass fishbowl example 91
reflections 27, 70
    Fresnel Effect 85
    pixel stretch 86
refraction 28, 70
    curvature of fishbowl 99
refractive index 70
Retro Ad Art
    resources for retro fonts and art 383
retro fonts
    resources 367
retro library 364
    backing up work 385
    color palettes 378
    custom shapes 367
    folder structure 384
    fonts 367
        font sample files 370
        previewing 370
    inspiration and material 380
        resources 380
    patterns 375
    shapes 364
    sorting through files with File Browser 384
    third-party custom shape sets 367
retro styles 330
    art deco 330
    art deco style exercise 331
    Bauhaus/constructivist styles 331
        exercise 358
    pop art 330
        Andy Warhol style exercise (part 1) 346
        Andy Warhol style exercise (part 2) 348
        Roy Lichenstein style exercise 340
    research resources 331
retro-style pizza poster exercise
    final image 356
    Grunge layer 351
        Add Noise filter 351
        adding Highlights option 353
        Clouds filter 351
        Diffuse Glow filter 352
        duplicate layer 353
        Emboss filter 352
        merge with duplicate 353
        setting foreground to black and background to
            white 351
    Grunge layer (duplicate)
        Palette Knife filter 353

Machine Wash Image Filters, examples of filters
        applied to 357
    Vintage Texture layer 354
        adding layer mask 355
        applying Clouds filter 355
        coloring yellow 354
reusability 68
reusable library creation
    Copy Merged option 190
    layer sets 191
RGB color mode
    reasons for using 9
Rounded Rectangle tool
    Add To Path Area button 279
    Add To Shape Area button 202
    adding shapes to mobile phone 281
    adding shapes to mobile phone outline 281
    Radius option 206
    Shape layers button 109
Roy Lichenstein style exercise 340
    adding black rectangle above image 345
    adding colorful border 343
    adding talk bubble 344
        adding text using Comix font 344
    cropping image 342
    Eyes layer 341
    Face layer 340
        applying Halftone Pattern filter 341
        painting with Brush tool 340
    Hair layer 341
    Line Art layer 340
        Multiply blending mode 340
    Lips layer 341
        applying Halftone Pattern filter 342

S
scanning, getting drawings into Photoshop 230
shading
    adding to body armor 249
    adding to body suit 245
    adding to Color Details layer set 242
    adding to gear straps 249
    adding to hair 250
    adding to skin 250
    pixel art 151
shadows 26
Shape drop-down menu 13
shape layer, creating 13
Shape tools 13
    benefits of using 213
shapes
    creating a reusable retro library 364
    reasons for creating 366

Shettlesworth, Patrick 235
shiny, happy emoticon exercise 218
    adding reflection 224
    Background layer 218
    creating angry emoticon 225
    Dimples layer 222
    Eyes layer 222
    Face layer 218
        Gradient Overlay layer style 219
        Inner Glow layer style 219
        Inner Shadow layer style 220
    Highlight layer 220
        foreground-to-transparent gradient 221
    Mouth layer 221
    Teeth layer 223
shortcuts
    changing brush sizes 237
    Copy Merged command 224
    subtracting selection 222
silhouette illustration 254
    compared to wireframe illustration 274
    definition 254
    extracting image from background 258
    golf apparel ad exercise 261
    outline of woman example 258
    Pen tool 258
    picking an image 255
        complexity 255
        composition 257
        creativity 257
        viewing angle 256
    reasons for using 254
        moods conveyed 254
Smith, Colin 5–6
    camera illustration 6
    guitar illustration 7
Smith, Jared 173
snowboarder exercise
    adding snow 316
    Background layer 314
        applying gradient 314
        applying LensFlare filter 314
    Cutout filter 313
spacebar shortcut
    navigating 137
stepped approach
    isometric perspective 140
Stroke dialog box
    settings 291
stroking paths with Brush tool 14
stuck in the rough example 40
    adding clouds 49
    adjusting opacity of mid grass layer 48
    adjusting saturation of distant grass layer 48

atmospheric perspective 48
blurring distant grass layer 48
blurring front grass layer 46
blurring mid grass layer 47
creating behind ball layer 45
creating distant grass layer 46
creating front ball layer 44
creating front grass layer 44
creating golf ball layer 40
creating mid grass layer 45
creating sky layer 41
stylistic paintings
    stylizing photographs as 308
stylizing photographs 308
    bringing out highlights and shadows 309
    picking a photograph 308
        complexity 308
        copyright issues 309
        hair 308
    portrait illustration exercise 316
    snowborder exercise 311
    techniques 308
subtracting selection
    shortcut 222
Swatches palette
    cartooning 231
    coloring hair 237
    Load Swatches option 232
    saving and using 231
    Small athumbnail option 378
    viewing 378
symbol fonts 372
    converting symbol into custom shape 373

T

text
    anti-aliasing 166
    pixel art 166
    pixel fonts 167
text exercise
    FFF Forward pixel font 168
    Type Color layer 172
        light source 172
    Type Outline layer 170
        merging outline layers 171
        two across, one up technique 170
text, adding to t-shirt exercise 301
    Background layer 301
    Circle layer 301
        adding text 304
    Color layer 302
    Outline layer 301
        coloring wireframe illustration 302

T-Shirt layer 301
texture mapping 71
Three D. *See* 3D
Threshold adjustment
    creating nose for portrait illustration 319
    stylizing photographs 309
Tool Presets
    creating Tool Preset for brush 43
Toolbox
    brushes 39
        Edit In ImageReady button 295
    Edit in Quick Mask Mode button 260
tools
    Add Anchor Point tool 78
    Blur tool 247
    Brush tool 14, 40, 50, 209, 237, 245, 246, 249, 250, 340
    brushes 39
    color modes 8
    Crop tool 343
    Direct Selection tool 78, 79, 280
    Ellipse tool 74, 75, 76, 109, 203, 205, 281, 365
    Elliptical Marquee tool 87, 90, 91, 92, 94, 97, 133, 157, 158, 161, 165, 213, 215, 217, 220, 221, 360
    Elliptical Shape tool 213, 218
    Eraser tool 154, 156, 164, 171, 188, 284
    Eyedropper tool 107, 108
    Forward Warp tool 54
    Free Transform tool 87
    Gradient tool 62, 90, 159, 160, 221
    Hand tool 137
    Horizontal Type tool 116, 304
    Lasso tool 11, 248
    Line tool 366
    Magic Wand tool 133, 134, 149, 154, 155, 163, 186, 337, 360
    Marquee tools 10
    Measure tool 140
    Move tool 122, 138, 143, 148, 152
    Path Selection tool 12, 77
    Pen tool 10, 11, 12, 14, 15, 17, 89, 107, 188, 206, 210, 218, 223, 258, 264, 277, 285, 287, 316, 321, 322, 323, 344, 364
    Pencil tool 119, 132, 147, 153, 160, 179, 185, 186
    Polygonal Lasso tool 217, 323, 334, 336
    Rectangle tool 122
    Rectangular Marquee tool 60, 85, 112, 121, 133, 190, 338, 345
    Rounded Rectangle tool 109, 202, 206, 279, 281
    Shape tools 13, 213
    Turbulence tool 56
    Type tool 168
    Warp tool 100

Transform menu
    Flip Horizontal option 320–321
true perspective compared to isometric perspective 139
Turbulence tool
    creating rippling flames 56
Tween dialog box, settings 297
tweening, description 297
two across, one up technique 170
    Pencil tool 171
Type tools 13
    anti-aliasing 168
    previewing fonts 370

V

vanishing point 25
vector illustrations
    stylizing photographs as 308
vector shapes 364
vertical lines 24
    isometric perspective 141
vintage art 330
    retro-style pizza poster exercise 351

W

Warp tool
    simulating refraction effect 100
Windows
    installing fonts 338
wireframe illustration 272
    blending wireframes images with real ones exercise 298
    compared to silhouette illustration 274
    creating outlines 276
        Pen tool 276
    definition of wireframe 272
    guidelines on picking an image 273
        complexity 274
        creativitity 275
        viewing angle 274
    history 272
    outlines with fill colors and animation exercise 284
    text, adding to t-shirt exercise 301
    uses 273
    wireframe basic drawing exercise 276
        hand holding a mobile phone example 277
work path
    as temporary path 276

Z

zooming, pixel art 134

friendsofed.com/forums

Join the friends of ED forums to find out more about our books, discover useful technology tips and tricks, or get a helping hand on a challenging project. *Designer to Designer*™ is what it's all about—our community sharing ideas and inspiring each other. In the friends of ED forums, you'll find a wide range of topics to discuss, so look around, find a forum, and dive right in!

■ Books and Information

Chat about friends of ED books, gossip about the community, or even tell us some bad jokes!

■ Flash

Discuss design issues, ActionScript, dynamic content, and video and sound.

■ Web Design

From front-end frustrations to back-end blight, share your problems and your knowledge here.

■ Site Check

Show off your work or get new ideas.

■ Digital Imagery

Create eye candy with Photoshop, Fireworks, Illustrator, and FreeHand.

■ ArchivED

Browse through an archive of old questions and answers.

HOW TO PARTICIPATE

Go to the friends of ED forums at **www.friendsofed.com/forums**.

Visit **www.friendsofed.com** to get the latest on our books, find out what's going on in the community, and discover some of the slickest sites online today!

friendsof
DESIGNER TO DESIGNER™
an Apress® company